D0931306

THE ASSOCIATION FOR SCOTTISH LITERARY STUDIES
NUMBER TWO

THE POEMS OF
JOHN DAVIDSON

THE ASSOCIATION FOR SCOTTISH LITERARY STUDIES

GENERAL EDITOR – MATTHEW P. MC DIARMID

THE POEMS OF
JOHN DAVIDSON

EDITED BY

ANDREW TURNBULL

VOLUME
ONE

SCOTTISH ACADEMIC PRESS

EDINBURGH & LONDON

1973

Published by
Scottish Academic Press Ltd.
25 Perth Street, Edinburgh 3
and distributed by
Chatto & Windus Ltd.
40 William IV Street
London W.C. 2

First published 1973
ISBN 7011 1988 8

Printed in Great Britain by R. & R. Clark Ltd., Edinburgh

PREFACE

I would like to acknowledge my indebtedness to the work of previous Davidson scholars, in particular Mr R. D. Macleod; Mr J. Benjamin Townsend, not only for his biographical and critical study of the poet but also for his industry in assembling the superb Princeton collection of Davidson material; Mr John A. Lester Jr., whose excellent bibliographical work has proved invaluable; and Mr W. M. Fisher of Milford, Connecticut, who very kindly allowed me to see his unpublished study of the poet.

I am obliged to the National Library of Scotland, and the university libraries of Yale, Leeds and Princeton, for permission granted to use and publish manuscript material in their possession. I owe a special debt to Aberdeen University Library, for its helpful purchase of Davidson material and the unfailing kindness of its staff.

Thanks are also due to many members of staff and postgraduate students in various departments at Aberdeen University who have given me the benefit of their expert knowledge. Above all, I must thank Mr Matthew P. McDiarmid, at whose suggestion this project was undertaken and without whose encouragement and advice it could not have been completed.

I am very grateful to Dr C. M. Grieve for allowing me to reproduce his poem 'The Caledonian Antisyzygy'.

The introduction to this book is no more than what it claims to be; bald statement concerning Davidson's thought and style has often had to take the place of argument, while many interesting and important aspects of the poet's work have not been discussed. These deficiencies will be more suitably supplied in a forthcoming study by the present writer.

CONTENTS

VOLUME ONE

viii

VOLUME TWO

x

INTRODUCTION

I

John Davidson was born on April 11, 1857, in Barrhead, Renfrewshire. His father, Alexander Davidson, was a minister of the Evangelical Union, and in 1860 took up the post of assistant to James Morison, the founder of the Union, at Dundas Street Church, Glasgow. Two years later he accepted a call from Nelson Street Church, Greenock, where the family remained till 1886, in, it would appear, fairly comfortable circumstances.

Of the quality of the poet's earliest years little is known beyond the bare facts. He attended the Highlanders' Academy, Greenock, till 1870, leaving to join the laboratory staff of Walker's sugar company, and later becoming assistant to the Greenock Public Analyst; while the years 1872-6 found him back in the Academy as pupil-teacher. We do know, however, that the boy was a voracious reader, at least in the field of well-established 'classics': Spenser, Shakespeare, Milton, Bunyan, Scott and Carlyle seem to have been his main diet, although we might guess that he was familiar with the Romantic poets, and, no doubt, Tennyson and Browning.

By the time he left school Davidson was already writing verse: 'On Sundays', he tells us, 'I generally made some blank verse about the universe. I wrote a hundred sonnets also, and various plays'. The only pieces to survive from this very early period are, however, 'Annie Smith', revised for *A Romantic Farce* (1878), and one of the poems in the collection *In a Music-Hall* – possibly 'A Sail' – written at the age of fifteen. We can probably assume that the 'various plays' were Shakespearian pastiche along the lines of *An Unhistorical Pastoral* which, though begun in 1874, was not completed until three years later.

During the early 'seventies, also, the young poet – described by a contemporary as 'reverently critical of his father's evangelical creed'[1] – seems to have finally rejected orthodox Christianity. Though Davidson's few published reminiscences of his father reveal that Alexander Davidson was, in his gentle kindliness, very far removed from the 'heavy father' presented to us by some commentators, and that he was admired and respected by his son – the word 'reverently' in the above quotation must not be ignored – there can be little doubt that young Davidson's views must have led to strained relations between him and his father. We have, however, no information as to the extent of this breach.

The poet's spell as pupil-teacher in Greenock was followed, in 1876, by a year at Edinburgh University where, the records indicate, he studied Latin and Greek. Davidson, however, appears to have found academic life uncongenial, spending most of his time during the second half of the session walking on Arthur's Seat. After this one session he left university to take up a teaching post at Alexander's Endowed School, Glasgow, and the next few years saw him in a succession of jobs as schoolmaster: Perth Academy (1878–81), Kelvinside Academy (1881–2) and Hutchison Charity School, Paisley (1883–4).

After his marriage, in 1884, to Margaret Macarthur, daughter of a Perth bobbin manufacturer, Davidson worked for a time in the Glasgow office of Clark's, a

[1] J. M. Sloan, 'A Rebel in Poetry', *John o'London's Weekly*, Sept. 26, 1926, p. 766.

Paisley thread firm. It seems likely that it was at this time that the poet first experienced those 'straitened circumstances' in which he was to live, more or less continually, for the rest of his life; while the birth of his two sons, Alexander (1887) and Menzies (1889), placed further demands on his undoubtedly slender purse. He had returned to teaching in 1885, at Morrison's Academy, Crieff, where he remained till 1888, while his last year of 'shameful pedagogy', the 'hellish drudgery' of schoolteaching, was spent at a private school in Greenock.

During his years in and around Glasgow Davidson apparently found time to attend classes, sporadically, at the University, becoming the friend and protégé of John Nichol, the Professor of English Literature. An admirer of Carlyle, 'with whose nature', according to a contemporary, 'his own had . . . not a few affinities',[1] Nichol's strongly philosophical approach to literature, his magnetic personality, his style of thought and his literary preferences – which included Swinburne and the so-called 'Spasmodic' poets, Sydney Dobell and Alexander Smith – no doubt made a lasting impression on the young poet. Noted also for his encouragement of those with literary ambitions, Professor Nichol probably proved a decisive factor in Davidson's determination to pursue a literary career, not least by introducing his young friend to the great Swinburne himself, who made encouraging gestures of a suitably grandiloquent nature. Though Swinburne's style had little influence on Davidson, the Scot's admiration for the older poet was deep and lasting.

The range of Davidson's literary work during the 'eighties is extensive, including the plays *Bruce* (1884), *Diabolus Amans* (published anonymously, 1885), *Smith* (1886) and *Scaramouch in Naxos* (1888); the novels *The North Wall* – Davidson's first published work, 1885 – and *Perfervid*, written at Crieff; a series of short stories, some of which later appeared in *The Great Men*; and most of the poems included in the *In a Music-Hall* volume. The private publication of *Scaramouch in Naxos*, *An Unhistorical Pastoral* and *A Romantic Farce* under the title *Plays* in 1889 drew a kind letter of encouragement from George Meredith, which sign of at least moderate approval from one of the 'great' may have been one of the immediate causes behind Davidson's decision to try for success in the London literary world as a full-time writer.

The new decade and the move to London, however, did little to alter Davidson's circumstances; he had now to eke out a living from another form of drudgery – that of journalism – contributing mainly to *The Speaker* and *The Glasgow Herald*. Nevertheless, he soon became involved in the literary life of the city; an associate, if not a member, of the Rhymers' Club from near its inception in 1891 he developed lasting friendships with literary figures as diverse as Richard Le Gallienne, Max Beerbohm and George Gissing. He was also becoming known as a poet, his artistic, if not financial, success being sealed by the appearance of two of his lyrics in the first number of *The Yellow Book*. Indeed, for a time it looked as though public as well as private acceptance would be his; though *In a Music-Hall* (1891), Davidson's first book of verse, had failed, the two following volumes, *Fleet Street Eclogues* (1893) and *Ballads and Songs* (1894), proved very popular with both critics and reading public.

But Davidson's success with the poetry-buying public was short-lived. Neither *A Second Series of Fleet Street Eclogues* (1896) nor *New Ballads* (1897) sold particularly well, while his prose – no less than eight volumes of novels, stories and essays were published between 1890 and 1896 – was never successful. *The Last Ballad* (1899), Davidson's final 'nineties volume of poems, sold almost as badly as his first. Even a promising return to drama with an adaptation of François Coppée's

[1] William A. Knight, *Memoir of John Nichol*, Glasgow, 1896, p. 181.

Pour la Couronne (*For the Crown*, 1896) which proved highly popular with London theatregoers, then indulging a *penchant* for romantic costume drama, failed to keep up its initial impetus: a second adaptation, *The Children of the King* (1897), closed after a two-week run, while the original plays *Godfrida* (1898) and *Self's the Man* (written 1899) never reached the stage.

As the decade progressed a note of desperation is sounded more and more frequently in the poet's letters. Financial worries are uppermost: in addition to the problem of supporting his wife and children, from his father's death in 1893 Davidson was forced to divert part of his meagre income to supplement that of his mother and sister, his brother – an alcoholic who later became insane – being totally unable to provide for them. Besides, or perhaps because of, his perennial financial difficulties he was increasingly troubled by ill-health: his letters continually report attacks of asthma, bronchitis or influenza, while, in 1898, he seems to have been severely incapacitated with a nervous complaint, possibly aggravated by a heart-attack brought on by cycling around the south of England in search of material for a series of travel-papers.

Nor were these Davidson's only problems; easily distracted, composing very slowly and with difficulty, he was forced to turn himself into a near-recluse to get any work done at all. To the naturally sociable poet who delighted in the variety and vitality of city life such enforced seclusion must have proved well-nigh intolerable. A move from London to Shoreham in Sussex, in late 1896 or early 1897, for reasons of both money and health, can only have intensified Davidson's frustration.

Luckily, the poet's friends proved staunch despite the abrupt pugnacity which he displayed, possibly as a result of his short stature and premature baldness – he wore a toupee during his early years in London. Davidson, indeed, stocky, bearded, and forthright, must have appeared an incongruous figure at these Rhymers' Club meetings where young poets worshipped at the shrine of pure art. Yeats himself has testified to the disconcerting effect the Scot had on this *fin de siècle* coterie. Richard Le Gallienne, however, one of the younger Rhymers, the man who, as reader for John Lane, had urged that publisher to accept Davidson's first volume of eclogues, became one of his closest friends. Le Gallienne's reminiscences of the Scots poet go some way towards explaining the quality which made his friendships few but deep:

> Someone has said that the '90s was a time of 'little giants'. The expression is a good one, and the man whom perhaps it especially fits was John Davidson, whose personality was rocky and stubborn and full of Scotch fight, with no little of Scotch pig-headedness. But with him, as with the lion in Holy Writ, within whose jaws the wild bees built their honeycombs, it was a case of *ex forte dulcedo*: for beneath his proud, rather pragmatic exterior, and that Highland manner which brings a suggestion of always going armed against offence, his nature was full of human kindness and repressed tenderness.[1]

One of Davidson's most loyal friends was Grant Richards, a fellow-journalist when the two met in the early 'nineties but later the publisher who, from 1901 to the poet's death, brought out Davidson's books despite substantial losses. Richards duly introduced Davidson to his uncle, Grant Allen – atheist, iconoclast and polymath. Allen, originally a classical scholar, who became, in turn, self-taught scientist, short-story writer and novelist, was a follower of Herbert Spencer and probably played a large part in determining the direction, if not the form, of

[1] Richard Le Gallienne, *The Romantic 90s*, London, 1951, p. 116.

Davidson's later thought. Certainly, he provided friendship and encouragement when the struggling poet most needed them.

Friends in need also were Edmund Gosse and Sir William McCormick – a friend from the Glasgow years – who exerted themselves to procure for Davidson, in 1899, a grant of £250 from the Royal Literary Fund. The same two continued in their efforts to help the poet, finally succeeding, in 1906, in obtaining for Davidson a Civil List pension of £100.

It will be apparent that the coming of the new century brought little change to the poet's fortunes. His abortive flirtation with the theatre continued: several adaptations from the French appeared previous to 1905 although only two survive – *Phèdre*, in typescript in NLS., and *Ruy Blas*, published as *A Queen's Romance* in 1904 and staged without success in the same year. The original play *The Knight of the Maypole*, written expressly for the theatre in 1900, was never put on and sold badly on its publication in 1903, while another original drama, on the subject of Lancelot, though commissioned for performance, was neither staged nor published and has since disappeared. It is possible that Davidson intended his next play, *The Theatrocrat*, for public performance, but the unstageable nature of the two surviving plays of his projected *God and Mammon* trilogy seems to reflect the poet's final realisation that the popular theatre was closed to him.

The style and thought of these three last poetic dramas parallel those of the series of long philosophical poems in blank-verse – the *Testaments* – that Davidson had been publishing since 1901. In that year had appeared the *Vivisector* and the *Man Forbid*, followed, in 1902, by the *Empire-Builder*, while *The Testament of a Prime Minister* came out in 1904. *The Testament of John Davidson*, the longest of the series and the last of the poet's books to be published in his lifetime, appeared in 1908. In addition to the 'Testaments and Tragedies' Davidson brought out, in 1903 and 1906 respectively, *A Rosary* – a miscellaneous collection of prose and verse – and *Holiday and Other Poems*, the only one of these many books to cover its publication costs.

During this last decade the poet's correspondence reveals a growing tendency to self-assertion and intolerance. Doubtless intensified by years of penury, ill-health and, above all, lack of the recognition he regarded as his due, this tendency, already apparent in the harsh bitterness of some of the verse of the later 'nineties, is reflected in the tone of the 'Testaments and Tragedies' – the medium through which Davidson hoped to convert the world to his dynamic, monistic 'philosophy'. The tone of the letters varies pathetically between bleak recognition of the totally unsaleable nature of his later work and blind insistence on the 'mint of money' to be tapped through the proper publication and advertisement of his books. Pathetic also is the tension apparent between his pose of proud isolation and his need for popular appreciation.

Davidson became more and more cut off from human contact. Though back in London from 1898 he discouraged visitors, partly because they distracted him and partly through shame at the poverty of his household. His isolation was increased by a move to Penzance in May 1907, necessitated by the state of both his health and his purse. Till his death he was to live in exile at Penzance, even giving up his membership of the Grosvenor Club – something he had retained even in his worst periods – in order to save the membership fee. In addition, he was still forced to rely on the journalism so repugnant to him.

Gradually the poet's increasing alienation from society led to an obsessive preoccupation with his self-appointed role as prophet of a new cosmology and social order – an obsession with his 'message' which produced a kind of defensive megalomania. The bleaker his prospects became, the more self-assertive and grandiloquent his public and private utterances. Clearly the poet, never pliable, was losing such resilience as he possessed; the bamboo, bending before the storm of poverty, illness and neglect, became the oak which can only break.

Davidson disappeared on March 23, 1909. Leaving the house to post a parcel of literary material to Grant Richards, he went to a local hotel where he had a glass of whisky and a cigar and was not seen again until his body was recovered from the sea six months later. Though his revolver and two cartridges had disappeared along with him, and the body carried marks, in the skull, of the possible entry and exit of a bullet, the inquest on the poet's death, through insufficient evidence, returned a verdict merely of 'Found Dead'.

There seems little doubt, however, that Davidson committed suicide. The preface to the posthumously published *Fleet Street and Other Poems*, the MS. of which came to light soon after his disappearance, hints strongly at the poet's intention of taking his own life:

The time has come to make an end. There are several motives. I find my pension is not enough; I have therefore still to turn aside and attempt things for which people will pay. My health also counts. Asthma and other annoyances I have tolerated for years; but I cannot put up with cancer.

Further statements in both Davidson's later poetry and his letters support this conclusion. Though there is no evidence that Davidson actually had cancer, the fear of such a disease, coupled with his other hardships, acting on an obviously unstable mind, could well have driven the poet to suicide.

Davidson, according to his own wishes, was buried at sea, some seven miles off Penzance, on September 21, 1909. He left an estate of a little over £319.

2

Davidson's ideas and attitudes, as revealed by his early work – in particular the plays – derive quite clearly from the staple Romantic positives of love and nature. Love is seen as a unifying power bringing both external and internal harmony; it breaks down barriers of rank, habit and convention, and develops into a kind of primal sympathy through which the individual is connected with 'the heart of the world', the deepest mysteries of nature. This concept remains fundamental to the poet's thought, though it gradually widens to take in the whole range of physical passion.

The importance of the unifying principle also characterises Davidson's attitude to nature. Associated with ideas of health, vigour and vitality, a sanative and redemptive power, the essential rightness of all the manifestations of nature is emphasised; the earth is seen as a 'pagan, as savage as fair', to which men mistakenly bring their own narrow moral discriminations. The poem 'Thoreau,' quoted above, is an early example of Davidson's view of nature as a complex and diverse unity, a 'pregnant, immaculate maid', no one aspect of which should be emphasised at the expense of another. Later attempts at 'laying the ghost of an unwholesome idea that still haunts the world – the idea of the inherent impurity of nature', include, for example, 'A Ballad of Tannhäuser' and 'A Ballad of a Nun' which celebrate the free indulgence of natural impulse, the rejection of moral precepts in the fulfilment of the deepest and strongest drives.

The themes of nature and physical passion are clearly inseparable in Davidson's work, the one being, as it were, a function of the other; love (ultimately all passionate feeling) being the most basic, the most natural impulse, is seen, on the one hand, as nature expressing itself through man who is thus united with the world on a purely instinctive level, and on the other as the means whereby man perceives nature's unity-in-diversity and his own relation to it. In this context it is interesting to note how frequently Davidson makes use of sexual imagery in his passages of natural description. Sexual imagery, of course, becomes increasingly important in the later, materialist phase.

These two concepts found in the work of the younger Davidson tend to appear as physical and sensual rather than spiritual and metaphysical: love is mainly extolled in highly sensuous terms, while the poet's 'pantheism' is based on an intuition of the physical unity of nature. It is significant that in 'Thoreau' it is the sensual side of that thinker that is most attractive to the poet – the earth-worshipping Thoreau who advocated 'a purely *sensuous* life' and who thought it a 'luxury to stand up to one's chin in some retired swamp for a whole summer's day'.[1] Though Davidson was not to emerge as a fully-fledged materialist till the early 1900s it is clear that the foundations were being laid much earlier.

Another concept fundamental to Davidson's thought also emerges in the earlier work alongside, and in conjunction with, the poet's attitudes to love, nature and instinct – that of the hero, the 'natural man'. Again a common feature of Romantic literature, Davidson's version of the hero is a man of instinct, spontaneous, who acts on impulse, listening to the 'treble notes' of his deepest natural promptings rather than the voice of shallow reason. The hero of *Smith* is the most complete realisation of this 'natural man' in Davidson's early work: dominant, rebellious, the embodiment of a strenuous union of emotion and intellect, of wide sympathies, he appears to his shallow contemporaries as 'a baby', 'uncultured', 'lacking the college stamp', 'a mere savage'; 'the kind of man that healthy girls/Yield to at once,' he falls in love instantly and spontaneously, and chooses to kill himself and his newly-discovered 'mate' rather than suffer being thwarted.

As he develops in Davidson's work the fundamental character of this 'natural man' emerges as self-reliance in the widest sense – the completely self-centred attitude of, say, 'The Outcast', which is not, however, to be confused with simple selfishness, being more a kind of individual integrity or 'truth to self', a refusal to act other than as directed by the promptings of one's own nature, a part of nature in the large. In this the Davidsonian hero seems to derive mainly from those of Carlyle (in, for example, the first essay on Jean Paul), Emerson[2] and Ibsen (one of the few writers to whom he acknowledges a debt). Obviously, also, the notion is connected with the idea of unity already emphasised with regard to earlier topics: the 'natural man' is essentially a unified self, united in 'blood and brain' by the 'still small voice' of nature. Hence, the Davidsonian hero does the 'right thing' automatically; all artificial barriers – habit, convention, public morality, traditional dualism and so on – being destroyed, he is directly connected with 'the heart of the world'. By becoming attuned to nature in himself he attains a deeper sympathy with the larger sphere.

This general type reappears in various guises throughout Davidson's work; the protagonists of most of the ballads are Davidsonian heroes, as are many of the materialist 'strong men' – though, at this later stage, the 'still small voice' becomes the literally elemental urge of matter towards self-consciousness through passionate feeling and action of an increasingly violent nature. Materialist heroes, like the Empire-Builder, the navvy in *The Testament of a Prime Minister*, or 'John Davidson', freed from the stifling trammels of 'civilisation' and 'culture', become more and more inflicters – and sufferers – of pain. Hence, in the materialist

[1] H. D. Thoreau, *Writings*, Boston and N.Y., 1906 , I, p. 408 and VII, p. 141.
[2] See note to 'The Outcast'.

heaven of the Empire-Builder and the Prime Minister are to be found the strong, the proud, the cruel, the warlike – all those

> Who took their stand upon the earth and drew
> Deep virtue from the centre, helped themselves,
> Desired the world and willed what Matter would.

The importance in Davidson's thought of a sense of wholeness and unity will be obvious. The origins of this tendency towards a world-view which attempts to weld unity out of diversity while preserving a sense of the rich variety and complexity of life lie both in the literary or cultural tradition of which Davidson was a part, and in certain environmental forces operating on the young poet. On the one hand, the intuitive apprehension of unity in nature and the universe, coupled with the intellectual perception of conflict, fragmentation and disunity, is one of the commonest Romantic experiences – an experience complicated in many cases by a divided emotional response consisting of both a need for wholeness and a delight in the sheer energy bred by conflict.

Goethe – whom Davidson must have opened at Carlyle's command – is, of course, with his concepts of *Polarität* and *Wiederholte Spiegelungen*, the *locus classicus* for this typical Romantic theme of unity-in-diversity, but similar intuitions are to be found in Carlyle himself. Important, also, in the development of this aspect of Davidson's thought were the 'Spasmodic' dramas to which he was introduced by Nichol. Centring around the character of an egotistical, satanic malcontent – a vulgarisation of Faust and the Byronic hero, the victim of an incurable thirst for experience in the pursuit of which he may commit innumerable crimes, finally seeking solace in nature and finding redemption through love – these formless, blank-verse 'Dramatic poems' vary stylistically from bombastic rhetoric to turgid prosiness; indulging at the slightest opportunity a penchant for incoherent metaphysic they mix a strong liberal interest in contemporary social questions with the most unmitigated individualistic self-absorption. Inspired originally by Philip James Bailey's *Festus* (1839), representative productions of the genre include J. W. Marston's *Gerald* (1842), Sydney Dobell's *The Roman* (1850) and *Balder* (1853), and Alexander Smith's *A Life-Drama* (1853).

Clearly, many attitudes found in these works find an echo in Davidson – for example, the emphasis placed on nature and love as redemptive powers – but, with reference to the topic under discussion, it is enough to indicate that, with their emphasis on extremes of sensation and their 'spasmodic' stylistic variation, coupled with an inevitable final picture of harmony and reconciliation, they embody a view of life as at once disturbingly complex and ultimately unified.

What, however, of the more immediately personal pressures acting on the young Davidson? It would not be going too far to point to the experience of contrast, even conflict, as perhaps the most important single factor in the poet's early background. There is, for example, the contrast between the boy's world of books – the romantic glamour of Scott, the linguistic exuberance of Carlyle – and the mundane, dull, rather parochial environment which was his day-to-day experience. Related to this is the contrast that appears later in the split between the young poet's ambition and his achievement: 'a singing bird of some description, and probable quality,' he calls himself, asserting that if 'I am what I take myself to be, my opinion carries great weight' – which egotism is in sharp contrast with his actual progress from pupil-teacher to junior master.

A much more important contrast, however, is that between town and country – specifically, between the ugliness of Greenock, by all accounts one of the more repellent of the Scottish industrial towns, and the beauty of its setting, the Firth of Clyde. The physical position of the Evangelical Union manse, between the town and the Firth, neatly symbolises Davidson's emotional position *vis-à-vis* these extremes: on the one hand he abhors the ugliness of the modern industrial town, 'the squalid thoroughfare, the sunless close', yet, on the other, he is willing to incorporate the town, a physical manifestation of power and energy, into his vision as another aspect of the profuse inventiveness of nature (in, for instance, the description of Greenock in 'A Ballad in Blank Verse'). Equally ambivalent is Davidson's attitude to the moral norms of modern capitalist society which accepted the contrast between extreme wealth and extreme poverty. Here the poet's reaction is similar to that of his mentor, Carlyle; appalled by the misery resulting from the development of industrial society, regarding commercial values with distaste – *Scaramouch in Naxos*, for example, is a satire on the 'divine institution of buying and selling', while 'The Gleeman' comments sadly on the limited values of the 'market place' – and contemptuous of bourgeois hypocrisy and philistinism, Davidson is again attracted by the energy potential of the 'captain of industry'.

Finally, young Davidson would have been faced with the contrast between the atmosphere of 'strong, believing prayer' that would have prevailed in his father's house and the air of the Public Analyst's laboratory: enthusiasm, belief, opposed to methodical exactitude and a sceptical outlook. It seems that it was an awareness of this conflict that first led the boy to question the revealed religion of his father. However, it would be wrong to see the immediate domestic surroundings of the poet's youth as the sole, or even the most important, reason for his lifelong dialogue, indeed dogfight, with religion. Equally, while it would be difficult to overemphasise the importance to Davidson's thought of his reaction against Christianity, to see this – as most commentators have tended to do – as springing mainly from the boy's sufferings at the hands of a harsh, narrowly bigoted, 'Calvinist' father (which one-sided picture seems far from the truth) is to wilfully ignore Davidson's place in the wider sphere of Victorian cultural history and to shift the emphasis from where it belongs: on the poet's attitudes as part of an important and pervasive nineteenth-century trend of feeling.

The Victorian age was a period of crisis for religion. The new climate of belief, the renewed emphasis on the spiritual life after almost a hundred years of rationalism – represented, in the literary sphere, by the Romantic movement – after its early exuberance soon began to run into difficulties, confronted by burgeoning industrialism with its attendant evils of mass poverty, slum-housing, and the 'cash-nexus', ruled by the seemingly 'iron laws' of political economy. This mechanised and mechanistic universe, the philosophic bases of which were implicit in post-Cartesian rationalism, could only be abhorrent to the Victorians, committed, as they were, to the idea of vital, creative divinity actively present in the individual and the natural world. Where in this system was there room for a just and compassionate deity?

Clearly the traditional religious palliatives were inadequate, the Church 'a lifeboat, warped and sunk' – a fact that became more apparent as the century progressed and revealed religion retreated before the theories of the 'new' science of biology. Beliefs previously regarded as either inarguable or irrelevant had to be strenuously examined and redefined or rejected; the 'will to believe' had to discover or create new objects of faith; the pattern of doubt, loss of faith, despair and conversion either to a refashioned form of traditional religious belief or a secular equivalent is repeated throughout the century in the spiritual history of figures as diverse as Carlyle and Mill, Tennyson and Samuel Butler. There is hardly an important literary work of the period that does not have a religious dimension – that does not contain an implicit or explicit attempt at self-definition *vis-à-vis* religion or some related ideological positive.

That Davidson has a place in the history of Victorian doubt is revealed by such early poems as 'The Voice' and 'No Man's Land' which exploit a vein of despair that recurs regularly in the poet's later work. A mood of gloomy questioning, an apprehension of the absurdity of life, is apparent in several of the eclogues: life comes to seem merely 'a naked precipice/O'erhanging death's deep sea', and time 'a dungeon vast/Where life lies rotting in the straw'. Davidson's acute awareness of the predicament of the Victorian doubter is nowhere more clear than in the portrait of Ninian in 'Lammas', though his probing of this mood continues through 'Epilogue to Fleet Street Eclogues' and 'Eclogue of the Downs' where the images of the Sphinx and the 'huddled city' on Truleigh Hill are powerfully expressive of the obscure, enigmatic, yet palpably inimical face presented by the universe to many men of the nineteenth century.

'Eclogue of the Downs' was based on prose pieces of 1898; early in the following year Davidson made public his own answer to 'the cat-call of the universe' in a series of letters to *The Speaker* – the principle of 'cosmic irony', a position that sees truth as emerging from conflict, paradox, and the tension between opposing forces, that, indeed, finds stability in the wholehearted acceptance of contradiction:

> Irony is centric, the adamantine axis of the universe. At its poles are the illusions we call matter and spirit, day and night, pleasure and pain, beauty and ugliness. By it our enterprises are whirled away from our most resolved intentions. . . . Irony is the enigma within the enigma, the open secret, the only answer vouchsafed the eternal riddle.

> Irony is not a creed. The makers of creeds have always miscalled, denied some part of the world. Irony affirms and delights in the whole. Consciously, it is the deep complacence which contemplates with unalloyed satisfaction Love and Hate, the tiger and the nightingale, the horse and the blow-fly, Messalina and Galahad, the village natural and Napoleon. Unconsciously, it is the soul of the Universe.

Though openly formulated only at a relatively late stage in the poet's career this position is, as we have seen, clearly adumbrated in much of his earliest work; opposition to 'creeds', an important – one might say the most important – aspect of Davidsonian irony is certainly implied in his attitudes towards love, nature, and the 'natural man', all of which imply a view of reality as diverse yet unified. The 'ironic' approach is, indeed, discernible throughout the poet's pre-materialist phase, even as far back as the 1870s and '80s: what, for instance, are poems like 'The Male Coquette' and 'The Rev. E. Kirk' but 'statements', as Davidson would put it, uncritical, dispassionate, of the characters almost as natural phenomena? The clearest example, however, of the existence in embryo of the ironic method in the poet's Scottish period is *Diabolus Amans* – Davidson's 'spasmodic' drama – which airs a veritable plethora of attitudes towards God and the world, mediated by the positives of love, nature and the hero, ending, as J. B. Townsend remarks, 'in a convenient compromise: Love . . . supersedes all faiths and resolves all differences'.[1]

It is to the work of the early 'nineties that we must look for the clearest statements of the position that Davidson was later to describe as 'ironic' – to 'St Valentine's Eve', for example, where pain and pleasure, love and hate, are seen as complementary, or to the anti-dogmatic 'Ballad in Blank Verse':

[1] J. Benjamin Townsend, *John Davidson: Poet of Armageddon*, New Haven, 1961, p. 98.

No creed for me! I am a man apart:
A mouthpiece for the creeds of all the world;
A soulless life that angels may possess
Or demons haunt, wherein the foulest things
May loll at ease behind the loveliest;
A martyr for all mundane moods to tear;
The slave of every passion; and the slave
Of heat and cold, of darkness and of light;
A trembling lyre for every wind to sound.
I am a man set by to overhear
The inner harmony, the very tune
Of Nature's heart . . .
                                        Within my heart
I'll gather all the universe, and sing
As sweetly as the spheres; and I shall be
The first of men to understand himself. . . .

It is his intuition of an 'ironic' universe that is largely responsible for the puzzlingly varied quality of Davidson's poetry, its incongruity and apparent caprice. To a mind which accepts the validity of all experience, all modes of thought, and regards truth as 'liker a diamond than a proposition: a brilliant, every facet and edge of which lightens with veracity', the contrast between, say, 'Coming' and 'The Hymn of Abdul Hamid' will not appear so incongruous. Hence, in Davidson's work we find what seems to be social criticism jostling the most blatantly élitist propaganda; seemingly sympathetic pictures of the underdog (as in 'A Northern Suburb') lie alongside poems, like 'The Aristocrat', which imply that strength is the only virtue; simple nature-poetry contrasts with the brash celebration of a steam-engine or city-life – poems which may themselves be followed by bleak pictures of slums or polluted rivers.

This 'ironic' trend of thought is evident not only in the subject-matter of Davidson's verse but also in his style. A very noticeable feature of his diction, the rapid juxtaposition of grave and comic, colloquial and artificial, prosaic and lyrical elements is, in part, intended as a linguistic embodiment of the poet's 'ironic' view of things and designed to communicate an impression of both multiplicity and inclusiveness. This is especially apparent in the eclogues – the first twenty lines of 'Michaelmas' is a good example – but is also a prominent feature of his later verse. The example of Carlyle again seems to lurk in the background, and, as in Carlyle's style, the effect of these incongruities of diction, though frequently not ineffective, often seems merely mannered.

In some of his imagery, also, Davidson attempts to embody, rather more successfully, that 'irony which is the soul of things'. One of the better-known passages from the poet's work, the evocation of Greenock and the Firth of Clyde at the opening of 'A Ballad in Blank Verse', exploits a strain of imagery which not only underpins the vigorous mood of the passage but also supplies a new dimension of meaning. Basically, the metaphoric texture of the lines conflates or intermingles town and country: natural scenery is described in terms of man-made commodities, particularly textiles – the firth is 'foam-embroidered', shores 'fringe the velvet tides', and so on; while the actual products of human industry are described in terms of animals or plants – ships have 'pinions' or, alternatively, 'iron limbs', the town is likened to a bird, factory chimneys are 'stalks', and the dead-metaphor in 'cranes' is brought to life. Similarly villages, hills and the seasons are described in human terms – among the latter, indeed, there are some very obvious town birds.

Finally, Davidson's use of form frequently mirrors his concept of 'irony'. This is apparent above all in the eclogues, where the dialogue – a favourite technique of Davidson's in his prose as well as his verse – enables him to present a wide variety of different opinions and aspects of a subject, to conflict with or complement each other, and occasionally to merge into a higher, more inclusive unity. The poet creates, in the talk of the individual journalists, each with clearly defined personality and opinions, a clash of character and idea; while, at the most superficial level, the incongruity of the implied identification of Fleet Street journalists with Arcadian shepherds must have appealed to him. The form of the eclogues is an emblem of the contrasting, multitudinous variety that Davidson found in the world and in his own mind – we might, indeed, apply to these poems Davidson's own observation on the main characters in *The Theatrocrat*: that they 'are made essentially out of the good and evil in myself'.

The Davidsonian concept of irony does bear a certain resemblance to the prevailing Paterianism of the 'eighties and early 'nineties: we might compare the Scot's advice to the artist 'to be open to all influences, to encounter the full stress of life' with Pater's dictum that we should be 'forever testing new opinions and courting new impressions, never acquiescing in a facile orthodoxy',[1] while the important passage in 'A Ballad in Blank Verse' where the protagonist adopts an 'ironic' standpoint echoes one of Oscar Wilde's early poems. However, Davidson's position owes more to the earlier Romantics; Goethe in particular, with his drive to unite apparent opposites, his acceptance of the mutual dependence of good and evil, truth and error, seems to lie behind many of Davidson's attitudes, although similar tendencies are present in much Romantic thought.

This mixture, or coming together, of old and new elements is a characteristic of Davidson's work. The importance in his early thought of what were, essentially, Romantic commonplaces has already been pointed out, but, on the other hand, his verse, from the 'eighties onward, has a place in the history of the opening up of new areas of subject-matter for poetry – townscape and the less savoury aspects of city life, the music-hall, the machine, the depiction of exotic or unbalanced states of consciousness, and a greater freedom in the treatment of sex.

A similar mixture of old and new elements is discernible in the poet's style. Though Davidson had a rather low opinion of the personal qualities of his Rhymers' Club colleagues their practice left an obvious mark on his verse in stylistic traits which it never entirely lost. This is most obvious in the poet's language and imagery, where a tendency towards artificiality, exoticism, and quirkiness – not, perhaps, surprising in a writer who, in his earliest years, believed 'Dictionaries, encyclopedias, &c.,' to be 'the proper source of a poet's vocabulary' – comes to full flower in the 'nineties. Davidson's verse abounds in the applied, artificial language beloved by the poets of the 'decadence'; Wilde, in particular, seems to lie behind the Scot's fondness for diction and imagery borrowed from the painter, the coutourier and the jeweller. Words like 'scrolled', 'embossed', 'lacquered', and 'diapered' constantly reappear, as do images derived from cloth or clothing, tapestry and embroidery. The macabre, *outré* imagery which the poets of the *fin de siècle* borrowed from Baudelaire and the Symbolists in their bizarre search for beauty in the unclean and unsavoury, an 'impressionist' fascination with effects of light – the 'perfect, only source of beauty' – a liking for synaesthetic effects, all are well represented in Davidson's work.

Yet Davidson, though associated with the Rhymers at an important stage in his career, was never really of them; there is always an 'apartness' about the Scot's work, despite the many 'decadent' trappings. He is, for example, while using most

Walter Pater, *The Renaissance*, London, 1912, p. 250.

of the lyric forms favoured by other 'nineties poets, much less obviously concerned with the kind of formal perfection desired by his Rhymers' Club acquaintances; by the same token, the kinds of verse most associated with Davidson's name, the eclogue and the tendentious ballad, though having a lyrical dimension are alien to the 'aesthetic' spirit, being adulterated by dramatic and narrative 'impurities'. Again, particularly in the latter form, Davidson's didactic purpose places his work apart from the protagonists of 'art for art's sake': even 'A Ballad of a Nun', regarded for a time as almost the archetypal 'decadent' poem, is, in its polemic against 'the bidding of priests and the behest of puritans',[1] more representative of Grant Allen's morally and socially committed 'New Hedonism' than that of Oscar Wilde.

The ballads, also, are a neat example of the backward-looking aspect of Davidson's work, ultimately deriving, as they seem to do, from Scott: not merely the Scott of the *Minstrelsy of the Scottish Border*, or, indeed, of the Scottish ballad imitations, but the Scott who was one of the first translators of the German Romantic poets. It is no great distance from Scott's 'William and Helen' – an 'imitation' of G. A. Bürger's 'Lenore' – to 'Alice' or 'The Queen of Thule', and from thence to 'A Ballad of Tannhäuser' or 'A Ballad of Euthanasia' (itself, perhaps, an ironic imitation of Bürger's ballad). Romantic echoes abound in Davidson's verse; Shelley, for example, seems to be the source not only of the 'procession' device used in 'A Ballad of the Exodus from Houndsditch' and, later, *The Testament of a Prime Minister*, but also of some of Davidson's favourite images and motifs – larks, clouds, fire. Later generations of Romantics have also left their mark on Davidson's verse. As J. B. Townsend remarks, a Pre-Raphaelite aura hangs about 'The Ordeal', an influence also apparent in the decorative medievalism that makes sporadic appearances in some of the lesser lyrics.

To some extent this peculiarity, this somewhat old-fashioned quality, may be ascribed to his early background. In 1878 he explains to Swinburne that the cultural isolation of his youth, the 'murky atmosphere' of Greenock, has prevented that poet's verse from having reached him in time to influence his own work. Certainly there can be little doubt that a Greenock minister's household would be isolated from the latest trends in art and literature; indeed, we have already seen that the young poet's reading, at this formative period in his life, was limited to a fairly restricted field. Paradoxically, however, this early isolation was probably responsible, in part, for Davidson's later surprising flashes of modernity. When he eventually found himself at liberty to satisfy fully his taste for books he developed a voracious appetite for reading and became – again, it would seem, due to his early enforced parochialism – rather indiscriminately enthusiastic over anything new; as Le Gallienne remarks:

> His temperament is one that will always, I think, respond sensitively to the last change in the intellectual and spiritual atmosphere; and his art may suffer for this characteristic to the end.[2]

Though deeper reasons will be suggested, it is not unlikely that it was partly due to this sensitivity to the latest trends that a gradual change in tone is noticeable in Davidson's work of the later 'nineties; from, roughly, the first appearance of 'St George's Day' the poet displays an increasing interest in the 'Imperial theme', his lyric rhythms become more insistent, and his advocacy of the physical life and the 'strong man' is more emphatic. This change in tone seems to reflect, to some extent, the shift in public taste towards the poets of the 'counter-decadence'

---

[1] Grant Allen, 'The New Hedonism', *Fortnightly Review*, March 1894, p. 384.
[2] Le Gallienne, *Retrospective Reviews*, London, 1896, II, p. 244.

– the group of poets who, in contrast with the group around Wilde and Arthur Symons, attempted to produce 'popular' verse of a politically conservative nature which beat the drum of Empire and lauded the 'manly' virtues of self-reliance, physical activity, loyalty to king and country, and acceptance of traditional norms of behaviour.

Most of the verse produced by this school – poets like Austin, Watson, Newbolt and Noyes – is quite as meretricious in its own way as the worst 'decadent' poetry, seldom rising above empty rhetoric, compounded of sentimental clichés about a non-existent 'Old England' and brassy, rabble-rousing doggerel. This side of Davidson's work comes to the fore in the first decade of the present century – in, for example, the execrable 'Song for the Twenty-Fourth of May', where the mindless jingle of the rhythm is, in its total insensitivity, perhaps the most appropriate medium for sentiments so grossly out of touch with reality. On the other hand, of course, such criticism must always be balanced by a recognition of the fact that this is Davidson at his worst, and that he could also produce poems like 'War-Song' which uncompromisingly reject the sentimental, religiose attitude to 'holy war' shared by most of the 'patriot' poets. In this latter piece the conclusion is that though war is inevitable, necessary, even 'right' – views typical of the 'counter-decadence' – we must have no illusions as to its horror, and reject those who would invest it with romantic glamour or a spurious religious aura. It is clear that, in 'War-Song', Davidson, again in sharp contrast with the Newbolts and Austins, has made a genuine attempt to come to grips with the 'savage antinomies' of existence and reached his ugly conclusion only after much conflict – a conflict reflected in the harsh power of the poem, the wholly appropriate staccato quality of its short lines, and its disciplined alliteration.

At its best, however, in the work of Henley and Kipling, the poetry of the 'counter-decadence' is by no means contemptible. Henley, indeed, who resembles Davidson in being too individual and gifted a writer to fit easily into a pre-arranged pattern, was a genuine metrical and linguistic innovator whose originality of form and language, springing from that exuberance which places him at the head of the robust 'counter-decadence', is shared by the Scottish poet. Though, despite appearances, the verse of the Prologue to 'In a Music-Hall' cannot have been influenced by the unrhymed stanza-forms of In Hospital, the very free stanza-forms of London Voluntaries, many of the Rhymes and Rhythms, and some of the hospital poems may have helped Davidson towards the rhythmic freedom of his later blank verse, or the metrical flexibility of poems like 'In the Isle of Dogs', 'Yuletide' and 'Apple Trees'. The language, also, of a poem like the 'Praeludium' to Henley's Hawthorn and Lavender is strongly reminiscent of Davidson's in its rich musical and synaesthetic imagery.

There is less resemblance between Davidson's verse and that of Kipling. Some of the former's more jingoistic verse may owe something to Kipling's characteristic rhythms, but the only real influence that can be detected is in 'Thirty Bob a Week' which, while using a Kiplingesque rhythm and exploiting his discovery of lower-class talk, deploys these elements in a manner much more flexible and restrained than that of Kipling himself.

Like 'War-Song', 'Thirty Bob a Week', in its not wholly successful attempt to incorporate metaphysical argument into a Kiplingesque framework, highlights the crucial differences between Davidson and the poets of the right-wing establishment. Intolerant of half-truth and opposed to all the ideological fabrications which he believed men use to hide from reality, Davidson took the assumptions underlying the sentimental conservatism and imperialism of the Right to their logical, ugly conclusion; what, asks the Empire-Builder, is he but 'tenfold a criminal' – 'No other name for Hastings, Clive, and me!' Behind this lies the relative depth of thought which ultimately separates Davidson from both of the main poetic schools of the time; he is, in fact, something decidedly old-fashioned in an age dominated, on the one hand, by the short 'impressionistic' lyric, and, on the other, by the portentous but essentially mindless 'patriotic' poem – a philosophical poet in the mould of Wordsworth and Shelley.

Though this 'philosophic' tendency, always strong in Davidson's writing from the plays of the 'eighties onwards, comes to its full flower with his development, early in the new century, of an all-embracing materialism, a more urgent inquiry into fundamental questions of existence and belief characterises his work of the later 'nineties. It must be remembered that Davidson was, at this time, going through something of a physical and mental crisis culminating in what appears to have been a complete breakdown. Lack of money, poor health, declining popularity, the strain of keeping two families, and the spiritual effect of his brother's madness, all combined to push the poet to the limits of his physical and mental endurance, to drive him back into himself, giving him a grudge against the world and building up a reservoir of frustration which eventually overflowed in harsh vituperation and the glorification of violence. The 'man apart' became 'the man forbid'.

It is hardly surprising that such a mood should force the poet into a deeper awareness of the 'cat-call of the universe' and compel him to formulate new answers to the questions 'what?' and 'why?' Out of his period of isolation at Shoreham, during which time he seems to have read deeply in philosophy, especially Nietzsche, Schopenhauer and possibly Ernst Haeckel, emerged Davidson's final, extreme version of the 'irony' which, though unformulated, had been present in his work since *Fleet Street Eclogues* – 'extreme' in the sense that the contradictions inherent in the universe are polarised to a greater extent, the dichotomy is more savage. This is particularly clear in 'Epilogue to Fleet Street Eclogues' where the existence of the 'Vale of Hinnom', Davidson's image for the mass of cast-off, diseased, poverty-stricken, failed 'human refuse', is accepted as a necessary counterpart to the strength and beauty of the world, a reflection of the universal order.

Nevertheless, it is clear that the poet was only temporarily satisfied with this position, or, at least, was still attempting to incorporate it in a wider, more totally unifying concept. Again 'Epilogue to Fleet Street Eclogues' hints at the final, materialist solution:

> We are fire,
> Cut off and cooled a while: and shall return,
> The earth and all thereon that live and die,
> To be again candescent in the sun,
> Or in the sun's intenser, purer source.
> What matters Hinnom for an hour or two?

Explicit adumbrations of Davidson's later, materialist position can, of course, be found as far back as the early and mid 'nineties in such poems as 'The Vengance of the Duchess' and 'Lammas'; but the poet's work of the period is full of frequently contradictory ideas which, though they obviously had caught his interest, were not necessarily accepted by him as true; indeed, his role of 'ironist' demanded this. Even in his first overtly materialist poem, *The Testament of a Vivisector*, he attempts to maintain this uncommitted façade, only admitting as late as 1903 that the materialist views expressed in the *Testaments* were his own.

It is probably fair to say, however, that the germ of some kind of materialist system was inherent in Davidson's work from very early in his career. The general tendency of his views on man and nature towards a monistic synthesis of spirit and substance is obvious, while, like Goethe who, 'because of the objective and sensuous character of his imagination',[1] was also unable to accept a transcendentalist world-system and attempted his own synthesis of mind and matter, Davidson's intense apprehension of the physical world, his almost visceral response to nature, made it altogether likely that his ideas should evolve towards a vitalistic monism of substance. There is also, of course, the early contact with, and interest in, the world of science – an interest which must have deepened under the influence of Grant Allen, himself a scientific journalist of some note. At any rate, after its long gestation period Davidson's materialism quickly reached adulthood: born in *The Testament of a Vivisector* it is in all essentials complete with the appearance of *The Testament of a Prime Minister* – a poem begun in 1902 and completed by mid-1903. Although *The Theatrocrat*, the Mammon plays and *The Testament of John Davidson* state the doctrine in fuller terms, adding minor refinements,[2] it is safe to say that with the *Prime Minister* Davidsonian materialism attained maturity.

Just as the foundations of his thought are constructed from not uncommon Romantic ideas, so the materialist edifice he raised upon them is built largely of no less common scientific theories – commonplaces of nineteenth-century physics. Particularly important in the poet's scheme was the theory of the ether, the extremely attenuated, imponderable substance filling the whole of space, which seemed a necessary postulate if the wave theory of light were not to founder on the problem of 'action at a distance'. The nebular hypothesis of Kant and Laplace, which put forward the view that planets condensed from a disc-shaped cloud of gas rotating about a solar nucleus, was the other main element of the poet's system. Both concepts, ironically enough, were already in the process of being discarded at the time of their wholehearted acceptance by the Scottish poet.

In the beginning then, according to Davidson, nothing existed but the eternal ether which, imbued with unconscious will and passion, its own 'innate desire' for self-consciousness, evolved electricity. This 'first analysable form of Matter' immediately reacted with the ether itself to produce hydrogen out of which the other elements were built up in the incandescent nebulae now filling the universe. In turn the nebulae condensed into stars and star-systems on the planets of which certain elements, notably carbon, hydrogen, oxygen and nitrogen, 'sensitive' but as yet 'unconscious', by means of 'chemical selection' and the 'intense and hungry chemical affinities', the vehicles of the inherent will of matter, evolved into conscious life. Finally, in man, the 'primeval aim' of matter is realised, self-consciousness; not, however, by the Darwinian process of natural selection, but through the ceaseless experimentation of matter's unconscious will. As ponderable matter is continually evolving from the ether, so is it continually devolving back into its original state; systems collapse, stars collide, scattering and breaking down their elements to become the source of future stars and solar systems which, in turn, will repeat the process. Matter being indestructible, the process is never-ending.

Into this basic materialist framework Davidson incorporated most of his earlier beliefs and obsessions. His political views – imperialist and totalitarian – are given a materialist rationale in *The Testament of an Empire-Builder* and the 'Ode on the Coronation of Edward VII', while his views on poetry find a similar basis.[3] As we have already seen, Davidson's view of the hero requires little modification in the last decade, although the poet's insistence upon the necessity for pain

[1] J.W. Beach, *The Concept of Nature in Nineteenth Century English Poetry*, N.Y., 1956, p. 276.
[2] See Appendix B.   [3] See Appendix A.

develops in importance: it is at the extremes of passion that we are most acutely conscious of our material being. Pain, then, the 'medium of Matter's consciousness', and the sexual act are of equal importance in Davidson's later philosophy, the latter, indeed, being elevated to the status of a fundamental principle: it is seen as having its origin in the poles of the primeval lightning, creator of ponderable matter, and later as manifesting itself in the phenomenon of chemical affinity.

The principle of 'irony', of course, remains an important feature of Davidson's thought, under a new name, however – 'immorality':

> . . . . . there is no moral order of the Universe . . . everything is constantly changing and becoming and returning to its first condition in a perpetual round of evolution and devolution; and this eternal tide of Matter, this restless ebb and flow, I call immorality. . . . It may also be called by as many metaphysics as there are properties and qualities in Matter, and in Matter's accomplishment, man. . . . It is a profoundly satisfying thought that no serious pursuit of man, no cherished conception, however erroneous in itself, is ever based in error.

Perhaps the ether itself, 'omnisolvent, omnicontinent, omnipresent, and omnipotent', was finally identified in the poet's mind with 'worshipful irony', 'the adamantine axis . . . the soul of the universe' that 'affirms and delights in the whole':

> Steep irony in Chaos, and the universe will string itself about it like crystals on a thread . . . I perceive the universe as a golden bough of irony, flowering with suns and systems.

It was certainly the continuing power of his 'ironic' view that led Davidson to explain the Christian myths as, in part, the mistaken interpretation of primeval material memories. The ideas of Heaven and Hell rise out of subconscious memories, present in every atom, of, respectively, the peace and stasis of the ether and the terrific forces released in the nebula when ponderable matter was in the process of creation. The idea of God has a twofold origin in, again, primeval memories of ethereal peace, and partly in the stirrings of matter's unconscious will; while the notion of the Trinity is seen as deriving from a subconscious apprehension of the 'triple form of the Universe' – ether, matter and energy. Sin, or rather consciousness of sin, Davidson explains as a result of an exhaustion, usually temporary in normal individuals but endemic in 'worn out stock', of the 'Material forces of Matter in man'; this is essentially a rationalisation, in materialist terms, of the mood expressed by Ninian in 'Lammas'. To Davidson, this discharge of material power, in 'passion and imagination', is 'the categoric imperative'.

This, of course, is not the poet's only explanation for the fact of religious belief, but constant in his thought is the view that what are believed to be revelations of divinity are, in fact, the efforts of the imagination, the power by which we are able to apprehend ultimate reality, to body forth its most penetrating intuitions as to the nature of the universe. 'The religious mood', he tells us, 'is the highest mood of the imagination', and while there is truth in religious belief – as there is in all belief – it is symbolic truth; but man has failed to recognise the 'metaphoric' nature of these intuitions, erecting them into actual dogma, fixed articles of belief, creeds which have distorted his view of reality and which he has used to hide from himself the real nature of things, propagating a false worship of weakness. Much of the immense body of religious imagery in Davidson's work may be interpreted as an attempt to restore religion to its metaphoric status, just as the ballads and certain of his other works refurbish, often with an 'ironic' twist, traditional myths and legends.

The very commonness of the scientific ideas underlying Davidson's materialism makes it difficult, if not impossible, to ascribe the roots of his system to any particular source. Scientific journalism was almost as popular in the late nineteenth century as it is today, and we can assume that the poet had been devouring books of popular science since his Greenock days. Nevertheless, J. B. Townsend may be correct in putting forward William Kingdon Clifford's *Lectures and Essays* (1879) as an influence, though the work of the German 'monist' Ernst Haeckel – in particular his *History of Creation* (1883), *Monism* (1895) and *Riddle of the Universe* (1900) – possibly has a stronger claim. Sources, however, are relatively unimportant, since it will be evident that, though his system uses the materials and discoveries of modern science, Davidson's method is far removed from that of the scientist.

In reality his position has far less in common with the scientific rationalism of Clifford, Haeckel, Spencer and Huxley, than with the individualistic intuitionism of the Romantic philosophers; his monism of substance is essentially little different from a monism of spirit – the idealism, for instance, of such Romantic egoists as Fichte and Max Stirner. Instead, however, of rejecting science, as many other Romantic irrationalists did, he poured science itself into a Romantic mould. It is significant how frequently references to alchemy and alchemical concepts crop up in the poet's work – both well before and long after 1900; the source of some of Davidson's most characteristic imagery, it casts indirect light on the peculiar quality of the 'poetic scientism' he espoused: 'science is still a valley of dead bones till imagination breathes upon them'. Proof lies, not in precise presentation and careful argument, but in unconscious, intuitive assent; science is advanced, conviction achieved, by something approaching a 'leap of faith'.

Given, then, that Davidson's views belong only superficially to the rational, scientific, empirical tradition it should not be altogether surprising that the philosopher whose thought seems to loom largest behind many of the poet's ideas is the idealist Arthur Schopenhauer. Even in their differences the two are related, many of Davidson's ideas being straightforward inversions of the pessimistic philosophy: for Schopenhauer, for instance, freedom is attained only through the renunciation of will, while, according to Davidson, it lies in wholehearted *identification* with the will of the universe. Again, while matter is to the German the purely phenomenal objectification of will, to Davidson matter is 'the thing in itself', will being an inherent property of substance. Davidson, indeed, unwilling to let anything evade that desire for integration and inclusiveness which seems to have been the basic motivating force behind his thought, attempts to do for metaphysics in general what he had done for religion; an inveterate magpie with a habitually analogical turn of mind he incorporates all systems into his own:

I perceive the identity of Spinoza's God, Hegel's Absolute, Fichte's Transcendental Ego, Schopenhauer's Will to Live, and Nietzsche's Will to Power. These all embracing categories are titles which Man in his madness has conferred on Matter.

This characteristic way of thinking – which lies behind the development not only of Davidson's 'irony' but also of his concept of matter, the ultimate principle, capable of assuming innumerable forms, continually changing yet remaining essentially the same – is reflected in an important group of images which, while present in the work of Davidson's Scottish period, gradually increases in importance from the early 'nineties onward. Smelting and forging, moulding, distilling, dissolving, weaving, and the alchemical strain already mentioned are the main, though by no means the only, components of this group of images: elements diverse enough, but linked by a process common to them all – that of change or transformation, coupled with a sense of strenuous activity. Often, this notion of change involves less a sense of complete transformation than of the exploitation or realisation of certain inherent possibilities; thus, the process of smelting realises the potential inherent in crude ore, distilling produces an essence or concentrate of the original substance, while weaving, by a process of synthesis rather than analysis, has a similar effect of exploiting the potential of materials, this time in the creation of a new form which includes the old.

So much, then, for the main outlines of Davidson's ideas, and how these ideas relate to his poetic practice. What, however, of his position as poet and thinker? Certainly, if we wish to make any important claims for the poet we must concentrate our attention on the work of his materialist period. Despite the attractive qualities of the best of his atmospheric 'nineties lyrics, poems which at least equal in quality those of the most accomplished 'decadent' poets, Davidson's work of this period, like that of Symons, Wilde, Johnson and the rest of their circle, remains essentially minor. The same might be said of the poet's experiments in 'popular' verse, such as the early 'In a Music-Hall', 'Thirty Bob a Week', and 'To the Street Piano', which go no further than Kipling and Henley; while the ballads and eclogues, though interesting from the point of view of their formal procedures, are, in general, artistically unsatisfying. In the last ten years of his life, however, Davidson's work embodies two related developments which were not only highly individual and prophetic – much of the poet's earlier work had been all of that – but, it could be argued, give the poetry something approaching major status. These added factors are his incorporation into poetry of the discoveries of science and his development of a highly distinctive blank verse.

The occasional use of scientific language and ideas was, of course, nothing new in Davidson's work, nor was it a new departure in nineteenth-century poetry: both the Romantics – notably Shelley – and the Victorian poets had attempted to treat earlier aspects of scientific discovery in verse, while the admired Goethe had managed to combine poetic genius and a spirit of scientific inquiry, turning the results of his research into poetry; but Davidson, in his materialist phase, goes very much further than any poet of the period, or before, not only in his use of the esoteric language of chemistry, biology, geology and astro-physics, but in using specifically scientific concepts as the very basis of his world-view.

At times – perhaps too frequently in the 'Testaments and Tragedies' – this can lead to a mere piling up of undigested scientific terminology in verse at once clotted and undisciplined, the impression being that Davidson regards the poetry as somehow inherent in the words and ideas themselves and not in any rigorous selection and arrangement effected by the poet; that Davidson felt that the words themselves had only to be written down in order to have the same profound effect on the reader that they evidently had on the poet himself is clear from his remarks in several prose works. For this reason his scientific verse, though locally successful in the *Testaments* (possibly entirely successful only in the *Vivisector*), is more consistently at its best in poems that he would probably have regarded as mere 'interludes'. These are works that explore themes similar to those of the 'Testaments and Tragedies' but – unhampered by that missionary zeal in the delivery of his 'message' which, while generating its own obsessive power, tends to flaw more 'serious' poems – exploit a vein of humour or whimsy in a tone sometimes loosely conversational, sometimes deliberately artful. Such a poem is 'Snow', deceptively slight at first glance, yet embodying several of the poet's more important ideas in form and language admirably tailored to the subject. Moreover, the ideas – the presence of the life-principle in all matter, the ultimate importance of the will to self-fulfilment, the fundamental relationship of apparently disparate phenomena, good and evil, beauty and ugliness – are allowed to emerge from the subject without being unduly forced.

In admitting that much of the later work is less assured than the earlier lyrics we must remember, however, that not only was Davidson aiming much higher in his materialist period, the occasions when he hit the mark making the effort all the more worthwhile, but that he was breaking new ground. Clearly, he felt the frustration of having new things to say while lacking a fully mature medium in which to say them. As we have already seen, many of the distinctive stylistic features, both linguistic and structural, apparent in Davidson's work are the result of attempts to embody his 'ironic' vision in verse; the poet's later blank verse is a similar attempt to embody that final view of the universe which combines the 'ironic' position with scientific materialism. His aim was the development of a highly flexible form, capable of rapid modulation, varying in tone and rhythm to accommodate a wide range of moods and themes – capable, in effect, of embodying in its own variety the variety of life itself.

Davidson, of course, was no stranger to blank verse, dramatic and non-dramatic; by the early 'nineties he had achieved a mature style, owing most, perhaps, to that of Alexander Smith, and already remarkably flexible. Already, also, most notably in parts of the eclogue 'Lammas' and 'A Woman and her Son', the poet's verse had shown a tendency towards a less obviously 'poetic' movement, corresponding more closely to the rhythms of everyday speech. Davidson himself suggests an analogy which, though prompted by the character of the work of the 'nineties, is even more closely applicable to the later blank verse:

I use blank verse newly as Wagner did music. If you take a chromatic score of Wagner's and attempt to play it in common time in one key you will have a terrifying result. You can't sing-song my blank verse.

Though the comparison here is between the extreme chromaticism, the constant modulation, of post-*Tristan* harmony and the subtle gradations of tone and stress that Davidson regards as distinctive features of his blank verse, an even more apt analogy might be the development of the Wagnerian vocal line which broke down and remodelled the conventional operatic distinctions between aria, recitative, ensemble and so on, modulating evenly from passages of great lyrical intensity to fairly dry declamation, always retaining its fluidity and feeling of continuous progression. We might extend the analogy: the freedom and flexibility of Davidson's later blank verse is due not only to its rhythmic freedom, being as much a matter of syntax, tone, verbal colour; just as Wagner, by sacrificing some local formal cohesion, changed opera from a sequence of self-contained dramatic structures to a form in which music and drama were welded into a larger, ultimately symphonic unity, so Davidson, in the interests of flexibility, tends to eliminate from his blank verse what might be called the more 'operatic' features of the traditional form – the formal, periodic structuring of the verse paragraph.

Davidson's later blank verse owes much of its 'roughness' to its deliberate lack of this kind of balance and periodicity. Clauses and sentences are piled up without a break, or with naturally occurring breaks that show little concern with traditional care in the placing of caesurae; furthermore, the distortions and compressions of syntax make for a quirky, knotted quality that contradicts our traditional expectations. Elsewhere, the verse, again with the aim of creating a more flexible, discursive medium, tends to accommodate itself more and more to the emphasis and cadence of ordinary speech; the opening lines of 'The Thames Embankment', for example, though technically quite regular blank verse, are not immediately experienced by the reader as such. In this general context we might point to the possible influence of Browning as well as to Davidson's practice of transforming passages from his prose journalism into verse.[1]

The Scot's blank verse is probably at its best when he manages to combine these two developments, striking a balance between the informal and the mannered. In 'The Crystal Palace', for instance, the poet's finest individual achievement, much of the effect – particularly in the superb opening paragraph, described as 'free verse' by A. E. Rodway[2] but, in fact, basically blank verse – springs from the tension between colloquial and artificial elements.

Finally, we must not ignore Davidson's influence on later writers. T. S. Eliot, for one, has admitted to a 'debt' to the Scot,[3] though 'Thirty Bob a Week', the poem which Eliot singles out for specific mention as having 'a very important place in the development of my own poetic technique', seems rather an odd choice since its exploitation of colloquial diction goes little further than that of Kipling, while Davidson's vein of 'dingy urban' imagery comes to the fore rather more strongly in later work. Some of the later blank-verse, such as the opening lines of *The Testament of an Empire-Builder*, seems to foreshadow much more clearly the distinctive Eliotesque tone and movement. Again, 'The Crystal Palace', with its interesting exploitation of significant juxtaposition and allusion – we might note in particular the 'sculpture' passages and the underlying religious imagery with its distinct allusions to Dante – anticipates the mature techniques of both Eliot and Pound, while the similarity of its thematic preoccupations to much of the work of these writers will be obvious.

Pound was, of course, acquainted with Davidson, as was D. H. Lawrence who, indeed, had read and admired some of the Scot's work. Other commentators, Priscilla Thouless in particular,[4] have remarked on the similarity of many of Davidson's ideas to those of Lawrence; both, for example, regard sexuality as a fundamental principle of the universe, and share a belief in the ultimately physical nature of thought and feeling. Both, also, subscribe to a dynamic, power-based, highly individualistic ethic. It is most unlikely, of course, that the Scot exerted any influence on the younger writer, but the similarity between the thought of Davidson and Lawrence is nonetheless interesting in that it serves to highlight the former's importance as a link between the earlier Romantic period and our own century.

This important function of Davidson's thought also comes out in its relationship to that of Hugh MacDiarmid. Both seem to share the same drive towards inclusiveness: Davidson's concept of 'irony', which underlies his whole intellectual outlook and which has its roots in the first Romantic movement, is very similar to the younger Scot's pursuit of a complex unity through deliberate eclecticism and the conscious juxtaposition of extremes. Nor is the resemblance restricted to their thought: in certain respects their poetic development displays interesting parallels. In what might be called their maturity both moved from a predominantly lyrical strain towards a similar kind of discursive, philosophical, rather experimental, 'prosaic' verse, producing long poems in which ideas predominate and which employ a wide linguistic mixture ranging from colloquialism through technical vocabularies and esoteric jargon to high-flown rhetoric. The rather more

[1] A selection of the more interesting of these passages will be found in the Notes.

[2] A. E. Rodway, 'The Last Phase', *Pelican Guide to English Literature: From Dickens to Hardy*, ed. Boris Ford, Harmondsworth, 1968, p. 404.

[3] In his Preface to *John Davidson: A Selection of his Poems*, ed. Maurice Lindsay, London, 1961.

[4] In *Modern Poetic Drama*, Oxford, 1934.

tendentious point might be advanced that it is in this later development that the ultimate importance of both poets lies, though, of course, MacDiarmid's great stature as a lyric poet is assured.

The latter's debt to Davidson has not gone unacknowledged.[1] Characteristically, MacDiarmid has emphasised Davidson's importance as a poet of ideas, drawing attention, in particular, to the older poet's pioneering work in versifying the discoveries of modern science. He has also, however, underlined Davidson's tendency to 'depoeticise' poetry, and it is in this aspect of Davidson's style – his attempt to mirror in language the incongruities and irregularities, even the ugliness and crudity, of life itself – that his affinity with MacDiarmid is most apparent. Indeed, MacDiarmid's apt characterisation, in verse, of the peculiarities of his own style might, in its essentials, serve as a fitting comment on the work of Davidson himself:

> I write now in English and now in Scots
> To the despair of friends who plead
> For consistency; sometimes achieve the true lyric cry,
> Next but chopped-up prose; and write whiles
> In traditional forms, next in a mixture of styles.
> So divided against myself, they ask:
> How can I stand (or they understand) indeed?
>
> Fatal division in my thought they think
> Who forget that although the thrush
> Is more cheerful and constant, the lark
> More continuous and celestial, and, after all,
> The irritating cuckoo unique
> In singing a true musical interval,
> Yet the nightingale remains supreme,
> The nightingale whose thin high call
> And that deep throb,
> Which seem to come from different birds
> In different places, find an emotion
> And vibrate in the memory as the song
> Of no other bird – not even
> The love-note of the curlew –
> > > can do![2]

3

This edition prints all of Davidson's non-dramatic verse, including the self-contained lyrics from his many original plays and his translations. All the lyrics from Davidson's novels and stories have also been included. Several of the poems have been hitherto uncollected, and some appear in print for the first time.

Where variants exist the text adopted is that of the last version to have been seen by the poet, although, in the case of obvious misprints in the preferred text, readings from earlier versions of the poems are occasionally adopted. Variant readings are normally shown in the footnotes, except in the case of unusually extensive reworking of a particular passage where the textual note will be found with the explanatory notes and commentary at the end of the volume. Minor variations in spelling are not noted, and punctuation variants are noted only if

[1] In, for example, an essay appended to Lindsay's *Selection*.
[2] MacDiarmid, 'The Caledonian Antisyzygy', *Collected Poems*, N.Y., 1967, p. 477.

they seem definitely to alter the meaning of a passage. In the compilation of the textual notes all available versions – book, periodical and manuscript – have been consulted; however, it seems likely that many more of the poems exist in undis-covered periodical versions. Furthermore, I have been unable to locate the manuscripts of *Ballads and Songs* and *Second Series of Fleet Street Eclogues*, both of which are probably still in existence. Though *Fleet Street and Other Poems* was printed after Davidson's death and hence has no textual authority, variants from that volume have been noted since it is the only published version of this collection.

The poems have been divided into five sections within which the order is, as far as that may be ascertained, chronological. Though this does not necessarily indicate actual dates of composition poems are generally dated by their first periodical appearance, or, occasionally, by references to contemporary events and other internal evidence. Where no periodical date is available the poems are printed in the order in which they appear in the separate volumes, following the last accurately datable poem in that volume: for example, the undatable poems from *The Last Ballad* (98–107) are printed after 'The Aristocrat' for which a date, that of its periodical publication, is available. The only real difficulties arise in the case of the poems of *In a Music-Hall*, covering the years 1872–90. A letter of Davidson's tells us that only one of these poems (unspecified) dates from as early as 1872, that 'In a Music-Hall' was written in 1884, and that 'In Grub Street' dates from 1890; 'The Rev. Habakkuk McGruther' can probably be taken as dating from 1879, 'The Queen of Thule' appeared in a periodical, and local references seem to assign a few poems to Davidson's years at Crieff (1885–8). Apart from this meagre information the only guidelines are aesthetic; thus, the order of these poems in this edition must not be taken as other than tentative.

The explanatory notes and commentary, at the end of the volume, besides covering certain textual points such as individual problems of dating, clarify some of Davidson's more obscure terms, indicate cross-references from poem to poem, and identify the more important allusions and sources. References are given to all of the prose sources in the poet's journalism, from which he quarried a great many of his poems; a selection of the more interesting of these sources is quoted in full. Wherever possible Davidson's own comments on, and correspondence concerning, individual poems have been included.

The afterword to *Holiday and Other Poems* and the Dedication to *The Testament of John Davidson* are printed as Appendices. Not only are they the only major 'prefaces' appended by Davidson to any of his volumes of poetry, but they give, respectively, a résumé of some of his more individual views on poetry itself in relation to the materialist philosophy, and a concise statement of that philosophy in its final form.

I

LYRICS, BALLADS AND SHORTER POEMS

1. A SAIL

The boat was pearl, the mast was gold
  And fretted with diamond-stone;
The sail was blue, of the azure hue,
  And silk of the finest tone.

The gold gave forth a golden sheen,
  The diamonds like suns gleamed bright,
And the silken sail shone as it had been
  Woven of starry light,
And the glow of the pearl was like the glow
  Of the moon in a summer night.   10

Beyond the range of the elfin lights,
  Over all a midnight gloom
Fearfully hung like a darkness sent
  From the place of eternal doom;
But round the boat the sea shone fair,
  Fair as a sunny sky;
And the channels between the islets green
  Like rainbow strips did lie.

The isles were surely isles of the blest:
  Luxuriance hid the soil;   20
Each fairer than Eden seemed,
Each brighter than heaven beamed;
  And the beings who bore the moil
Were fairy creatures whose joyous features
  Seemed to know nothing of toil.

They brought us food, and they brought us wine
  From the Edens all around;
The food of the gods and their nectarous drink
  Were never more luscious found.

Among the trees, along the shores,
    And within the silken sail,
A nameless wind sweet-smelling blew
    A long, voluptuous wail.

The boat slid on like a sledge on ice;
    The lights they never grew dim;
The wind ever blew, and the fairy crew
    Had never a weary limb.

O softly, slowly, swingingly
    Along the serpentine sea!
Between the isles for miles on miles,
    And ever more merrily!

On purple cushions of taffeta
    With tassels of golden thread,
Beneath a canopy of silk
    My sweetheart laid her head;
And I scarce could tell where her bright hair fell,
    Which was the hair or the thread.

She lay in a robe of gossamer,
    So fine that her gentle limbs
Shone through the white, and gave it a tint
As delicate as e'er was lent
    To the rose-leaves' waxy rims;
And through her lashes her dark eyes shone
    Like diamonds upon the mast;
And her bosom was bare, and the charmëd air
Made a music in it with her flowing hair,
    And mine shook with a passionate blast.

2. THE SWING

We sat on the swing together;
    At the end of the orchard-close,
A hill with its budding heather
    Like a purple dome arose.

On the heavily-ivied chapel
    The sun for the windows sought;
In the shadows of pear-tree and apple
    The daisies were crowded and caught.

And this was her thirteenth summer,
    And I was as old as she; 10
But love is an early comer;
    He came to her and me.

O, silently, slowly swinging,
   Till a star peered half afraid,
And the chapel-bell was ringing,
   And the shadows were lost in shade!

3. BETROTHED

He: Betrothed to one who loves me dearly,
    Who is the most enskyëd lady
    In sight of every wild and staid eye,
  That knows her body's beauty merely,

  Yet is delight a dead thing to me;
    She whom I worshipped now I love not;
    I am worse than dead if death will move not
  To save me while it does undo me.

  And she is fairer, stronger, vaguer,
    Than any perfect, splendid statue   10
    That looks in neutral marble at you:
  She has no soul within to plague her.

  And she is sweeter than the portrait
    Of any tender, sweet Venetian,
    Painted in deathless tints by Titian;
  But she is dead – surely a sore trait!

  I looked; and lo, her wondrous beauty!
    I loved; and lo, she glowed with passion!
    I reached to heaven; she clung to fashion;
  She is its queen; I, slave to duty.   20

  She was still-born; death nursed her, fed her;
    She is a miracle that's common,
    A lovely, loveless, soulless woman:
  The world's sepulchral palace bred her.

  She loves me? Well, wants to be mated.
    Married? I must be married to her.
    She will not see what, were I truer
  She should be told, that I am sated

  With all her divers ways of pleasing;
    Yea, of her very beauty too, sick   30
    As one who tires of verse or music,
  And bound to keep my ache increasing.

She: He loved me once, but now he's feigning.
    I loved him not when most I thought it;
    But from his passing fire I caught it:
  Now like the moon's my fire is waning.

I would have one whose love would seize me,
Light me, inspire me, put life in me,
And from the mouldy dead world win me.
He loves me not; he shall release me!   40

4. 'MAKE ME A RHYME TO STARLIGHT'

Your eyebrows are indistinct,
　But your eyes are the kindliest gray;
　　They are wells of fire and dew,
　The marriage of April and May,
Laughter and tears interlinked.

　Your brow is lowly and true;
　Your hair is dusky and gold;
Your lips are curved and red,
　And soft and warm, and they fold
　　A flock of the pearliest hue.   10

When passion had made you its bed –
　A flame waking up in a lamp –
　　Through the mist of the world like a far light,
　You beaconed me forth from the damp,
Dark life, where I lay as one dead.

　Of all heavenly creatures that are bright,
　Your spirit's the noblest and purest;
And your voice, which is love sublimed,
　Is the slowest to speak but the surest,
　　And as piercing and soft as the starlight;   20
And that last's the rhyme you wish rhymed.

5. DECEMBER

The heartless, sapless, dying year
　With icy fingers
Clutches the earth in mortal fear;
　And while life lingers

Within his veins that swelled with spring,
　And glowed with summer,
And now are poisoned by the sting
　Of that old-comer,

Who comes to all to end their days,
　Whom men call Death,   10
He breathes upon the earth's wan face
　His chilly breath,

If it may be to strike her dead
　For company;
To die alone he is afraid;
　And some there be

4

Of men and flowers as old and frail,
    With blood as sere,
And some both young and sweet, as pale
    As is the year,   20

Who will be buried in the snow
    With him to sleep;
Their souls come from and now must go
    To the unknown deep.

But those lives are dwelling still
    In lively frames
Are full of mirth, and take their fill
    Of works and games:

Make love, make wealth, gain fame, gain power,
    As if for ever,   30
Forget that life is but an hour,
    A sea-bound river,

And warm with sport laugh at the cold;
    Yet is it true
If they live long they will grow old –
    I mean not you;

Not you, nor me: we only know
    Our blood is fire
Can melt the longest winter's snow,
    And not expire.   40

6. FOR LOVERS

When in the morning I awaken first,
I find your head upon my shoulder laid,
Its clustered wealth of golden treasure burst
Forth of the band wherewith 'tis nightly stayed.
I hear the swallows twittering in their nest
In our wide-open, southern window hung,
And eke the lark, tired out with love and rest,
Shouting that song he has so often sung;
And many a lusty cock crows long and loud;
The languid, strolling breeze into our room   10
Flings stolen sweets from every flower and bud,
Easing his heavy burden of perfume.
Anon your eyes heave up their skyey lids
Welling with dawn; my raptured gazing bids
A blush auroral to your bright cheek speed,
A smile breaks forth, and it is day indeed.
    Then forth to spend the pleasant summer day
That holds such infinite, supreme delight,
It makes us blame the sun's most lengthened stay
In summer's noon, and curse the scowling night,   20

Even as we pouted at the early beams
That darkened dismally our loving dreams.
   Along the brown, crisp, withered woodland way
Bestrewn with greenest moss and maiden-hair,
That like an aisle's thick matting winding lay
Between the trees that pillar the blue air,
Hand clasped in hand and voice attuned to voice,
Chanting in borrowed words our own true love
With such divine, enraptured, Sapphic noise
As stills to listen blackbird, merle, and dove,   30
And with a tread heart-lightened to such ease
As would have added grace to Dian's bearing,
With eyes that lighten, locks free to the breeze,
Two waves of love, full-breasted, onward faring,
Through all the wood and swift across the lea
We hurry downward to the happy sea,
And cast ourselves on ocean's boundless stream,
Even as we have been flung into time's dream.
We lie and listen to the hissing waves,
Wherein our boat seems sharpening its keel,   40
Which on the sea's face all unthankful graves
An arrowed scratch as with a tool of steel.
We gaze right up into the simple blue,
We watch the wheeling, diving, sailing mew.
Oh then, we think if ever on our love
Vulture calamity shall flap his wing,
We will not wait until we have been hove
Half-eaten to despair, that wolfish thing;
But while our eyes are yet undimmed with tears,
And ere hope's ague has become quotidian,   50
We will forestall despair and blighting fears,
Sheltering in death our love's unstooped meridian:
For in our boat even at the sun's midnoon,
Like two discoverers we will straight embark,
And sail within his shadow, that bright boon,
A voyage parallel to his great arc,
And then in his red, western winding-sheet
Sink down with him to death's rest, deep and sweet.
   Then in our naked godhood hand in hand
Into the joyous element we spring: 60
So light we are, thereon we almost stand,
But the sea clings us like a living thing.
And you are lovely swimming in the sea,
And like a creature born and bred therein;
But never did a thing so fair and free
Inhabit there, nor ever shall, I ween.
I bear you on my back a little way;
For meed you sing an ocean melody,
So sweetly in the splendour of the day
That all the rippling waves move silently;   70
And round about the air intensely listens,
And from his pride an eagle stoops to hear,

The sun your face with all his wonder glistens
And earth stands still; eternity is near;
Amazëd eyes of fish through ocean's wrinkles
Peer out like scattered stars in noon of night;
Nor air, nor bird breathes note, no wavelet tinkles;
All Nature is death-still to hear aright.
   Enrobed again we set our sails for shore,
And having landed, in an arbour dine.   80
Then forth we bound – scarce half the day is o'er –
Our restless spirits more elate with wine.
We listen to the mowers' cheery song;
We laugh at clownish, soul-less labourers,
And shout upon the dead to come along
And leave their filthy shrouds and sepulchres.
Through narrow field-paths, threading close-ranked wheat,
And tasselled oats, and heavy-scented beans,
And beadsmen barley in obeisance meet
Sloping their cowlëd heads before the means   90
Of life in everything, the mighty sun;
Along rough roads where sweet wild roses blow
To-day in pomp, to-morrow dead and done;
Where in the ill-dug ditches cresses grow;
By hedges that have been unbarbered long;
Across a bridge the Romans built of yore
The river's banks buttressing, 'tis so strong,
With ancient ivy wholly mantled o'er,
We stray. You gather as we pass along
Wheat-ears, and barley-ears, and tinted vetches;   100
Wild rose-buds that the nightingale's sweet song
Ne'er listen to full-blown, for – beauteous wretches! –
The sun's kiss that the scent rapes from their breasts
And opes their blushing bosoms, kills them too;
Bride-bed of gnats, woodbine, that hedges vests;
Forget-me-nots, scarce as your eyes so blue;
A lone spring primrose waning now in June
As Hesper pales when onward comes the moon;
And little earnest daisies, single-eyed,
That worship heaven with faces glorified.   110
With fairy fingers than the flowers more fragrant
This spoil of fields you link into a chain;
On shaggy rocks with groping foot and vagrant,
I search for berries and a hatful gain.
With berries crushed we make ourselves shame-faced;
With berries pierced you string a grassy thread;
Then with your flower-wove chain I gird your waist,
And wreath your flower-outshining, golden head,
And on my knees fall down and worship Thee,
My berry-stained, flower-crownëd deity!   120
While from the very highest heaven of song,
And highest welkin-height a wing has measured,
Relays of larks their love-songs loud prolong
In surging notes that are in heaven treasured.

7

And then each quick descends from heaven's height;
His spirit swoons in such a high-pitched flight;
His serviceable wings, his tongue of fire,
His sun-enduring eyes wax faint and tire.
Where in the universe then must he wend?
Why, to that clime where languid poets use,   130
His mate's sweet bosom – she, his only muse,
As I to you my wearied spirit bend,
And drink deep draughts from those sweet fountains twin,
Your eyes, Castalia and Hippocrene.
    Within a pool, deep in a pebbly strand,
The purest of the diamonds that are strung
Upon the glen, a bracelet of the land,
We see the heavens as in a mirror hung.
Oh, then we wonder upon what great loom
The warp and woof of heaven's tent were wrought!   140
Who reared its poles and gave such spacious room,
Who hung its deathless lamps, their bright fire brought?
I wonder at your beauty's perfectness;
I wonder at the blueness of the sky;
I wonder at the sun's bright steadfastness;
I wonder at the breeze that wanders by;
I wonder at the larks constantly singing,
And at the proper motion of the stream;
I wonder at the still, green grass up-springing,
And what sweet wonder fills your sweet day-dream;   150
I hear the rolling music of the spheres,
Wondering, and wondering at the cloven dell;
I wonder at the floating gossameres;
I see creation is a miracle.
    We climb a hill, and there behold the sun
Sink down aglow with work serenely done.
And while we watch his orb fast disappearing,
Lo, from behind us like a sable sprite,
A lonely crow sails past, right sunward steering,
A seeming, silent pioneer of night;   160
Down the ravine a screaming curlew flies;
We are transfigured by the crimson skies.
    Night comes and brings its honey-laden hours;
The pillaging wind flies with its scented spoil
Up from the robbed and sweetly moaning flowers;
Your silk hair nets it in a golden toil;
Love's night recedes, and love's day nearer lowers;
Love is the world's life-blood, and you and I
Two pulses throbbing in one melody.
    Hark, from afar the corn-crake's mellowed call.   170
Hush, in the grove the nightingale is singing!
The stars throb fast as they to earth would fall,
In their inwoven spheres love's music ringing.
Subdued almost, our sense can hardly tell
The music from the odour; it perceives
A sweetly-scented tune, a sweet-toned smell;

8

Love mingles everything its soul receives.
Lo, you and I with God are all alone,
And you and I with Him will now be one.

7. A MAY MORNING

A distant cock crows loud and clear;
  The larks are singing loftily;
The cloudless sun his noon is near;
  A southern wind blows o'er the lea.

On every grass-green blade is hung
  The morning's diamond dewy order;
The shadows of the hills are flung
  Head-foremost o'er the river's border.

The river flows with stately ease;
  The high-heaved firmament of blue –   10
Does it reflect the azure seas,
  Or do the waters take its hue?

The dells are rich with primroses;
  The leas are white with snow of daisies;
And every streamlet's rim knows this –
  It soon will win love's dearest praises,

For ever the waves seem murmuring,
  'When are you coming, blue flowery skies?
When will you shine on us here while we sing,
  Sweetly shine with your sunny eyes?   20

'Are you lighting the fairies' gloomy grots,
  Delicate, fairy chandeliers?
Where are you shining, forget-me-nots?
  When are you coming to dry our tears?'

'Summer is coming,' the bee is humming,
  Humming with honey-sweet hum
That sweetens the air, for summer is coming –
  Coming! – the summer is come!

8. THE NAIAD

The Naiad sings within her well:
  'My waves are crystal clear;
My voice is like a tinkling bell;
  My banks are never sere.

'I comb my rippling locks of gold,
  And then with violets blue
I twine a wreath their braids to hold,
  Some fashion, quaint and new.

'Each little blue flower-universe
    That nestles in my hair,
Enskies a thousand dewy spheres;
    Each sphere, a rainbow fair.

'My grotto in the sweltering noon
    Is cool as tongue can tell;
I sing all day my naiad-rune,
    And tend my bubbling well.

'And when the sun at eventide
    Has loosed his fiery yoke,
I haste to dance in meads unspied
    With other fairy folk.'

9. THE TRIUMPH OF LOVE

'Love, your love – speak low –
    Now, give it now to me.
Your pride? Let it go, let it go.
    Your wealth? Let it sink in the sea.
Women like you should be poor;
    Gold upon beauty is vain:
Love, O lady, be sure
    Is loveless without some pain.
Let the triumph of love be seen;
    Come poor to me, poor, my queen.'

The lady rose at length,
    And looked to earth and sky;
She laughed in her loving strength,
    And flung her bracelets by;
She scattered her wealth abroad,
    She donned a homespun gown,
And said, as she took the road:
    'Now, sweetheart, we shall go down
Where poverty reigns as queen,
That the triumph of love may be seen.'

10. 'WHEN THE WAYS WITH MAY-FLOWER WHITEN'

'When the ways with May-flower whiten,
    And before the lilac blooms,
When the songs and feathers brighten
    In the forest's bridal rooms;
Though your beauty should forsake you,
    And your love itself decay,
I will come, my own, to take you,
    If I have to fight my way.'

So her heart at peace reposes
　　Till the winter-time shall go;　　　　　　　10
But the lilac and the roses,
　　And the fruit came, and the snow;
And the years came, and age took her;
　　All her beauty did decay;
For her lover false forsook her;
　　But her love shall last for aye.

11. IS LOVE WORTH LEARNING?

Is it worth the learning
　　This love they bless –
Pale lovers yearning
　　For happiness?
Why do they glory in the night?
What dream is theirs of proud delight?
　　Is it worth the learning?

My heart is burning;
　　It cries to me.
Is it worth the learning　　　　　　　　　10
　　What this may be?
Why do I walk alone all day?
'She is in love,' the maidens say.
　　Is love worth learning?

Was it worth the learning?
　　He kissed my hand!
Is love worth learning?
　　I understand,
Though love may come and love may go,
It is the only thing to know:
　　Love's worth the learning.　　　　　　　20

2 bless –) praise? IMH.　　4 happiness?) happy days, IMH.　　5 For happy
days and happier nights, IMH.　　6 For waking dreams of dear delights? IMH.
9 cries to) scorches IMH.

12. AYRSHIRE JOCK

I, John Auld, in my garret here,
　　In Sauchiehall Street, Glasgow, write,
Or scribble, for my writing-gear
　　Is sadly worn: a dirty white
　　My ink is watered to; and quite
Splay-footed is my pen – the handle
　　Bitten into a brush; my light,
Half of a ha'penny tallow-candle.

A little fire is in the grate,
   Between the dusty bars, all red –   10
All black above: the proper state
   To last until I go to bed.
   I have a night-cap on my head,
And one smokes in a tumbler by me:
   Since heart and brain are nearly dead,
Who would these comforters deny me?

Ghosts lurk about the glimmering room,
   And scarce-heard whispers hoarsely fall:
I fear no more the rustling gloom,
   Nor shadows moving on the wall;   20
   For I have met at church and stall,
In streets and road, in graveyards dreary,
   The quick and dead, and know them all:
Nor sight nor sound can make me eerie.

Midnight rang out an hour ago;
   Gone is the traffic in the street,
Or deadened by the cloak of snow
   The gallant north casts at the feet
   Of merry Christmas, as is meet;
With icicles the gutter bristles;   30
   The wind that blows now slack, now fleet,
In every muffled chimney whistles.

I'll draw the blind and shut – alas!
   No shutters here! . . . My waning sight
Sees through the naked windows pass
   A vision. Far within the night
   A rough-cast cottage, creamy white,
With drooping eaves that need no gutters,
   Flashes its bronze thatch in the light,
And flaps its old-style, sea-green shutters.   40

There I was born. . . . I'll turn my back;
   I would not see my boyhood's days:
When later scenes my memories track,
   Into the magic pane I'll gaze.
   Hillo! the genial film of haze
Is globed and streaming on my tumbler:
   It's getting cold; but this I'll praise,
Though I'm a universal grumbler.

Now, here's a health to rich and poor,
   To lords and to the common flock,   50
To priests, and prigs, and – to be sure! –
   Drink to yourself, old Ayrshire Jock;
   And here's to rhyme, my stock and rock;
And though you've played me many a plisky,
   And had me in the prisoners' dock,
Here's my respects t'ye, Scottish whisky!

That's good! To get this golden juice
    I starve myself and go threadbare.
What matter though my life be loose?
    Few know me now, and fewer care.   60
    Like many another lad from Ayr –
This is a fact, and all may know it –
    And many a Scotchman everywhere,
Whisky and Burns made me a poet.

Just as the penny dreadfuls make
    The 'prentice rob his master's till,
Ploughboys their honest work forsake,
    Inspired by Robert Burns. They swill
    Whisky like him, and rhyme; but still
Success attends on imitation   70
    Of faults alone : to drink a gill
Is easier than to stir a nation.

They drink, and write their senseless rhymes,
    Tagged echoes of the lad of Kyle,
In mongrel Scotch: didactic times
    In Englishing our Scottish style
    Have yet but scotched it: in a while
Our bonny dialects may fade hence:
    And who will dare to coin a smile
At those who grieve for their decadence?   80

These rhymesters end in scavenging,
    Or carrying coals, or breaking stones;
But I am of a stronger wing,
    And never racked my brains or bones.
    I rhymed in English, catching tones
From Shelley and his great successors;
    Then in reply to written groans,
There came kind letters from professors.

With these, and names of lords as well,
    My patrons, I brought out my book;   90
And – here's my secret – sold, and sell
    The same from door to door. I look
    My age; and yet, since I forsook
Ploughing for poetry, my income
    Comes from my book, by hook or crook;
So I have found the muses winsome.

That last rhyme's bad, the pun is worse;
    But still the fact remains the same;
My book puts money in my purse,
    Although it never brought me fame.   100
    I once desired to make a name,
But hawking daily an edition
    Of one's own poetry would tame
The very loftiest ambition.

13

Ah! here's my magic looking-glass!
　　Against the panes night visions throng.
Lo! there again I see it pass,
　　My boyhood! Ugh! The kettle's song
　　Is pleasanter, so I'll prolong
The night an hour yet. Soul and body!　　　　　110
　　There's surely nothing very wrong
In one more glass of whisky toddy!

13. THE REV. HABAKKUK McGRUTHER
OF CAPE WRATH, IN 1879

God save old Scotland! Such a cry
　　Comes raving north from Edinburgh.
It shakes the earth, and rends the sky,
　　It thrills and fills true hearts with sorrow.
'There's no such place, by God's good grace,
　　As smoky hell's dusk-flaming cavern?'
Ye fools, beware, or ye may share
　　The hottest brew of Satan's tavern.

Ye surely know that Scotland's fate
　　Controls the whole wide world's well-being;　　　10
And well ye know her godly state
　　Depends on faith in sin's hell-feeing.
And would ye then, false-hearted men,
　　From Scotland rape her dear damnation?
Take from her hell, then take as well
　　From space the law of gravitation.

A battle-cry for every session
　　In these wild-whirling, heaving last days:
'Discard for ever the Confession;
　　Abolish, if you choose, the Fast-days;　　　　20
Let Bible knowledge in school and college
　　No more be taught – we'll say, "All's well."
'Twill scarcely grieve us, if you but leave us
　　For Scotland's use, in Heaven's name, Hell.'

14. THOREAU

I tell you who mock my behaviour,
　　There is not a desert in space;
Each insect and moss is a saviour,
　　And Nature is one thing with Grace.

Who called me a hermit misprized me;
　　I never renounced a desire;
The thought of the world has disguised me,
　　And clad with a vapour my fire.

But soon in the night of my dying
    The pillar of cloud will be lit,   10
And the dark world, ashamed of its lying,
    Behold I am fairer than it.

'He is terrible; no one can love him;
    His virtue is bloodless and cold;
He thinks there is no soul above him;
    His birthright it was to be old.'

O scandalous worldling, self-centred,
    Can you love what you cannot descry
With a vision the light never entered?
    Is your conscience less dreadful than I?   20

Close-sucking the bone and the marrow
    Where life is the sweetest, I fed
Like an eagle, while you, like a sparrow,
    Hop, hunting the streets for your bread.

As freshly as at the beginning,
    The earth in green garments arrayed,
In the dance of the universe spinning,
    A pregnant, immaculate maid,

Looks up with her forehead of mountains,
    And shakes the pine-scent from her hair,   30
And laughs with the voice of her fountains,
    A pagan, as savage as fair.

15. THE VOICE

When it comes like a levin-brand
    You must not evade the voice;
Die manfully where you stand,
    But receive the shaft of its choice.

It is this that now blinds my soul's sight:
    We are motes in a ray of God's eye;
But he knows not we dance in his light,
    He is blind as the sun in the sky.

It is this that now slaughters my soul:
    We are not worth damning to hell,   10
Or rewarding with heaven. That's the whole
    Harsh word of the voice from the well.

What star shines there in the gloom?
    Who speaks? Is it God? Is it I?
Who shouts through the trumpet of doom?
    'It's a lie, it's a damnable lie!'

As I do live, these things I tell
    Are true and written with my hand. –
Like Lucifer from heaven I fell,
    And dropped at night in No Man's Land.
    My feet took root in shifting sand,
Whose grains were broken bones of men;
    But from that ghastly grinding strand
I writhed my body free again.

I came upon a grove of fir,
    And found a cone-ypaven street   10
Which led where scented juniper
    Did hedge an arbour warm and sweet,
    For goddesses' appointments meet.
There were old roses, autumn-proof,
    And violets sleeping at my feet,
And woven woodbine made the roof.

Sleep wound me in her purple zone,
    And laid me on a bed of moss
Like dark green taffeta that's sewn
    With golden lace of rusted gloss.   20
    No need had I to turn and toss:
I slumbered like a babe new-born;
    But knew the moon had struck across
My head when I awoke at morn.

I dipped my face among the dew;
    The rosy odours were my food;
I knelt where valley-lilies blew,
    And agates all the channel strewed,
    To drink with birds; I was endued
With power to understand their notes;   30
    They lauded love as lovers should,
With eager hearts and trembling throats.

As through the wood I took my way
    And flew along from tree to tree,
And cheered me with their roundelay;
    And I was glad as I could be.
    But when I heard the moaning sea,
And reached the forest's bourn, they fled,
    And left me on an upland lea,
An empty heaven overhead.   40

And straightway then I understood
    That it was evening; half an hour
Had seemed my journey through the wood,
    And yet a day had passed; the bower,
    The birds, the time were in the power
Of some enchantment, as I thought;

I wondered whose could be the dower
Of witchcraft that this thing had wrought.

Soon I was ware who wove the spell:
    There stood between me and the west   50
That burned with sunset, on the swell
    Of the high lea, a woman, dressed
    In crimson, with a golden vest;
A crescent crown, with jewels proud,
    Among her hair, half-loose, half-tressed,
Sat like a rainbow on a cloud.

Her head upon her shoulder hung,
    As she undid her hair; one arm
Was naked; to herself she sung:
    And that is how she works her charm   60
    On souls of men to do them harm.
I shook, and shrieking would have gone,
    But natheless all my soul's alarm,
With her bright eyes she drew me on.

Low, low she laughed and kissed my mouth,
    Then wrapped me in her golden hair.
She was a sorceress in sooth,
    And held me with a mother's care
    Close to her bosom pressed; and there
Her strong heart did the charm conclude,   70
    Entuning mine until it bare
A burden to her beating blood.

She took me to a curtained cave,
    Where lamps, like moonlight, white and still,
Shed perfumed lustre. The bright wave
    That furthest dares when great thoughts fill
    The ocean's heart of love, and spill
In swelling tides, stole up and laid
    One kiss upon the cavern's sill,
Then shrank away as if afraid.   80

At moments music, soft and rich,
    From hidden minstrels came in gusts;
Anon the rainbow-crested witch
    Sang piercing songs of loves and lusts;
    And once she spake: 'Behold where rusts
The armour of an elfin kinght!
    Behold! with thrice three deadly thrusts
I killed him: he defied my might.'

Night sank: the moon hung o'er the wave,
    But such a radiant flood was thrown   90
Across the waters from the cave,
    The moon was like a ghost – her own;

No palest star beside her shone;
And pageants through that bright sea-room
    Whose heaven-high walls were night, swept on
From gloom to glare, from glare to gloom.

I saw the ocean fairies float;
    And Venus and her island passed;
I saw Ulysses in his boat –
    His struggles bent the seasoned mast.   100
    I, too, prayed madly to be cast
Among the waves, when close in-shore
    The Syrens, singing, came at last;
But the witch wove her spell once more.

I saw a ship become a wrack;
    Charybdis laughed, and Scylla bayed;
Arion on the dolphin's back,
    By Nereids courted, sang and played;
    And Proteus like a phantom strayed;
Old Neptune passed with locks of white;   110
    When Dian came, the heavenly maid,
I saw the moon had vanished quite.

Then voices rose and trumpets rolled;
    And broidered, silken sails appeared,
And crowded decks, and masts of gold,
    And heavy, blazoned banners reared –
    The burning eye, the swarthy beard,
The glittering arms with gems inlaid,
    The starry swords the Paynim feared,
The glory of the first crusade.   120

Straight came a storm; from thunder-clouds
    The golden lightning streamed and flashed,
And fired the twisted, silken shrouds,
    And gilt the foam; the thunder crashed,
    And rain like arrows stung and lashed
The pallid knights, whose armour rang;
    Ship smote on straining ship and thrashed
The waves, and shrill the wild wind sang.

Then suddenly the sun arose,
    And from her cave she made me pack,   130
That wanton witch, with gibes and blows.
    I prayed her to be taken back
    And see more visions, when – alack! –
Fast rooted in the grinding strand
    I found myself, the human wrack,
The ghastly verge of No Man's Land.

Osiris, Apis, Isis, gods indeed!
   Their temples have been closed since I was crowned,
And still the sun and moon their journeys speed,
   And that fat, crescent-fronted bull has found
The goad stronger than god, if he be that.
   Now am I king, powerful as liberty
From counsel, law, religion, can estate
   The monarch of the mightiest monarchy
While life is mine: there is the filthy fly
That spoils my dainty dish – Cheops must die.   10

And shall I then inhabit bird or beast?
   I'd be a bird to live a life on high;
Of dew to drink, on luscious fruit to feast;
   Some splendid, noble bird – the Phoenix, I!
In Araby the blest my home shall be,
   Where balmy winds caress each spicy grove,
And dally sweetly with the smiling sea,
   Where all the elements are linked in love.

There shall be shining crest and beauteous neck
   Of purple feathers gemmed with golden ones,   20
My snow-white tail with here and there a fleck
   Like evening crimson, and my seeing suns
Flash on the blue of heaven when noon is bright,
And gleam a gorgeous spectre in the night,
The wonder of the world, the theme of seers,
For countless leases of a thousand years.

Methinks I'd sooner be a beast or bird
   Than enter once again a human frame;
For spirits are in human flesh interred
   Not wedded unto strength, or winged with flame: 30
And use and wont, fate's angels, have disposed
   Even of Cheops' life, though less than more:
But wherefore should there be on me imposed
   One subtle bond; wherefore should I deplore
A thought unproved, a wish ungratified,
Because of anything to be defied?
Why should I sympathise at all with men?
   The world and its inhabitants exist
For kings alone: to use my chattels then,
   Clogging humanity being thus dismissed.   40

The race of men hath issued none knows where,
   Even like a locust-cloud in harvest-time;
And when its pasture, earth, is nibbled bare,
   It shall fare homeward to some unknown clime.
The greater part of time to gain the less

Men spend in toil and sleep, two kinds of death,
And momentarily their lives possess
  In feeding, laughing, breeding; not in breath.
Each generation passes, living, dying,
  And thinks itself somewhat – yea, so much worth,   50
That the successive ages magnifying
  The individual life have seen far forth
To a mirage of immortality,
Imaged from life's lasting reality.

O foolish men who think yourselves so great,
  Ye are but fires that burn a little bout,
And being used to mould some toy by fate,
  Transmit your flames, then go for ever out.
Proud-blooded men, I'll teach you what ye are;
  I'll stop your spring-like health, and blast your flowers;   60
I'll set your petty happiness ajar;
  Ye shall no more have any happy hours:
I will be fate, and ye shall be my jests,
Things merely to fulfil all my behests.
Ye shall be lashed to work, and worked to death
  At labour neither beautiful nor good.
Useful, good, beautiful? – these words are breath,
  And all is vanity. Hold firm my mood,
And Egypt that believes itself so wise,
Shall bear the cost and sorely agonise,   70
To rear avowedly what now it makes
Unwittingly, huge nothing.
            ('Whereupon he planned a pyramid')

18. THE MAHDI

Islam is living! Follow me,
  God's champion against the world!
A new crusade time shall not see;
  But lo, our battle-flag unfurled!

The pestilence shall stalk about,
  And fleet-winged Azrael shrilly sing:
The heavens shall hang their meteors out
  And streams of blood in deserts spring.

Shetan's chief slave shall lead a host;
  And Gog and Magog issue forth: 10
A grisly smoke, hell's swartest boast,
  Shall coil about the stifled earth.

God's wrath burns like a desert when
  Harmattan blows: to quench its heat
From adamantine hearts of men
  Our scimitars a fount shall beat.

Our counsel shall be swift and wise;
    Our motion shall be mystery;
Death-shafts shall dart forth of our eyes
    From victory to victory.   20

Then shall the great Archangel blow
    The trump of doom, and at the sound
The shrivelled rivers cease to flow,
    And ocean's bed be naked ground.

A second blast; and like a light
    Blown by a wind the sun shall stream
And wither out; and in that night
    The heavens shall vanish as a dream.

A spectral silence, felt, unknown,
    Shall haunt the weltering chaos, till,   30
With bloodless cheeks, and trembling tone,
    Wet eyes, sad heart, and feeble will,

The angel faintly blow again:
    Yet Adam in his grave shall hear
The deepest dead shall rise amain;
    And Hell and Paradise appear.

The terrors of the dread abyss,
    The shrieking throngs by demons lashed
Over the brink with fiery hiss,
    We shall behold, awed, unabashed,   40

A moment. Then our happy feet
    Along the keen and star-bright thread,
Al-sirat's filmy bridge shall fleet;
    And sure shall be our feathery tread.

Mohammed beckons at the gate!
    Up, follow me in ways he trod!
The languid, green-robed houris wait!
    Hear, and obey the word of God.

19. IN A MUSIC-HALL

Prologue.

In Glasgow, in 'Eighty-four,
I worked as a junior clerk;
My masters I never could please,
But they tried me a while at the desk.

From ten in the morning till six
I wrote memorandums and things.
I indexed the letter-books too,
When the office-boy wasn't about.

21

And nothing could please me at night –
No novels, no poems, no plays,
Hardly the talk of my friends,
Hardly my hopes, my ambition.

I did as my desk-fellows did;
With a pipe and a tankard of beer,
In a music-hall, rancid and hot,
I lost my soul night after night.

It is better to lose one's soul,
Than never to stake it at all.

Some 'artists' I met at the bar,
And others elsewhere; and, behold,
Here are the six I knew well.

I. *Mary-Jane MacPherson.*

He thinks I'm a governess still,
    But I'm sure that he'll pardon my choice;
I make more, and rest when I'm ill,
    And it's only the sale of my voice.

I doubt it is sinful to dream;
    The World's the true God-head, I fear;
Its wealth, power, iniquity seem
    The mightiest Trinity here.

And this on a leaf of its book,
    Which is life, and is ne'er out of date,
Is the passage I see when I look
    As in Virgil for tidings of fate:

'You must each undergo a new birth;
    You must die to the spirit, and be
A child of the lord of the earth,
    Of our Saviour, Society.

'Get wisdom of worldly things,
    And with all your getting, get gold;
Beware of the tempter who sings
    Of other delights than are sold.

'But of all things a poor girl should shun,
    It is the despising of pelf;
And another as notable one
    Is the loving a lad like herself.

'Because while she dreams day and night
    Of love, and good fortune, and bliss,
Oppression, disgrace, and despite,
    Glad fiends that are never remiss.

'The world's evil angels of wrath
    Pursue him she loves with their rods,   30
Till he falls overcome in the path;
    For the World's the most jealous of gods.'

Then I read in my heart, and I see
    The heresy taught by my dear;
Before he was parted from me,
    He whispered it into my ear:

'I go to make money, my sweet;
    I'll join the gold-worshipping crew,
And soon bring the world to my feet,
    For I'll worship and labour for you.   40

'Your work is to dream, dearest heart,
    Of the happiest, happiest life.'
I whispered, 'I'll manage my part;
    I'll dream day and night I'm your wife.'

But that is so long, long ago,
    Such daily eternities since;
And dreaming is sinful, I know,
    And age all my poor darling wins.

Time patiently weaves from his sands
    My life, a miraculous rope: 50
I would sever the cord in his hands
    And die; but I hope, and I hope.

II. *Tom Jenks.*

A fur-collared coat and a stick and a ring,
    And a chimney-pot hat to the side – that's me!
I'm a music-hall singer that never could sing;
    I'm a sort of a fellow like that, do you see?

I go pretty high in my line, I believe,
    Which is comic, and commonplace, too, maybe.
I was once a job-lot, though, and didn't receive
    The lowest price paid in the biz., do you see?

For I never could get the right hang of the trade;
    So the managers wrote at my name, 'D.B.,'   10
In the guide-books they keep of our business and grade,
    Which means – you'll allow me – *damned bad*, do you see?

But a sort of a kind of a pluck that's mine
    Despised any place save the top of the tree.
I needed some rubbing before I could shine,
    Some grinding, and pruning, and that, do you see?

So I practised my entrance – a kind of half-moon,
    With a flourishing stride and a bow to a T,
And the bark and the yelp at the end of the tune,
    The principal things in my biz., do you see?   20

Oh, it's business that does it, and blow all the rest!
    The singers ain't in it alongside of me;
They trust to their voices, but I know what's best –
    Smart business, like clockwork and all, do you see?

I'm jolly, and sober, and fond of my wife;
    And she and the kids, they're as happy as me.
I was once in a draper's; but this kind of life
    Gives a fellow more time to himself, do you see?

III. *Lily Dale.*

She's thirty, this feminine cove,
    And she looks it at hand, you'll allow.
I was once on the streets. By Jove,
    I was handsomer then than now.

Thin lips? Oh, you bet! and deep lines.
    So I powder and paint as you see;
And that's belladonna that shines
    Where a dingier light ought to be.

But I'm plump, and my legs – do you doubt me? –
    You'll see when I go on the stage!   10
And there isn't a pad, sir, about me;
    I'm a proper good girl for my age!

I can't sing a bit, I can't shout;
    But I go through my songs with a birr;
And I always contrive to bring out
    The meaning that tickles you, sir.

They were written for me; they're the rage;
    They're the plainest, the wildest, the slyest;
For I find on the music-hall stage,
    That that kind of song goes the highest.   20

So I give it them hot, with a glance
    Like the crack of a whip – oh, it stings!
And a still, fiery smile, and a dance
    That indicates naughtiest things.

And I like it. It isn't the best:
    There are nurses, and nuns, and good wives;
But life's pretty much of a jest,
    And you can't very well lead two lives.

But sometimes wild eyes will grow tame,
    And a voice have a tone – ah, you men! –30
And a beard please me – oh, there's my name!
    Well? I take a week's holiday then.

IV. *Stanley Trafford.*

This of me may well be said –
    Of a host as well as me:
'He held himself as great; he made
    His genius his own protégé.'

I loved the beauteous star-veiled truth,
    I strove and failed, and strove again.
I wrote some verses in my youth,
    And knew two noted poets then.

Now I wear a tinsel dress,
    Now I strum a gilt guitar;
For I made my first success
    As 'The Sentimental Star.'

I could be more glad than most,
    I was born for happiness.
Since despair began to boast,
    No one ever tasted less.

The sun, the stars, the moon, the sea –
    I say no word of these – a sign,
A little good sufficed for me,
    A rose's scent made heaven mine.

But most some old thing newly thought
    By some fresh thinker pleased my sense,
And strong, sweet words with rapture wrought,
    And tempered with intelligence.

I craved not wealth, I craved not fame,
    Not even a home; but only time
To dream the willing dreams that came,
    And keep their record in a rhyme.

Wherefore I starved, and hither fell,
    A star in this the nether heaven.
Without, I shine; within, is hell.
    What might have been had I still striven,

Had I not sold my soul for bread!
    But what is this? I'm dull to-night;
My heart has quite seduced my head;
    I'm talking poetry outright.

Ha, ha! I'll sing my famous song,
   I feel I can recall its tone;
The boy's dream suits the gas-lit throng!
   Mark – 'Words and music all my own.'   40

And then, oh, then! Houp-la! Just so!
   Selene, Lily, Mary-Jane?
With which, I wonder, shall I go
   And drown it all in bad champagne?

V. *Selene Eden.*

My dearest lovers know me not;
   I hide my life and soul from sight;
I conquer all whose blood is hot;
   My mystery is my mail of might.

I had a troupe who danced with me:
   I veiled myself from head to foot;
My girls were nude as they dared be;
   They sang a chorus, I was mute.

But now I fill the widest stage
   Alone, unveiled, without a song;   10
And still with mystery I engage
   The aching senses of the throng.

A dark-blue vest with stars of gold,
   My only diamond in my hair,
An Indian scarf about me rolled:
   That is the dress I always wear.

And first the sensuous music whets
   The lustful crowd; the dim-lit room
Recalls delights, recalls regrets;
   And then I enter in the gloom.   20

I glide, I trip, I run, I spin,
   Lapped in the lime-light's aureole.
Hushed are the voices, hushed the din,
   I see men's eyes like glowing coal.

My loosened scarf in odours drenched
   Showers keener hints of sensual bliss;
The music swoons, the light is quenched,
   Into the dark I blow a kiss.

Then, like a long wave rolling home,
   The music gathers speed and sound;   30
I, dancing, am the music's foam,
   And wilder, fleeter, higher bound,

And fling my feet above my head;
   The light grows, none aside may glance;
Crimson and amber, green and red,
   In blinding baths of these I dance.

And soft, and sweet, and calm, my face
   Looks pure as unsunned chastity,
Even in the whirling triple pace:
   That is my conquering mystery.   40

VI. *Julian Aragon.*

Ha, ha, ha! ho, ho, ho! hee, hee, hique!
I'm the famous Californian Comique!
   I'm as supple as a willow,
   And as graceful as a billow,
I'm handsome, and I'm strong, and I've got cheek.

Cheek's nothing; no, by Jingo! I'm obscene!
My gestures, not my words, say what I mean
   And the simple and the good,
   They would hiss me if they could,
But I conquer all volition where I'm seen.   10

I twist, contort, distort, and rage and rustle;
I constrain my every limb and every muscle.
   I'm limber, I'm Antæan,
   I chant the devil's pæan,
I fill the stage with rich infernal bustle.

I spin, and whirl, and thunder on the board;
My heart is in my business, I'm encored;
   I'm as easy as a sprite,
   For I study day and night,
I dream, devise – I travail, by the lord!   20

'My nature's a perennial somersault,'
So you say, and so I think; but whose the fault?
   If I don't know good from evil,
   Is it wrong to be a devil?
You don't get lime-juice cordial out of malt.

But I'm plump, and soft, and strong, and tall, and sleek,
And I pocket twenty guineas every week;
   I journey up and down,
   I've sweethearts in each town,
I'm the famous Californian Comique.

Epilogue.

Under the earth are the dead,
Alive and asleep; overhead
Are the angels, asleep and dead.

Not even shadows are we,
But the visions these dreamers see.

These dreamers below and above –
The dream of their dreams is love.

But we never will count the cost;
As dreams go, lusty and stout,
We make us a heaven and hell.   10

There are six dreams I knew well;
When I had sung them out,
I recovered my soul that was lost.

20. THE MALE COQUETTE

I have a heart; pray, do not go,
    Sweet ladies, all and some.
It beats for you 'Plan-plan!' for, lo,
    'Tis hollow as a drum!

Behold my soft and softening eyes!
    The fading star of morn
Hangs not so sweetly in the skies:
    Why blaze yours then with scorn?

My tongue drops honey like a hive;
    My hands are soft and small.   10
What! I am only five feet five!
    Well, some are not so tall.

Look at the diamonds on my breast,
    My golden chain and locket,
My many suits, all of the best –
    And never mind my pocket.

Pathetic songs of love I sing,
    And you may have your choice:
I play; I flash my diamond ring;
    Falsetto is my voice.   20

I tread a higher walk of art
    Than he who plights his troth,
Then breaks it, and the maiden's heart:
    Such clumsy work I loathe.

A gold and silver mine for me
    Is every blooming maid;
With tongue and eye I work, and she
    Scarce feels the pick and spade.

28

To strike a tender, golden vein,
   And draw it from the eyes 30
In glowing glances; with a chain
   Of welded words and sighs

To raise a blush upon the face;
   Or with dynamic power
Explode the thought's most hidden place;
   And at the parting hour

To gain a little fluttering sigh:
   These are my art's high aims;
And in its practice I will die
   In spite of nasty names. 40

A male coquette? Well, be it so:
   The pig delights in dirt,
The poet in his verses' flow;
   And I was born to flirt.

21. THE REV. E. KIRK, B.D.

So here I have by happy chance
   A rambling tower of Babel,
A crow-stepped, roof-bent, rough-cast manse
   With fruit on every gable.

My glebe is fifty acres round,
   And there my corn is growing;
My poultry cluck with cosy sound;
   I hear my cattle lowing.

Above the plane-trees, gray and high
   My solid steeple rises; 10
It looms between me and the sky
   Like other earthly prizes.

But I have clear and without fail,
   Or trust in harvest's ripe end
For fiars' prices, on the nail,
   Five hundred pounds of stipend:

And naught to do, the truth to speak,
   Save sit and sip my toddy,
And write a sermon once a week,
   And bury anybody. 20

Some half-dozen marriages
   Come in the pairing season;
I visit sick folk if they please –
   Or anything in reason.

The world is here some ages late,
    And stagnant as a marish:
I thank my stars it is my fate
    To have a country parish;

For wearing done with constant use
    For me has no inducement,   30
And city charges play the deuce
    With all a man's amusement.

The sheep are few: somehow to God
    I'll answer how I fed mine . . .
And there's my gallant salmon-rod,
    And there my famous red-line.

With these last autumn on the Earn
    I killed the thirty-pounder
That seemed amid the lapping fern
    No glossier, nor rounder,   40

Than cased in glass it looks there – see,
    Beneath my gun and pipe-rack –
The gun the earl presented me,
    My seasoned pipes, a ripe stack.

My single life contents me yet;
    I have some oats to scatter:
A barmaid or a ballet-pet
    Is no such deadly matter,

When one is on the sunny side
    Of thirty and an athlete: 50
At thirty-five I'll take a bride,
    And make the narrow path meet,

As many a man has done before,
    The broad one: it will lead me
To live in health and see fourscore,
    And have my son succeed me.

22. KINNOULL HILL

We sat on the verge of the steep
    In a coign where the east wind failed.
In heaven's top, cradled, asleep,
The young sun basked, and deep
    Into space the universe sailed.

And eastward the cliff rose higher,
    And westward it sloped to the town,
That smoked like a smouldering fire
Built close about spire after spire;
    And the smoke was pale-blue and brown.   10

The smell of the turf and the pine
   Wound home to our heart's warm core;
And we knew by a secret sign
That earth is your mother and mine;
   And we loved each other the more.

And out of the rock, scarred and bare,
   The daws came crying in crowds,
And tossed themselves into the air,
And flew up and down, here and there,
   And cast flying shadows, like clouds.   20

We heard not the lark, but we heard
   The mellow, ineffable tune
Of a sweet-piping, wood-haunting bird.
Our heart-strings were stricken and stirred,
   And we two were happy that noon.

23. WINTER IN STRATHEARN

She crumbled the brown bread, she crumbled the white;
The snow lay deep, but the crumbs lay light:
The sparrows swept down like withered leaves;
The starlings sidled with scarlet greaves,
And burnished, black-green harness scrolled
With damaskings of dark old gold;
The gallant robin, he came not nigh,
But a tom-tit sparkled a frightened eye;
The blue blackbird with his saffron bill
Hopped with the crowd; and the finches sped   10
With their scarves of white and their vests of red
From the sea-green laurels; and out of the hill,
Where the steep Blue-rocks stood, stark and gray,
A jackdaw flew; and the carrion crow
Frightened them now and again away,
Swooping down on the bloodless prey
All in the powdery snow-white snow.
She crumbled the brown bread, she crumbled the white,
She fed them morning, noon, and night.
They fought and scolded till supper was done,   20
Then wing after wing went away with the sun.

The twinkling Earn, like a blade in the snow,
The low hills scalloped against the high,
The high hills leaping upon the low,
And the amber wine in the cup of the sky,
With the white world creaming over the rim,
She watched; and a keen aroma rose,
Embodied, a star above the snows;
For when the west sky-edge grows dim,
When lights are silver and shades are brown,   30
Behind Torlum the sun goes down;

And from Glenartney, night by night;
The full fair star of evening creeps;
Though spectral branches clasp it tight,
Like magic from their hold it leaps,
And reaches heaven at once. Her sight
Gathers the star, and in her eyes
She meekly wears heaven's fairest prize.

24. JOHN BALIOL AT STRATHCATHRO

A gorgeous flourish as of victory,
And Baliol entered, vested like a king,
Crowned, sceptred, almost looking like a king.
Before went portly mace-bearers; behind
His son came first, and then the Constable
Bearing the sword of state; and after him
A train of shamed and sullen ministers.
'What pageantry is this?' King Edward cried.
'Rather what mockery?' said Annandale.
But Baliol, heeding not, spake solemnly: 10
'My sovereign liege, high peers, and friends and foes,
I come to do my kingly obsequies.
A royal spirit did inflate my life
Which I mistook for an attendant sprite
With me incorporate when Norway's maid,
A wan, cold pearl, the hungry sea received
To glimmer in its unsearched treasure-house.
This genius first embraced me when a boy:
High manners of command among my mates
Seemed warnings of what fate was wooing me.   20
Our feudal households all are little courts;
But in the regiment and discipline
Of my retainers and my family
There did exist a true monarchial style
More perfect than the Scottish Court could boast.
Thus ever entertained I kingly state,
And loved it chastely, unexpectantly;
And when I was made king my heart was glad.
But oh! the tarnished and inglorious crown
Proved triple what are all kings' diadems,   30
A thorny torment, and no fortune-cap.
Lo! when I walked between two holy men
To be anointed in the holy place,
Even as an infant's first supported steps
Start in upon its journey to the tomb,
So then began with me this sorry end.
An infant has a king within itself,
Whose fleshy vesture as it wears, grows fair
To perfect manhood; thence sweet, mellowing age
Ripens it on to hoary majesty;   40
The which thrown off, forth steps the kingly soul,
The veiled informer of the graceful flesh.

But I, when I have doffed my kingly dress,
Disgraced and ugly shall be all-despised.'
King Edward here broke in on him, and said:
'An histrionic king! What say you, lords,
Shall he speak on, or go out sighing now?'
The Earl of Annandale took up the sneer:
'Nay, let him speak, while memory prompts his tongue:
I warrant it was practised in a glass!'   50
But Baliol like a stag at bay replied:
'Lord Annandale, your taunt is envy-bred.
Remember when you stand, as I stand now,
Which very well may chance, how I resigned
My majesty, and imitating me,
Worthily do a most unworthy deed.'
'The unworthiest deed was to accept a crown
Which was not yours.' But Edward cried: 'No more!
You come, Lord Baliol, to resign the crown,
The kingdom, your ill-government has wrecked.'   60
'The rocks I struck upon were English rocks
Alluring with false beacons. Macers, come,
Lay down these clubs; they have beat out my eyes.'
Then stepping forward to Lord Annandale,
'Proud Earl, this is the sceptre; scan it well.
It is of silver; lo! a lovely stalk
All barked about with gold. It blossoms, too,
Like Aaron's rod; look, there are fleurs-de-lis;
And here are thistles of rare workmanship;
And images of sacramental cups;   70
Medusa-heads that strike each other dead;
Hours could be spent in following this foliage
Winding and interwinding: see, three knobs
Divide the shaft: it is a candlestick,
And from its capital there rises out
A taper, clasped and held by imaged saints,
Ending and flaming in a crystal ball:
Alas! it only lit my own dark shame.
A kingly sceptre, a magician's wand,
Powerful and subtle! So I hoped: it made   80
A double ell of weakness in my hand:
It was my wife, but ne'er possessed by me;
So now I yield it wholly to that priest
Who made me cuckold as he married us.'
And slow at Edward's feet he laid it down.
Then taking off his crown the weary king
His sad apostrophes began again.
'The crown imperial, a splendid gem!
Thy weight shall never more oppress my brow.
I coveted thy gold-knit jewel-walls,   90
And for a day delighted me in thee
When thou becam'st the palace of my brain.
I scan thy triple rampire wonderingly;
Thy fair, broad base, so rich with varied stones.

33

Look at these slabs of oriental pearl,
These topazes, and amethysts and rubies,
And hyacinths, and emeralds, and garnets,
Shining like faces in their golden collars!
Look at them, lords! they gleam like very suns;
Your eyes like moons do borrow of their fire,   100
And flash it back, giving and taking light,
With all the wistful eagerness of love.
Sapphires and diamonds form the second storey,
And twenty golden turrets tipped with pearl:
In them too there's a syren witchery
Of singing, gentle sighing, snaring scent.
Fair crosses, flowered of pearls and diamond dust,
Build up the third cirque; and from it four arcs,
Curiously chased and figured, meet and close,
Enamelled blue and powdered o'er with stars,   110
Crowned with a cross. The walls are softly hung
With tire of purple velvet, diamond-laced.
Alas! my lords, this noble gorgeous dome
My head has found a blank immuring jail;
Its velvet tire like sackcloth flayed by brows,
And on its cross my soul was crucified.
Here, take the crown.' King Edward took it up
And put it on, saying: 'I will wear it too.'
Then Baliol, reaching out a trembling hand:
'Give me the sword. Shall I unsheathe it? There;   120
Five feet of steel panged full of angry fire,
And tempered to a mood most murderous.
Give it a bloody scabbard, shall I now,
Within your bosom, king? That were a deed!
I am no doer. Back into thy bed,
Thy dainty crimson-curtained resting-place,
A lair too lovely for so fierce a brute:
I lay it at your feet, not in your heart.'
King Edward girt him with the sword, and said:
'Thou art as sure a madman as a fool.'   130
'Madmen are sometimes simply overwise;
All men are fools, yea, very full of folly;
Folly is ignorance, and every soul
Can have a knowledge such a little share,
Omniscience sees a gross and foolish world;
The greatest fool is he who cannot know.
Adversity has taught me many things;
I am content to be a fool and mad.'
'That last was sensible: I like you now.'
He heeded not, but doffed his robe and said: 140
'Off, purple dress! I cast theee from me here
With hundredfold the joy I did thee on.
Methinks the martyr, tortured, wrenched, and broke,
From his torn mortal garb escapes at last
To find less ease than now my being feels.
The seal! the seal! Lord Chancellor, the seal!

So; now I sign my own enfranchisement:
The kingly slave is now a noble freeman;
Now I'll betake me to some decent life.'
Then up King Edward rose and took his turn.   150
'Tarry a little. Think you that our power
Defied and now triumphant will endure
To pass unpunished your rebellion?
This your submission is most politic,
But you must not depart hence unrebuked.
Sir William Ormesby, we commission you
To write a paper of this Earl's transgressions;
His weakness and his folly; his French league.
Set down therein that he acknowledges
The perfect justness of our present war;   160
And that he sorrows deeply for his crimes;
And begs not pardon, merciless to justice,
But humbly for such sentence as may please
Our injured and insulted sovereignty.
This shall he read armed with a snowy wand,
The mocking baton of black criminals,
Before our deputy and all the peers:
Which being finished, shall in part atone;
And for the rest, imprisonment of him
And of his son while it shall be our will.'   170
'Alas! I see submission, mild and meek,
Turning when one is struck the other cheek,
But rouses ire in heartless dignities,
Who batter mouth, brow, and beseeching eyes.
I gave up all, and having nothing, lo,
The nothing that I had is stolen so!'
Then soldiers led him and his son away,
While Annandale to Edward softly said:
'My liege, I think you promised me a crown;'
And got for answer, loud and mockingly,   180
'Good Earl, think you that we have nought to do
But conquer crowns, and hand them o'er to you?'

25. A WOOD IN AUTUMN

I wandered in a wood upon a day
    In ripe October, and the corn was reaped.
Beyond the mossy boles in fair array
    The builded sheaves appeared in sunlight steeped;
Their drooping ears no gentlest wind assailed;
    Each long, rough shadow reached the other's base;
On some dark stake they seemed to be impaled,
    Or strung like beads the sloping field to grace.
Behind them through the trees the reddening west,
    But faintly blushing yet, told to the world   10
The time was coming on it loves the best,
    When to its deeps the warm sun should be hurled.

All suddenly the silence of the wood,
    Then only by the insects' humming broken,
With wailing was fulfilled even as I stood.
    No motion made they as a warning token;
But each tall tree and bush that rooted there,
    Shook, to a breath of its own breathing trembling;
For each had found a tongue, and on the air,
    Without artistic flourish or dissembling,   20
But simply from its core sent forth a song,
    All in the burden joining tunefully,
Whenas the thorn with voice that echoed long,
    Had sung a verse of that sad melody.
The dark and secret pine beat time to them;
    The strong old oak took up a mighty bass;
The mountain-ash and beech with fluted stem
    Warbled the tenor; and the treble's place,
Besides the thorn, the gentle birch fulfilled;
    While all the saplings sang an alto strong,   30
Making such harmony I was well-willed
    To listen ever to that greenwood song.

I knew the meaning of the sounds they sang
    Then as I listened; but when they were done,
There did about my aching memory hang
    A sounding echo, all the meaning gone.
Whether they mourned their tarnished, ragged dress,
    Fast leaving them with bare, unsheltered backs,
Or for their long-lost Hamadryades,
    Or comrades fallen before the woodman's axe,   40
Or other still more lamentable thing,
    I know not; only this, I heard them sing.

26. ON A HILL-TOP

The airy larks ceased shouting in the lift
    With fearless voice pitched at the utmost height,
Attendants of the sun, the steadfast, swift,
    And mighty hunter of the thronging night,
What time a wanderer from a mountain-crest
Beheld the mist-hung, crimson-lighted west.

A hectic village – pleasure's summer daughter –
    A bay with boats, a frith most like a lake,
With ruby stain spilled on the hither water,
    And on the further, shade in mass and flake,   10
Between the mountain and the mountains lay
Unseen by him. His eye's enchanted ray

Burnished the sunset with a melting glance
    Of more ethereal fire, that leapt along
The serried summits like the golden lance
    The cloudy champion, thundering, flings among

The huddled, quaking hills. The west obeyed
The summons of his eye, and quick repaid

His gift of added splendour, opening wide
   The gate between the two eternities.   20
Forth issued first a streaming billowy tide
   Of dulcet music as of psalteries,
Crested with fierier sound; with it broke out
Flushes of throbbing colour like the shout

Of people newly freed, with trumpets, gongs,
   Drums, clarions – their hues so pulsed and lived;
From far within there floated gusts of songs
   Sung by sweet voices. Then his soul received
In that baptismal flood of resonant light
And luminous sound the gift of second-sight.   30

Dreams are the blossoms borne by rooted thought;
   And visions watched by mightiest seers have been
Bright shades of meditative fancies caught
   On some midnight's immaculate, black screen;
But he beheld his lady in the sky;
And all the heroes whom he loved passed by.

They issued shadowy from the glowing door,
   And swept like regal clouds with lofty gait,
Bending before her. On the azure floor
   Enthroned she sat in sweet and solemn state   40
Above both day and night, where time is heard
Singing soft snatches like a far-perched bird.

27. THOMAS THE RHYMER

Home from the wedding of the king
   The earl rode late and soon.
A wizard's strain sang in his brain;
   And in the afternoon
He met the wizard by the sea –
   Thomas of Ercildoune.

'And this,' said then the scornful earl,
   'This is your stormiest day!
The clouds that drift across the lift
   Are soft and silver-grey;   10
One sail, too near to be a bird,
   Glides o'er to Norroway.

'A blush is on the weather-gleam,
   The sun sinks low and lower;
The gloaming fills the cup he spills,
   The faint moon bending o'er
The sleepy waves, reluctant, poised,
   Drop peacefully ashore.'

The elfin lord of Ercildoune,
    That weary wizard, said:
'Tell me, I pray, what chanced that day
    The King of Scots was wed.
An uninvited bridal guest,
    They say, came from the dead.'

'They truly tell. The king led forth
    His bride to head the dance;
And in her mood fair maidenhood
    Had summoned every lance
Of nameless, gracious witchery,
    Of matchless smile and glance,

'For one last conquest of mankind.
    A shout rang to the roof;
Each star-bright eye shone eagerly
    To weave the viewless woof
Of airy motion through the warp
    Of music. Swift reproof

'Fell on us; for a soundless wind
    Blew purple every light;
The dancing ceased; the dancers clasped
    Each other's hands; each knight
Before his trembling lady stood,
    Blanched, breathless, at the sight.

'An odour, chill, sepulchral, spread,
    And lo, a skeleton!
A creaking stack of bones as black
    As peat! It seemed to con
Each face with yawning eyeless holes,
    And in a breath 'twas gone.'

Three times aloud laughed Ercildoune,
    He laughed a woeful laugh.
'A sign!' he cried. 'Say not I lied
    Till night-fall.' With his staff
He wrought grotesquely in the air,
    Then said: 'Our land must quaff

'The bitterest potion nations drink;
    This token is the last.
Recall, my lord, the weltering horde
    Of loathly worms that passed
Northward, and like a filthy sponge
    Wiped greenness off as fast

'As west winds wash the snow; that orb
    That shook its spear of awe

Beside the brand Orion's hand
 Is still in act to draw,
A hideous star – these eyes of mine
 Its glare at noonday saw;

'The floods that swamped flocks, fields, and towns,
 While men in throngs were slain;
Earthquakes that took the land and shook
 The meads beneath the main –   70
Shells gleamed by drenched flowers, tangle clung
 Like snakes about the grain:

'Herewith strange fire from heaven fell,
 Mayhap for priestly crimes,
On abbeys fair; the hinds still stare,
 And mutter saving rhymes,
At belfries in fantastic heaps
 Resoldered by their chimes.

'I rede these signs to mean a storm:
 That storm shall break to-day.'   80
With face on flame a rider came.
 'It's herald, by my fay!'
The Rhymer said, and sudden swept
 His robe and beard away.

Said then the panting messenger
 'The King of Scots is dead!'
The earl grew white. 'The King! – Alight.'
 But he rode on ahead.
'The heir's a baby over seas:
 In truth are we stormstead!'

28. ANSELM AND BIANCA

Even in her passion's lofty tide,
 When nothing seemed too hard to dare,
When earth's most lowly lot, her pride
 With Anselm had been proud to share,
A shadow started at her side,
 A ghostly whisper clove the air,

Down fluttered dead her high-flown dream.
 When Anselm hoarsely pled: 'Be mine!'
'No, no!' she answered. 'Though I seem
 To have no thought that is not thine,   10
I dare not wed. I sadly deem
 Marriage for us is death's dark shrine.'

And looking like the twilight skies,
 That now unbosom, now conceal

39

Their meaning stars in rhythmic sighs,
    She made his anguished being feel
Love's keenest pain, saying, with closed eyes:
    'Beseech me not; my senses reel.'

A time there came when Anselm ceased,
    Save by his looks that helpless pled,   20
To urge her. Then her love increased
    As pity deepened; nameless dread
Had prisoned love; but love, released,
    Grew free and fearless as the dead.

'Make me your bride, and if,' she said,
    'Our wedding day be Doomsday, then
We'll end time now.' So they were wed,
    Even as she wished, that day. And when
Homeward Anselm Bianca led,
    Trees seemed to her as walking men: 30

Her bridal vision far outran
    The swiftest sight of mighty seers:
She failed to note time's dainty span,
    But saw the day beyond the years,
And highest God, the shadow of man,
    And man, the image of his fears.

And like a little child she thought:
    'If all the world had only dared
To seize the pleasure that it sought,
    Earth had been heaven.' And Anselm shared   40
Her mystic mood: their souls had caught,
    As souls that have in hell despaired,

Or souls that have in heaven hoped,
    Catch ever that green ray revealed
Only to who have soared or groped . . .
    The wedding-bells panted and pealed
Like happy hearts; and evening coped
    A monumental day love built.

Night's monogram, the twilight star,
    In silver wrought upon the hem   50
Of pallid gold that flickered far –
    The border of the sky – for them
Throbbed like two passionate flowers that are
    Lit in one bloom on one fair stem.

Their hearts the only music made,
    Until their golden ringing felt
The dulcet, lowly serenade
    That lowly friendship sweetly dealt
For gentle dealing. 'Love,' she said,
    'Speak, or my happy eyes will melt!   60

'Say if you like the music, sir.'
　　She blushed like one that is too bold.
'Yes, very well,' he answered her.
　　'My love,' she said, 'I have been told
Music is like Arabian myrrh,
　　That yields what scent the senses hold.'

'Or like a diamond,' Anselm mused.
　　'From rippling notes a desperate mind
Draws sweeter sadness; mirth is fused
　　To liquid smiles; and lovers find   70
Their ladies' words; the latch is loosed
　　Of heaven's gate, and saints made blind.

'The tune breaks forth in showers of light,
　　But one beam strikes each listener's sense.
Oh, sweetheart, could we hear aright
　　The deep tone, shy as Proteus, whence
Melodious sound takes birth, more bright,
　　More vital than this hour intense,

'Our future would appear.' 'And we
　　How much the wiser? Ah! I fear   80
To see the future, love, would be
　　Only a vision of our bier.'
She said this quaintly. Archly, he:
　　'What is your meaning? Let me hear.'

'I mean were we our last hour told,
　　Though day to day, like rhyme to rhyme,
Re-echoed joy – an age of gold –
　　Death, like a hideous gifted mime,
Would haunt us, dumb with meaning, bold,
　　Careless as one who knows his time.   90

'So not to know is better, dear,
　　That knowledge that we must disown.
Let us not talk of death. What? Here!
　　My love!' But on the instant blown,
A strident note crashed through the clear
　　And tinkling music, like a stone

Breaking the murmur of a stream;
　　And after came the trumpeter,
A herald, with plume of foaming cream,
　　And stood before them. 'Noble sir,   100
Prince Florio sends me, and thy theme
　　Is recompense. Deliver her,

'Your bride, to him.' 'A monstrous jest!'
　　'An old jest, sir, from death's jest-book.

Your father, Anselm, was the best
    Who ever played it, when he took
Prince Florio's mother, and the rest
    From lord to knave, drowned in the brook,

'That hissed with blazing beams, and frothed
    About the burning tower.' 'He seized   110
His own true wife, to him betrothed,
    But rapt away.' 'My lord was pleased
To bid me hold no words.' 'This loathed,
    Unfellowed insult! What! Appeased

'By just my bride! You – hellish one!' –
    Tell him – unworthy to be man –
Your lord, I'll strip him in the sun,
    And whip him dead.' 'My master's plan
To do as by his sire was done
    Is well' – 'Away!' The herald ran.   120

Bianca sobbed: 'Where shall we fly?'
    'Nowhither, love; we'll fight. Be still,
Be patient, pray.' Her fearful eye
    Clung to him piteously, till
She stood alone; then sigh on sigh
    Like incense rose; and on the sill

Of life her soul beheld the soul
    Of destiny. 'Then this it was.'
She thought, 'that did our talk control
    Deathward. When most without a cause   130
They seem, our thoughts leap at the goal.
    Merciful God, bid horror pause!'

Anselm returned, white as the dead.
    'Take all your jewels. Bravely, dear!
Our festal friends, our men – all fled!
    The tower's besieged; but do not fear:
The stair within the wall will stead.
    Be quick! I'll help you, love.' 'Hush! hear!

'They beat the gate!' 'One afternoon –
    Listen – (I travelled years ago   140
In Italy) – I heard a tune,
    And thought to see a boy; but, lo!
Rounding a knoll, I lighted soon
    Upon an ancient, lying low

'Beneath a wild vine, clustered ripe.
    I laughed to scorn the pastoral.
He nodded, fingering his pipe;
    Then said: "There is no life at all
But love: so after many a stripe
    Deserved and undeserved, I call   150

42

'"With music back my love, my youth.
   My spring, my summer burnt to ash –
Which is the sifted soul of truth –
   I sit without the din and crash
Of drudging life; and memory's tooth
   Bites golden apples." This was trash,

'But now the old man's steady gaze
   Across the blue lake, bossed with isles,
The green and golden slopes, the haze
   That veiled with purple serried files   160
Of snow-capped mountains, and the ways
   That crawled through flowers, and leapt the stiles,

'Are balm to me. That lake's our bourne.
   Come, love, sweet love.' He spoke no more;
For having touched the spring to turn
   The quaintly graven, secret door,
Hidden behind a curtained urn
   That came from Tuscany, a roar

Of fierce, exulting voices burst,
   With iron tread and armour's clang,   170
Out of the opened wall. And first
   He kissed her; then his bright sword rang
Scabbardless, and he stood. None durst
   Approach his guard until he sprang

Upon them. Two foes fell; then, he.
   He staggered to his feet, and bled,
Leaning against the wall. But she,
   Haled from before her unpressed bed
At which she knelt, strained to be free,
   And 'Save me, save me!' hoarsely said.   180

Back surged his life; that breath of woe
   Summoned it back. He made one stride,
Shook free his eyes, and saw his foe
   With sword advanced before his bride.
He rushed upon the steel – even so!
   And plunged his own deep in her side.

29. ALICE

The paynims seized her in the wood
   Where shadows moved alive,
Where steep rocks made a well of shade,
   And no sweet flowers might thrive.

One from her hair the pearl-strings tore:
   She seemed as fair again;
The pearls, the only gems she wore,
   Lost all their lustre then.

43

A cry she cried: 'Help, help, dear love!'
  They gagged her with her lace;   10
Her scarf – white silk, like foaming milk –
  They bound across her face.

Pale, dumb with lust, they rent her robes;
  She thanked God for her hair.
White in the wood, unsheathed she stood,
  The only flower there.

But when she felt her nakedness,
  These wolves she clasped and clung;
Their eyes devoured her sweet distress,
  And low their laughter rung.   20

The ruthless paynims then cast lots
  Who should possess her first.
'Hark, Alice! hist! I keep my tryst!'
  And in her lover burst.

He fought the three, and felled each foe,
  That none should ever rise;
Then stood. She loosed her scarf; and lo,
  Their souls were in their eyes.

Right as her quickened spirit rose
  Her shuddering body dawned;   30
Her arms would veil the tinted snows,
  Her sight restore its bond.

But shame, the body's false friend, died –
  Flame in the sun's clear frown:
Only her virgin soul he eyed;
  Her arms hung meekly down.

He leapt the space between; her eyes
  Held his with trembling power.
No word they spoke; wrapped in his cloak,
  He bore her to her bower.   40

30. THE GLEEMAN

The gleeman sang in the market-town;
The market-folk went up and down.

His blue eyes waned when thronging thought
Would not obey as visions ought;
Then flashed and flung their radiance straight –
Availing prayer – at heaven's gate;
And thought and word chimed with the tune.
His scarlet cloak and sandal shoon,

His tunic with the silver fur,
Of forest green and minever,
His golden brooch and carcanet,
Was not the garb that gleemen get.
So said the dames; the dreamy girls
Gazed only on his golden curls;
The sapless ancients sneered and frowned;
The young men with a spell were bound,
And eyed his gleaming, studded belt,
The scabbard and the jewelled hilt.

But no one praised the harp of gold
    His fingers deftly rang,
Or listened to the things he told;
    But this is what he sang:

'Loose your knotted brains awhile,
    Market-people, sore bested;
Traffic palsies all your isle;
    Hear a message from the dead.

'Though the sultry flood of life
    Brims my veins; though starry truth
Still maintains a changing strife
    With the purple dreams of youth;

'Songs the master-maker wrought –
    Who are now the guests of death,
Lulled by echoes of their thought –
    Fill me with their eager breath.

'What! You stare with horny eyes,
    And my singing-robes you scan?
You would make my sword your prize?
    Maidens only see the man?

'Learnëd clerk with icy sneer,
    Must I strike a lower clef?
Hear, O heaven, and earth, give ear,
    I will sing though men be deaf!

'And the throbbing sky shall list,
And the rivers cease to bound,
Startled mountains pierce the mist,
    Happy valleys drink the sound.

'Earth is fairer than we know:
    Shining hours and golden beams!
Lilies sigh, and roses glow,
    And the beasts have noble dreams.

45

'Lo! the youngest soul is scarred,
   Blanched with tears and dyed with stains,
For the world is evil-starred,
   But the vision still remains:

'Plenty, from her bounteous horn,
   Dealing bread instead of stones;
Golden lands of nodding corn
   Lusty labour reaps and owns;

'Fearless suns, and no sick star,
   No more maiden moons ashamed,   60
Cities sweet as forests are,
   Sin unthought, unknown, unnamed;

'Babes that wail not in the night,
   Wretched heirs of poisoned lives;
No young souls that long for light,
   Festering in scholastic gyves;

'Not a damsel made the tomb
   Of a thousand loves unchaste;
Woman mistress of her womb,
   Never bound to be embraced;   70

'Man by hunger unsubdued,
   Conqueror of the primal curse,
Master of his subtlest mood,
   Master of the universe.'

He wrapped his cloak about his face,
And left the bustling market-place.
The juggler had an audience,
The mountebank drew showers of pence,
The pardoner cheapened heaven for gold:
I ween the market-folk were sold.   80

31. NOCTURNE

The wind is astir in the town;
It wanders the street like a ghost
In a catacomb's labyrinth lost,
Seeking a path to the heath.
Broad lightnings stream silently down
On the silent city beneath.
But haunting my ear is the tune
Of the larks as they bathe in the light;
And I have a vision of noon
Like a fresco limned on the night: 10
I see a green crescent of trees;
A slope of ripe wheat is its foil,

46

The cream of the sap of the soil,
Curdling, but sweet, in the breeze.
The sun hastes, and evening longs
For the moon to follow after;
And my thought has the tenderest scope:
Tears that are happy as laughter,
Sighs that are sweeter than songs,
    Memories dearer than hope.   20

32. THE QUEEN OF THULE

The Queen of Thule loved a lord
    As poor as poor could be:
Her people pled with her to wed
    The Prince of Orcadie.

She thought her strength of love at length
    Would make their wishes fade;
And night by night the lovers met
    Deep in a forest-glade.

A streamlet like a wind-blown lyre
    Now paused, now murmured soft;   10
The moon came like a lily on fire
    With love, and watched them oft.

She played eaves-dropper to their talk;
    From heaven she bent her head,
And in her star-attended walk
    She pondered what they said.

Why is the Queen alone to-night?
    'Come, come,' she cries, 'to me.
O wind, breathe low! – 'Tis Harold! – No;
    The Prince of Orcadie!   20

'What brings you here?' 'A pliant fate
    Puts you into my hand;
So yield you now: Heaven knows my vow
    To rule you and your land.'

'You told me that you loved me, sir;
    And sure it made me rue
That you must pine; for love of mine
    Can never be for you.

'Sir, you must leave me.' 'Thus, alone?
    That were a gentle deed!'   30
'What make you here?' 'I chased the deer
    All day upon my steed.

19 My Harold? – No! SAR.   27 for) since SAR.

47

'Three dark brown hinds I killed, and then –
    My heart still pants withal –
I killed a gallant stag of ten:
    His horns may grace your hall.'

'I like you not, dark man; your brow
    Is heavier than the night.
Away, away! Come, Harold, now,
    And end my woman's fright!'   40

'Cry louder, Queen; your voice must rend
    The grave, or find instead
The trump of doom if you would send
    A message to the dead.

'An hour we fought; the fight was hot –
    I flung away the sheath:
Here on my sword his blood lies cold;
    His corpse, upon the heath.'

'Why did you this?' 'For love of you.'
    'Then with your wicked sword   50
Mix my life's flood with that sweet blood
    Of him my soul adored.'

'Not so; I did your people's will:
    Now you must be my wife.'
'What! murder on my heart's door-sill
    My only love, my life,

'Then rouse up with your bloody sword
    The love you have bereft,
And straight demand my heart and hand!
    Is there no lightning left?'   60

'My Queen, I saw his thievish glance,
    The untimely smile, the fear;
I saw his vision like a lance
    Pierce him who had your ear.

'I marked him gaze till he could feast
    His eyes your eyes upon,
Like that ecstatic orient priest
    Who watches for the dawn.

'And when your whisper blessed his ears,
    I saw his soul rejoice,   70
Like some far traveller who hears
    The dusky Memnon's voice.

54 must you SAR.   64 who) that SAR.

48

'And when your hand touched his for joy,
    Or in the press by luck
Blown like a lily, I saw the boy
    Reel like one lightning-struck.

'And when your breath of Eastern spice –'
    'O God, give o'er!' cried she.
'Such sights,' he said, 'would melt raw ice
    To fiery jealousy.   80

'What more? I struck young Harold dead
    In fair fight at a stone,
Whereon I laid his golden head;
    And there he lies alone.

'Two streams meet there and softly prate
    Of all their wandering ways,
Like children when their hearts are great
    With deeds of holidays.

'They heeded not when we two fought;
    They heed not that pale lord –'   90
'Is it his blood that wanders there
    Upon your dreadful sword?'

She took the sword; it made her reel;
    Her tears came in a flood;
They fell upon the ruddy steel,
    And mingled with the blood.

Then with her raven hair she wiped
    The tear-drenched blood away;
A moonbeam strayed along the blade,
    And left it cold and gray.   100

'Now, hell-brand, do your work!' she cried,
    And ran him through and through.
The sword stood quivering in his side,
    But still his breath came true.

'Prince, are you dead?' she hoarsely said.
    He smiled upon the Queen:
'No, I am dying for your love,
    As I have always been;

'So, give me now your hand to kiss.'
    She gave the Prince her hand.   110
'This steel is cold; take, now, good hold,
    And pluck away the brand.'

79 raw) cold SAR.   83 laid) placed SAR.   85 softly) sweetly SAR.
100 And) Then SAR.

49

She plucked it out and let it fall;
　His soul had not yet passed;
'The sword I slew with, slays me too,'
　He said, and gripped it fast.

And then he ground between his teeth,
　'Before my soul can part,
This thirsty sword must have a third,'
　And stabbed her through the heart.　　　　120

In snowy white the pale moon rolls
　As in a winding-sheet
Three corpses pale; and three new souls
　Are at the judgement seat.

117 ground) gasped SAR.　　120 through) to SAR.　　123 corpses) bodies SAR.

33. FROM GRUB STREET

Rondeau

My love, my wife, three months ago
　I joined the fight in London town.
I haven't conquered yet, you know,
And friends are few, and hope is low;
　Far off I see the shining crown.

I'm daunted, dear; but blow on blow
With ebbing force I strike, and so
I am not felled and trodden down,
　　My love, my wife!

I wonder when the tide will flow,　　　　10
Sir Oracle cease saying 'No,'
　And Fortune smile away her frown.
　Well, while I swim I cannot drown;
And while we sleep the harvests grow,
　　My love, my wife.

Roundel.

My darling boys, heaven help you both!
　Now in your happy time of toys
Am I to die? How I am loth,
　My darling boys!

My heart is strong for woes or joys;
My soul and body keep their troth,
　One in a love no clasping cloys.

Why with me is the world so wroth?
　　What fiend at night my work destroys?
Has fate against me sworn an oath,　　　　10
　My darling boys?

50

Villanelle.

On her hand she leans her head,
   By the banks of the busy Clyde;
Our two little boys are in bed.

The pitiful tears are shed;
   She has nobody by her side;
On her hand she leans her head.

I should be working; instead
   I dream of my sorrowful bride,
And our two little boys in bed.

Were it well if we four were dead?   10
   The grave at least is wide.
On her hand she leans her head.

She stares at the embers red;
   She dashes the tears aside,
And kisses our boys in bed.

'God, give us our daily bread;
   Nothing we ask beside.'
On her hand she leans her head;
Our two little boys are in bed.

34. A BALLAD OF HELL

'A letter from my love to-day!
   Oh, unexpected, dear appeal!'
She struck a happy tear away,
   And broke the crimson seal.

'My love, there is no help on earth,
   No help in heaven; the dead-man's bell
Must toll our wedding; our first hearth
   Must be the well-paved floor of hell.'

The colour died from out her face,
   Her eyes like ghostly candles shone;   10
She cast dread looks about the place,
   Then clenched her teeth and read right on.

'I may not pass the prison door;
   Here must I rot from day to day,
Unless I wed whom I abhor,
   My cousin, Blanche of Valencay.

'At midnight with my dagger keen
   I'll take my life; it must be so.
Meet me in hell to-night, my queen,
   For weal and woe.'   20

51

She laughed although her face was wan,
　　She girded on her golden belt,
She took her jewelled ivory fan,
　　And at her glowing missal knelt.

Then rose, 'And am I mad?' she said;
　　She broke her fan, her belt untied;
With leather girt herself instead,
　　And stuck a dagger at her side.

She waited, shuddering in her room,
　　Till sleep had fallen on all the house. 　　　　30
She never flinched; she faced her doom:
　　They two must sin to keep their vows.

Then out into the night she went,
　　And stooping crept by hedge and tree;
Her rose-bush flung a snare of scent,
　　And caught a happy memory.

She fell, and lay a minute's space;
　　She tore the sward in her distress;
The dewy grass refreshed her face;
　　She rose and ran with lifted dress. 　　　　40

She started like a morn-caught ghost
　　Once when the moon came out and stood
To watch; the naked road she crossed,
　　And dived into the murmuring wood.

The branches snatched her streaming cloak;
　　A live thing shrieked; she made no stay!
She hurried to the trysting-oak –
　　Right well she knew the way.

Without a pause she bared her breast,
　　And drove her dagger home and fell, 　　　　50
And lay like one that takes her rest,
　　And died and wakened up in hell.

She bathed her spirit in the flame,
　　And near the centre took her post;
From all sides to her ears there came,
　　The dreary anguish of the lost.

The devil started at her side,
　　Comely, and tall, and black as jet.
'I am young Malespina's bride;
　　Has he come hither yet?' 　　　　60

'My poppet, welcome to your bed.'
　　'Is Malespina here?'
'Not he! To-morrow he must wed
　　His cousin Blanche, my dear!'

'You lie, he died with me to-night.'
    'Not he! it was a plot.' 'You lie.'
'My dear, I never lie outright.'
    'We died at midnight he and I.'

The devil went. Without a groan
    She, gathered up in one fierce prayer,   70
Took root in hell's midst all alone,
    And waited for him there.

She dared to make herself at home
    Amidst the wail, the uneasy stir.
The blood-stained flame that filled the dome,
    Scentless and silent, shrouded her.

How long she stayed I cannot tell;
    But when she felt his perfidy,
She marched across the floor of hell;
    And all the damned stood up to see.   80

The devil stopped her at the brink:
    She shook him off; she cried, 'Away!
'My dear, you have gone mad, I think.'
    'I was betrayed: I will not stay.'

Across the weltering deep she ran;
    A stranger thing was never seen;
The damned stood silent to a man;
    They saw the great gulf set between.

To her it seemed a meadow fair;
    And flowers sprang up about her feet.   90
She entered heaven; she climbed the stair
    And knelt down at the mercy-seat.

Seraphs and saints with one great voice
    Welcomed that soul that knew not fear;
Amazed to find it could rejoice,
    Hell raised a hoarse half-human cheer.

35. A BALLAD OF HEAVEN

He wrought at one great work for years;
    The world passed by with lofty look:
Sometimes his eyes were dashed with tears;
    Sometimes his lips with laughter shook.

His wife and child went clothed in rags,
    And in a windy garret starved:
He trod his measures on the flags,
    And high on heaven his music carved.

53

Wistful he grew but never feared;
    For always on the midnight skies   10
His rich orchestral score appeared
    In stars and zones and galaxies.

He thought to copy down his score:
    The moonlight was his lamp: he said,
'Listen, my love;' but on the floor
    His wife and child were lying dead.

Her hollow eyes were open wide;
    He deemed she heard with special zest:
Her death's-head infant coldly eyed
    The desert of her shrunken breast.   20

'Listen, my love: my work is done;
    I tremble as I touch the page
To sign the sentence of the sun
    And crown the great eternal age.

'The slow adagio begins;
    The winding-sheets are ravelled out
That swathe the minds of men, the sins
    That wrap their rotting souls about.

'The dead are heralded along;
    With silver trumps and golden drums,   30
And flutes and oboes, keen and strong,
    My brave andante singing comes.

'Then like a python's sumptuous dress
    The frame of things is cast away,
And out of Time's obscure distress,
    The thundering scherzo crashes Day.

'For three great orchestras I hope
    My mighty music shall be scored:
On three high hills they shall have scope
    With heaven's vault for a sounding-board.   40

'Sleep well, love; let your eyelids fall;
    Cover the child; goodnight, and if . . .
What? Speak . . . the traitorous end of all!
    Both . . . cold and hungry . . . cold and stiff!

'But no, God means us well, I trust:
    Dear ones, be happy, hope is nigh:
We are too young to fall to dust,
    And too unsatisfied to die.'

He lifted up against his breast
    The woman's body stark and wan;   50
And to her withered bosom pressed
    The little skin-clad skeleton.

54

'You see you are alive,' he cried.
    He rocked them gently to and fro.
'No, no, my love, you have not died;
    Nor you, my little fellow; no.'

Long in his arms he strained his dead
    And crooned an antique lullaby;
Then laid them on the lowly bed,
    And broke down with a doleful cry.   60

'The love, the hope, the blood, the brain,
    Of her and me, the budding life,
And my great music – all in vain!
    My unscored work, my child, my wife!

'We drop into oblivion,
    And nourish some suburban sod:
My work, this woman, this my son,
    Are now no more: there is no God.

'The world's a dustbin; we are due,
    And death's cart waits: be life accurst!'   70
He stumbled down beside the two,
    And clasping them, his great heart burst.

Straightway he stood at heaven's gate,
    Abashed and trembling for his sin:
I trow he had not long to wait,
    For God came out and led him in.

And then there ran a radiant pair,
    Ruddy with haste and eager-eyed
To meet him first upon the stair –
    His wife and child beatified.   80

They clad him in a robe of light,
    And gave him heavenly food to eat;
Great seraphs praised him to the height,
    Archangels sat about his feet.

God, smiling, took him by the hand,
    And led him to the brink of heaven:
He saw where systems whirling stand,
    Where galaxies like snow are driven.

Dead silence reigned; a shudder ran
    Through space; Time furled his wearied wings;   90
A slow adagio then began
    Sweetly resolving troubled things.

The dead were heralded along:
    As if with drums and trumps of flame,
And flute and oboes keen and strong,
    A brave andante singing came.

55

Then like a python's sumptuous dress
    The frame of things was cast away,
And out of Time's obscure distress
    The conquering scherzo thundered Day.   100

He doubted; but God said 'Even so;
    Nothing is lost that's wrought with tears:
The music that you made below
    Is now the music of the spheres.'

36. FOR HESPER JOYCE LE GALLIENNE

What boat is this comes o'er the sea
From islands of eternity?

A little boat, a cradle boat,
The signals at the mast denote;

And in the boat a little life:
Happy husband, happy wife!

1 *See Notes.*

37. A CINQUE PORT

Below the down the stranded town,
    What may betide forlornly waits,
With memories of smoky skies,
    When Gallic navies crossed the straits;
When waves with fire and blood grew bright,
And cannon thundered through the night.

With swinging stride the rhythmic tide
    Bore to the harbour barque and sloop;
Across the bar the ship of war,
    In castled stern and lanterned poop,   10
Came up with conquests on her lee,
The stately mistress of the sea.

Where argosies have wooed the breeze,
    The simple sheep are feeding now;
And near and far across the bar
    The ploughman whistles at the plough;
Where once the long waves washed the shore,
Larks from their lowly lodgings soar.

Below the down the stranded town
    Hears far away the rollers beat;   20
About the wall the seabirds call;
    The salt wind murmurs through the street;
Forlorn the sea's forsaken bride,
Awaits the end that shall betide.

18 The larks from lowly lodgings soar. PMG.   19 stranded) brooding PMG.

38. IN ROMNEY MARSH

As I went down to Dymchurch Wall,
  I heard the South sing o'er the land;
I saw the yellow sunlight fall
  On knolls where Norman churches stand.

And ringing shrilly, taut and lithe,
  Within the wind a core of sound,
The wire from Romney town to Hythe
  Alone its airy journey wound.

A veil of purple vapour flowed
  And trailed its fringe along the Straits;   10
The upper air like sapphire glowed;
  And roses filled Heaven's central gates.

Masts in the offing wagged their tops;
  The swinging waves pealed on the shore;
The saffron beach, all diamond drops
  And beads of surge, prolonged the roar.

As I came up from Dymchurch Wall,
  I saw above the Downs' low crest
The crimson brands of sunset fall,
  Flicker and fade from out the west.   20

Night sank: like flakes of silver fire
  The stars in one great shower came down;
Shrill blew the wind; and shrill the wire
  Rang out from Hythe to Romney town.

The darkly shining salt sea drops
  Streamed as the waves clashed on the shore;
The beach, with all its organ stops
  Pealing again, prolonged the roar.

39. LONDON

Athwart the sky a lowly sigh
  From west to east the sweet wind carried;
The sun stood still on Primrose Hill;
  His light in all the city tarried;
The clouds on viewless columns bloomed
Like smouldering lilies unconsumed.

'Oh sweetheart, see! how shadowy,
  Of some occult magician's rearing,
Or swung in space of heaven's grace
  Dissolving, dimly reappearing,   10

57

Afloat upon ethereal tides
St. Paul's above the city rides!'

A rumour broke through the thin smoke
   Enwreathing abbey, tower, and palace,
The parks, the squares, the thoroughfares,
   The million-peopled lanes and alleys,
And even-muttering prisoned storm,
The heart of London beating warm.

12 St. Paul YB.

40. SPRING

I

Over hill and dale and fen
   Winds adust and roving strum
Broken music now and then
   Out of hedges, lately dumb,
Snow enshrouded; for again,
   Here and now the Spring is come.

Hungry cold no more shall irk
   Beast or bird on hill or lea;
Rivers in the meadows lurk,
   Whispering on the flowers to be;   10
Rustics sing about their work;
   Spring is come across the sea.

Pink and emerald buds adorn
   Squares and gardens up and down;
Madge, quite early in the morn,
   Gads about in her new gown;
Daisies in the streets are born;
   Spring is come into the town.

II

Certain, it is not wholly wrong
   To hope that yet the skies may ring
With the due praises that belong
   To April over all the Spring:
If one could only make a song
   The birds would wish to sing.

The beggar starts his pilgrimage;
   And kings their tassel-gentles fly;
The labourer earns a long day's wage;
   The knight, a star of errantry,   10
With some lost princess for a page
   Strays about Arcady.

10 knight, a star) knightly star PMB   12 about) over PMB.

58

Now fetching water in the dusk
   The maidens linger by the wells;
The ploughmen cast their homespun husk,
   And, while old Tuck his chaplet tells,
Themselves in spangled fustian busk,
   And garters girt with bells.

Maid Marian's kirtle, somewhat old,
   A welt of red must now enhance;   20
Oho! ho ho! in silk and gold
   The gallant hobby horse shall prance,
Sing hey, for Robin Hood the bold;
   Heigh ho, the morris-dance!

Oh foolish fancy, feebly strong!
   To England shall we ever bring
The old mirth back? Yes, yes; nor long
   It shall be till that greater Spring;
And some one yet may make a song
   The birds would like to sing.   30

29 may) shall PMB.   30 like) wish PMB.

III

Foxes peeped from out their dens;
   Day grew pale and olden;
Blackbirds, willow-warblers, wrens
   Staunched their voices golden.

High, oh high, from the opal sky,
   Shouting against the dark,
'Why, why, why must the day go by?'
   Fell a passionate lark.

But the cuckoos beat their brazen gongs,
   Sounding, sounding, so;   10
And the nightingales poured in starry songs
   A galaxy below.

Slowly tolling, the vesper bell
   Ushered the shadowy night:
Down-a-down in a hawthorn dell
   A boy and a girl and love's delight.

14 shadowy) stately YB.

IV

By lichened tree and mossy plinth
   Like living flames of purple fire,
Flooding the wood, the hyacinth
   Uprears its heavy-scented spire.

The redstart shakes its crimson plume,
    Singing alone till evening's fall
Beside the pied and homely bloom
    Of wallflower on the crumbling wall.

Now dandelions light the way,
    Expecting summer's near approach;   10
And, bearing lanterns night and day,
    The great marsh-marigolds keep watch.

41. IN MEMORIAM MILDRED LE GALLIENNE

Where do the dead folk go?
Where is this white soul glowing
Serene and sweet?
How shall we rest, not knowing?
How can we know?
And shall we meet,
Where the dead folk do go?

What of the darkness? Ah! he sang it well,
And now he needs his song.
But this – we cling to this, however long   10
In Time's dark night we dwell:
A lamp of light once lit not Death itself can quell.

Our songs are sweeter far,
The flowers about our feet
Sweet and more sweet,
And every star
Is starrier,
Because of her.

42. SONG OF A TRAIN

A monster taught
To come to hand
Amain,
As swift as thought
Across the land
The train.

The song it sings
Has an iron sound;
Its iron wings
Like wheels go round.   10

Crash under bridges,
Flash over ridges,
And vault the downs;
The road is straight –
Nor stile, nor gate;
For milestones – towns!

60

Voluminous, vanishing, white,
The steam plume trails;
Parallel streaks of light,
The polished rails.   20

Oh, who can follow?
The little swallow,
The trout of the sky:
But the sun
Is outrun,
And Time passed by.

O'er bosky dens,
By marsh and mead,
Forest and fens
Embodied speed   30
Is clanked and hurled;
O'er rivers and runnels;
And into the earth
And out again
In death and birth
That know no pain,
For the whole round world
Is a warren of railway tunnels.

Hark! hark! hark!
It screams and cleaves the dark;   40
And the subterranean night
Is gilt with smoky light.
Then out again apace
It runs its thundering race,
The monster taught
To come to hand
Amain,
That swift as thought
Speeds through the land
The train.   50

24 But the sun is run Sp.   25 *om.* Sp.   29 Forests Sp.

43. TO THE STREET PIANO

I. *A Labourer's Wife*
Tune – 'Ta-ra-ra-boom-de-ay'.
All the day I worked and played
When I was a little maid,
Soft and nimble as a mouse,
Living in my father's house.
If I lacked my liberty,
All my thoughts were free as free;
Though my hands were hacked all o'er,
Ah! my heart was never sore.

61

Oh! once I had my fling!
I romped at ging-go-ring;
I used to dance and sing,
And play at everything.
I never feared the light;
I shrank from no one's sight;
I saw the world was right;
I always slept at night.

What a simpleton was I
To go and marry on the sly!
Now I work and never play:
Three pale children all the day
Fight and whine; and Dick, my man,
Is drunk as often as he can.
Ah! my head and bones are sore,
And my heart is hacked all o'er.

Yet, once I had my fling;
I romped at ging-go-ring;
I used to dance and sing,
And play at everything.
Now I fear the light;
I shrink from every sight;
I see there's nothing right;
I hope to die to-night.

21 Tom, Sp.

II. *After the End.*
Tune – 'After the Ball'.

Oh sorry meaning! Oh, wistful sound!
Lilted and shouted, whistled and ground,
Still in my brain you will waltz and beat?
Haunt me no longer, tune of the street!
Standing between the quick and the dead,
I buy you off with a word of dread:
What will it matter who danced at the ball,
Or whose heart broke at the end of all?

After the end of all things,
    After the years are spent,
After the loom is broken,
    After the robe is rent,
Will there be hearts a-beating,
    Will friend converse with friend,
Will men and women be lovers,
        After the end?

Roses and dew, the stars and the grass,
Kingdoms and homes like fashions must pass,
Seedtime and harvest, sunshine and rain
Cease and be welcomed never again;

3 brain) ears Sp.

62

But passion and power, courage and truth,
Grace and delight and beauty and youth,
Will they go out like the lights at a ball
With sun, moon and stars, at the end of all?

    After the spheral music
        Ceases in Heaven's wide room,
    After the trump has sounded,
        After the crack of doom,
    Never will any sweetheart
        A loving message send,
    Never a blush light the darkness   30
        After the end?

44. THIRTY BOB A WEEK

I couldn't touch a stop and turn a screw,
    And set the blooming world a-work for me,
Like such as cut their teeth – I hope, like you –
    On the handle of a skeleton gold key;
I cut mine on a leek, which I eat it every week:
    I'm a clerk at thirty bob as you can see.

But I don't allow it's luck and all a toss;
    There's no such thing as being starred and crossed;
It's just the power of some to be a boss,
    And the bally power of others to be bossed: 10
I face the music, sir; you bet I ain't a cur;
    Strike me lucky if I don't believe I'm lost!

For like a mole I journey in the dark,
    A-travelling along the underground
From my Pillar'd Halls and broad Suburbean Park,
    To come the daily dull official round;
And home again at night with my pipe all alight,
    A-scheming how to count ten bob a pound.

And it's often very cold and very wet,
    And my missis stitches towels for a hunks;   20
And the Pillar'd Halls is half of it to let –
    Three rooms about the size of travelling trunks.
And we cough, my wife and I, to dislocate a sigh,
    When the noisy little kids are in their bunks.

But you never hear her do a growl or whine,
    For she's made of flint and roses, very odd;
And I've got to cut my meaning rather fine,
    Or I'd blubber, for I'm made of greens and sod:
So p'r'aps we are in Hell for all that I can tell,
    And lost and damn'd and served up hot to God.   30

5 on leek, YB.   15 suburban YB.   23 the wife YB.   25 *her* YB.
28 *I'm* YB.

I ain't blaspheming, Mr. Silver-tongue;
    I'm saying things a bit beyond your art:
Of all the rummy starts you ever sprung,
    Thirty bob a week's the rummiest start!
With your science and your books and your the'ries
        about spooks,
    Did you ever hear of looking in your heart?

I didn't mean your pocket, Mr., no:
    I mean that having children and a wife,
With thirty bob on which to come and go,
    Isn't dancing to the tabor and the fife: 40
When it doesn't make you drink, by Heaven! it makes
        you think,
    And notice curious items about life.

I step into my heart and there I meet
    A god-almighty devil singing small,
Who would like to shout and whistle in the street,
    And squelch the passers flat against the wall;
If the whole world was a cake he had the power to take,
    He would take it, ask for more, and eat them all.

And I meet a sort of simpleton beside,   50
    The kind that life is always giving beans;
With thirty bob a week to keep a bride
    He fell in love and married in his teens:
At thirty bob he stuck; but he knows it isn't luck:
    He knows the seas are deeper than tureens.

And the god-almighty devil and the fool
    That meet me in the High Street on the strike,
When I walk about my heart a-gathering wool,
    Are my good and evil angels if you like.
And both of them together in every kind of weather
    Ride me like a double-seated bike.   60

That's rough a bit and needs its meaning curled.
    But I have a high old hot un in my mind –
A most engrugious notion of the world,
    That leaves your lightning 'rithmetic behind:
I give it at a glance when I say 'There ain't no chance,
    Nor nothing of the lucky-lottery kind.'

And it's this way that I make it out to be:
    No fathers, mothers, countries, climates – none;
No Adam was responsible for me,
    Nor society, nor systems, nary one: 70
A little sleeping seed, I woke – I did, indeed –
    A million years before the blooming sun.

48 them) it YB., BS.

I woke because I thought the time had come;
    Beyond my will there was no other cause;
And everywhere I found myself at home,
    Because I chose to be the thing I was;
And in whatever shape of mollusc or of ape
    I always went according to the laws.

I was the love that chose my mother out;
    I joined two lives and from the union burst;   80
My weakness and my strength without a doubt
    Are mine alone for ever from the first:
It's just the very same with a difference in the name
    As 'Thy will be done.' You say it if you durst!

They say it daily up and down the land
    As easy as you take a drink, it's true;
But the difficultest go to understand,
    And the difficultest job a man can do,
Is to come it brave and meek with thirty bob a week,
    And feel that that's the proper thing for you.   90

It's a naked child against a hungry wolf;
    It's playing bowls upon a splitting wreck;
It's walking on a string across a gulf
    With millstones fore-and-aft about your neck;
But the thing is daily done by many and many a one;
    And we fall, face forward, fighting, on the deck.

79 *I* YB.   80 *I* YB.

45. AUTUMN

I

All the waysides now are flowerless;
    Soon the swallows shall be gone,
And the Hamadryads bowerless,
    And the waving harvest done;
But about the river sources
    And the meres,
And the winding watercourses,
    Summer smiles through parting tears.

Wanderers weary, oh, come hither
    Where the green-leaved willows bend,   10
Where the grasses never wither,
    Or the purling noises end;
O'er the serried sedge, late blowing,
    Surge and float
Golden flags, their shadows showing
    Deep as in a castle-moat.

10 leaved) plumed Sp.

Like a ruby of the mosses
　Here the marish pimpernel,
Glowing crimson, still embosses
　Velvet verdure with its bell;20
And the scallop-leaved and splendid
　Silver-weed,
By the maiden breezes tended,
　Wears her flowers of golden brede.

Water-plantain, rosy vagrant,
　Flings his garland on the wave;
Mint in midstream rises fragrant,
　Dressed in green and lilac brave;
And that spies may never harass
　In their baths30
The shining naiads, purple arras
　Of the loosestrife veils the paths.

II

Aftermaths of pleasant green
　Bind the earth in emerald bands;
Pouring golden in between,
　Tides of harvest flood the lands.
Showers of sunlight splash and dapple
　The orchard park;
And there the plum hangs and the apple,
　Like smouldering gems and lanterns dark.

Let no shallow jester croak!
　Fill the barn and brim the bowl!10
Here is harvest, starving folk,
　Here, with bread for every soul!
Rouse yourselves with happy ditties,
　And hither roam,
Forsaking your enchanted cities
　To keep the merry harvest-home.

Surely now there needs no sigh!
　Bid the piper bring his pipe;
Sound aloud the harvest-cry –
　Once again the earth is ripe!20
Golden grain in sunlight sleeping,
　When winds are laid,
Can dream no dismal dream of weeping
　Where broken-hearted women fade.

More than would for all suffice
　From the earth's broad bosom pours;
Yet in cities wolfish eyes
　Haunt the windows and the doors.

Mighty One in Heaven who carvest
  The sparrow's meat,
Bid the hunger and the harvest
  Come together we entreat!

30

Aftermaths of pleasant green
  Bind the earth in emerald bands;
Pouring golden in between
  Tides of harvest flood the lands.
Let the wain roll home with laughter,
  The piper pipe,
And let the girls come dancing after,
  For once again the earth is ripe.

40

46. A BALLAD OF A NUN

From Eastertide to Eastertide
  For ten long years her patient knees
Engraved the stones – the fittest bride
  Of Christ in all the diocese.

She conquered every earthly lust;
  The abbess loved her more and more;
And, as a mark of perfect trust,
  Made her the keeper of the door.

High on a hill the convent hung,
  Across a duchy looking down,
Where everlasting mountains flung
  Their shadows over tower and town.

10

The jewels of their lofty snows
  In constellations flashed at night;
Above their crests the moon arose;
  The deep earth shuddered with delight.

Long ere she left her cloudy bed,
  Still dreaming in the orient land,
On many a mountain's happy head
  Dawn lightly laid her rosy hand.

20

The adventurous sun took Heaven by storm;
  Clouds scattered largesses of rain;
The sounding cities, rich and warm,
  Smouldered and glittered in the plain.

Sometimes it was a wandering wind,
  Sometimes the fragrance of the pine,
Sometimes the thought how others sinned,
  That turned her sweet blood into wine.

Sometimes she heard a serenade
Complaining sweetly far away:
She said, 'A young man woos a maid;'
And dreamt of love till break of day.

Then would she ply her knotted scourge
Until she swooned; but evermore
She had the same red sin to purge,
Poor, passionate keeper of the door!

For still night's starry scroll unfurled,
And still the day came like a flood;
It was the greatness of the world
That made her long to use her blood.

In winter-time when Lent drew nigh,
And hill and plain were wrapped in snow,
She watched beneath the frosty sky
The nearest city nightly glow.

Like peals of airy bells outworn
Faint laughter died above her head
In gusts of broken music borne:
'They keep the Carnival,' she said.

Her hungry heart devoured the town:
'Heaven save me by a miracle!
Unless God sends an angel down,
Thither I go though it were Hell.'

She dug her nails deep in her breast,
Sobbed, shrieked, and straight withdrew the bar:
A fledgling flying from the nest,
A pale moth rushing to a star.

Fillet and veil in strips she tore;
Her golden tresses floated wide;
The ring and bracelet that she wore
As Christ's betrothed, she cast aside.

'Life's dearest meaning I shall probe;
Lo! I shall taste of love at last!
Away!' She doffed her outer robe,
And sent it sailing down the blast.

Her body seemed to warm the wind;
With bleeding feet o'er ice she ran:
'I leave the righteous God behind;
I go to worship sinful man.'

She reached the sounding city's gate;
No question did the warder ask:
He passed her in: 'Welcome, wild mate!'
He thought her some fantastic mask.

30

40

50

60

70

Half-naked through the town he went;
  Each footstep left a bloody mark;
Crowds followed her with looks intent;
  Her bright eyes made the torches dark.

Alone and watching in the street
  There stood a grave youth nobly dressed;
To him she knelt and kissed his feet;
  Her face her great desire confessed.   80

Straight to his house the nun he led:
  'Strange lady, what would you with me?'
'Your love, your love, sweet lord,' she said;
  'I bring you my virginity.'

He healed her bosom with a kiss;
  She gave him all her passion's hoard;
And sobbed and murmured ever, 'This
  Is life's great meaning, dear, my lord.

'I care not for my broken vow;
  Though God should come in thunder soon,   90
I am sister to the mountains now,
  And sister to the sun and moon.'

Through all the towns of Belmarie
  She made a progress like a queen.
'She is,' they said, 'whate'er she be,
  The strangest woman ever seen.

'From fairyland she must have come,
  Or else she is a mermaiden.'
Some said she was a ghoul, and some
  A heathen goddess born again.   100

But soon her fire to ashes burned;
  Her beauty changed to haggardness;
Her golden hair to silver turned;
  The hour came of her last caress.

At midnight from her lonely bed
  She rose, and said, 'I have had my will.'
The old ragged robe she donned, and fled
  Back to the convent on the hill.

Half-naked as she went before,
  She hurried to the city wall,   110
Unnoticed in the rush and roar
  And splendour of the carnival.

No question did the warder ask:
  Her ragged robe, her shrunken limb,
Her dreadful eyes! 'It is no mask;
  It is a she-wolf, gaunt and grim!'

She ran across the icy plain;
    Her worn blood curdled in the blast;
Each footstep left a crimson stain;
    The white-faced moon looked on aghast.   120

She said between her chattering jaws,
    'Deep peace is mine, I cease to strive;
Oh, comfortable convent laws,
    That bury foolish nuns alive!

'A trowel for my passing-bell,
    A little bed within the wall,
A coverlet of stones; how well
    I there shall keep the Carnival!'

Like tired bells chiming in their sleep,
    The wind faint peals of laughter bore;   130
She stopped her ears and climbed the steep,
    And thundered at the convent door.

It opened straight: she entered in,
    And at the wardress' feet fell prone:
'I come to purge away my sin;
    Bury me, close me up in stone.'

The wardress raised her tenderly;
    She touched her wet and fast-shut eyes:
'Look, sister; sister, look at me;
    Look; can you see through my disguise?'   140

She looked and saw her own sad face,
    And trembled, wondering, 'Who are thou?'
'God sent me down to fill your place:
    I am the Virgin Mary now.'

And with the word, God's mother shone:
    The wanderer whispered, 'Mary, hail!'
The vision helped her to put on
    Bracelet and fillet, ring and veil.

'You are sister to the mountains now,
    And sister to the day and night;   150
Sister to God.' And on the brow
    She kissed her thrice, and left her sight.

While dreaming in her cloudy bed,
    Far in the crimson orient land,
On many a mountain's happy head
    Dawn lightly laid her rosy hand.

47. NOVEMBER

Long-loitering yet, with warmth and wet,
   Autumn outstays its time to pass.
Crimson and gold, in wood and wold,
   The dead leaves diaper the grass;

And twirled and twined by wave and wind,
   As by a master-craftsman's hand,
They damascene the olive-green
   O'erbrimming brooks that flood the land.

At shut of eve the elm-trees weave
   Athwart the pallid lavender   10
Of clouds that dye the city sky,
   A net of boughs where sparse leaves stir.

Soon comes the dark: in square and park,
   In misty streets, like fiery flakes
The lamps are lit; the hansoms flit,
   Uncouth, phantasmal: London wakes.

48. TO MY FRIEND

What is between us two, we know:
Shake hands and let the whole world go.

49. TO MY ENEMY

Unwilling friend, let not your spite abate:
Help me with scorn, and strengthen me with hate.

50. TO THE NEW WOMEN

Free to look at fact,
Free to come and go,
Free to think and act,
Now you surely know
The wrongs of womanhead
At last are fairly dead.

Abler than man to vex,
Less able to be good,
Fiercer in your sex,
Wilder in your mood,   10
Seeking – who knows what?
About the world you grope:
Some of you have thought
Man may be your hope.

Soon again you'll see,
Love and love alone,
As simple as can be,
Can make this life atone.

Be bold and yet be bold,
But be not overbold,   20
Although the knell be toll'd
Of the tyranny of old.

And meet your splendid doom,
On heaven-scaling wings,
Women, from whose bright womb
The radiant future springs!

51. TO THE NEW MEN

Heat the furnace hot;
Smelt the things of thought
Into dross and dew;
Mould the world anew.

More than earth and sea
Is a heart and eye:
Gird yourselves, and try
All the powers that be.

Wicked, cease at once
Troubling; wearied eyes,   10
Rest you now, while suns
Dawn and moons arise.

'Stablish heaven to-day;
Cleanse the beast-marked brow;
Wipe all tears away:
Do it – do it now!

Love, and hope, and know:
Man – you must adore him:
Let the whole past go:
Think God's thought before Him.   20

Knowledge is power? Above
All else, knowledge is love.

Heat the furnace hot:
Smelt the world-old thought
Into dross and dew;
Mould the earth anew.

He glowed and flamed with faith in Heaven and Hell,
　　And travailed for his Church in thought and deed;
They cast him out because he preached too well
　　His peremptory creed.

He hid himself among the northern heights;
　　He watched the misty torrents, thundering, fall;
He watched the shortening days, the lengthening nights;
　　And heard the Lord God call,

'Go back, and noise abroad the wrath to come;
　　Ask no man's help; proclaim me in the crowd;　　10
Shall my anointed minister be dumb,
　　When all my foes are loud?

He hastened to the city: in a square
　　He preached the gospel. 'Fellowmen,' he cried,
'Jehovah speaks through me; you shall not dare
　　To laugh or turn aside.

'I preach no system nebulous and new;
　　God is, or is not: I have not to sell
Cosmetics for the soul: I offer you
　　The choice of Heaven or Hell.　　20

'Heed not bellettrist jargon, nor the rant
　　Of wanton art and proud philosophy;
But purge your reason of the subtlest cant,
　　And listen now to me.

'These are the grievous times that Paul foretold:
　　Men have become self-lovers, moneyers;
Boastful and haughty; scorners of the old;
　　Thankless, unholy; worse

'Than apes in lusts unspoken that appal
　　Sweet love; of dissolute fantastic mood;　　30
Egoists, artists, scientists; and all
　　Haters of what is good.

'Be warned ye sceptics, poets – fools; refrain
　　Who lick the lip and roll the lustful eye;
Repent, ye rich, that for your pleasures drain
　　The heart of labour dry.

'Reformer, bishop, knowledge-monger, quack –
　　Kill-Christs! – I am to every mortal sent;
But chiefly to the wise and good, alack!
　　I cry, repent! repent!　　40

73

'Ye gentle-hearted, lofty-sprited ones
　　Who dream, who hope, who think, and who design,
And who perform humane things for men's sons,
　　　Denying things divine,

'Ye labour nobly, asking no reward;
　　But I pronounce unselfishness a crime,
And tell you that the Great Day of the Lord
　　　Brags in the womb of time.

'Soon shall the elements with fervent heat
　　Melt, and the stars be shed like withered leaves;　　50
And ye shall stand before the judgement-seat
　　　With murderers, liars, thieves.

'Repent! repent! and shun your awful fate!
　　Why were your souls to your own bodies lent
But for your own first care! Men, good and great,
　　　I say, repent! repent!

'And turn to Christ who put his glory by,
　　And suffered on the cross that anguish fell;
If you will not believe before you die,
　　　You shall believe in Hell!'　　60

The chill wind whispered winter; night set in;
　　Stars flickered high; and like a tidal wave,
He heard the rolling multitudinous din
　　　Of life the city lave,

And burst in devious streams and eddying wreaths,
　　To fill the halls its glowing surges stain,
And hidden nooks wherein it clangs and seethes,
　　　And spends itself in vain.

A glittering-eyed and rosy boy that way
　　Went past and gravely gazed; a minstrel thrummed　　70
His banjo strings; 'Ta-ra-ra-boom-de-ay,'
　　　A happy harlot hummed.

Then from a shadowy corner of the square,
　　A phantom stole and took the preacher's hand,
And led him swiftly east to Houndsditch where
　　　The Aldgate once did stand.

A vapour sank, ill-smelling and unclean,
　　Over the orient city; and writhed and curled
Up Houndsditch like a mist in a ravine
　　　Of some fantastic world,　　80

Where wild weeds, half-way down the frowning bank,
　　Flutter like poor apparel stained and sere,
And lamplike flowers with hearts of flame their rank
　　　And baleful blossoms rear.

74

Nothing he noted of the ceaseless roar
    Of wheels and wearied hoofs and wearied feet,
That sounded hoarse behind 'twixt shore and shore
    Of brimming Aldgate Street.

He only heard a murmur gathering fast,
    Of hidden multitudes in wrath and pain;   90
Anon a visionary pageant passed,
    Through the high-shouldered lane.

But first the bleared and beetling houses changed
    To ivied towers and belfries old and gray,
And pointed gables, antic chimneys, ranged
    In order disarray.

Then in the midst of Houndsditch one appeared,
    Panting with haste, and bearing heavily
A massive cross; but not as one that feared:
    Rather he seemed to be   100

With desperate courage flying an event,
    Most woful, unexpected, undesigned,
Born of immaculate heroism, meant
    Wholly to bless mankind.

He sped along a path of cloud and flame,
    That spanned the city, looking ever back
With pity and with horror, till he came
    Where an abyss yawned black.

Straightway he raised the cross high in the air;
    Its shadow darkened space: into the deep   110
He threw it: then his terrible despair
    Fell from him, as a sleep

Falls from a young man on a summer morn:
    Wondering and glad a lowly way he took
By pastures, flowers and fruit, and golden corn,
    And by a murmuring brook:

The while were heard descending from the skies
    Or out of future times and future lands,
A bruit low and whispers, shadowy cries
    Of joy and clapping hands.   120

But this scarce-heard applause, so far, so faint,
    Like happy tears shed in a stormy sea,
Sudden was lost in the deep-voiced complaint,
    The shouts of victory,

Of hope and woe, that with discordant stress
    Tempestuously filled the phantom street,
As from its doors there issued forth a press
    Of folk with noiseless feet,

That hurried like a torrent through a strait,
   And o'er the magic path of flame and cloud – 130
Arms, voices, of that silent-footed, great
    And many-mannered crowd!

Above the street the Holy City hung,
   Close as a roof and like a jasper stone
Lit by the Lamp of God; while seraphs sung
    And saints adored the Throne.

Beneath, the sewers, flaming suddenly,
   Bore down, like offal, souls of men to swell
The reeking cess-pool of humanity,
    The hideous nine-orbed Hell. 140

Templars and warrior-bishops hewed and hacked
   Christian and Pagan; kings and priests at feud
Each other smote; king, king – priest, priest attacked;
    Creed, creed – zeal, zeal pursued

With thumbscrews, racks, strappadoes, cord and stake;
   And victims passed: live folk like tired-off toys
Broken and burned – women on fire! Christ's sake!
    And tortured girls and boys!

And there came also gentle counsellors,
   And some announced that discord now should cease; 150
But every blessing rotted to a curse
    Upon the lips of peace.

Then cloth-yard shafts and knightly panoplies
   Gave place to ordnance and the musketeer;
And evermore pealed hymns and battle-cries,
    And shrieks of pain and fear.

The king o'erthrew the priest; the folk did tame
   The king; and, having nobly played the man,
Bowed to the yoke again, while God became
    A sleek-haired Anglican. 160

And still the motley pageant thundering poured
   Along the Heaven-roofed and Hell-drained street –
Priest, trooper, harlot, lawyer, lady, lord,
    And all with noiseless feet.

Because the way with living flesh was paved,
   With men and women, stifled, broken, bruised,
Whose blood the thresholds of the Churches laved,
    And stood in pools, and oozed,

And spirted high like water in a land
   Of mire and moss, at every hoof and foot 170
Spattering the snowy alb, the jewelled hand
    Of priest and prostitute.

Voiceless and still the human causey lay,
    Until the City of God began to pale,
And Hell grow cold; then from that dolorous way
    Broke forth a feeble wail;

And here and there some sign of life appeared –
    A lifted arm; and faces quick or dead
Surged in the bloody plash; and one upreared
    A ghastly, shrieking head,   180

That straightway fell, brained by a ruthless hoof:
    But the live stones grew stormier evermore,
As dim and dimmer waned the Heavenly roof,
    And Hell burned low and lower.

Prone, or half-raised, or upright, desperate blows
    By these down-trodden ones were dealt about;
At last the whole live road in wrath arose,
    And smote the wanton rout.

Straightway a blood-red fog darkened and shone
    And hid the street. . . . Was it the crimson stain   190
Of morn alone? Or must the New Day dawn
    O'er mountains of the slain?

The mist dissolved: Lo! Nature's comely face!
    No Hellish sewer poisoning the air,
No parish Heaven obliterating space,
    But earth and sky so fair –

Infinite thought, infinite galaxies;
    And on a daisied lawn a shining throng
Of noble people sweetly sang: here is
    The burden of their song: 200

        'With love and hope we go;
          We neither fear nor hate;
        We know but what we know;
          We have become as Fate.'

Then suddenly the winter fog unclean
    Sank o'er the orient city, and writhed and curled
Up Houndsditch like a mist in a ravine
    Of some fantastic world,

Where wild weeds halfway down the frowning bank
    Flutter like poor apparel stained and sere,   210
And lamplike flowers with hearts of gold their rank
    And baleful blossoms rear.

The preacher, ghastlier than the phantom, cried
    'Get thee behind me, Satan!' clutched the night,
Staggered, ran on, shrieked, laughed, fell down and died
    Of that strange-storied sight.

Few marked his death amid the ceaseless roar
Of wheels and wearied hoofs and wearied feet,
That sounded hoarse behind 'twixt shore and shore
Of brimming Aldgate Street.   220

53. THE VENGEANCE OF THE DUCHESS

The sun of Austerlitz had dawned and shone and set in blood,
When to Illyria Sigismund rode home by fell and flood.

'What news, what news, Duke Sigismund?' the Duchess Agnes cried.
'Heavy – an avalanche of lead,' Duke Sigismund replied.

'Across the astonished land the sun comes conquering from the west –
Napoleon's banners, purpled in the blood of Europe's best.'

'Heavy – an avalanche of lead!' she echoed in dismay.
'Take heart,' he said. But she, 'Ah me! this was our wedding-day

'Five years ago! – Oh! that base churl, and unimagined thief,
That kingdom-breaker! Give me words, or I shall die of grief!   10

'Our wedding-day, and Europe fallen! How comes it that earth stands!'
She paced the room across, along, and wrung her jewelled hands.

At last a new thought dyed her cheek and set her eyes on fire:
'Husband, upon my wedding-day, grant me my heart's desire.

'I have a thing to do. Take horse. – You're tired, my love? Drink wine –
But come – you must – and ride with me to Idria's poisonous mine.'

By circling paths adown the hill they rode, a toilsome way;
And came where in a cup-like gap the town of Idria lay.

Far in the hideous mine the haughty Duchess Agnes found
The thing she sought for buried quick a mile beneath the ground: 20

A ghastly shape of palsied bones across the lamplight dim,
Scarce held together by the chains that bound him limb to limb.

While on the earthy slate quicksilver globed itself like dew,
He struck the sulphurous cinnabar with feeble blows and few.

A clammy sweat welled over him and drenched his ragged sash;
Upon his back appeared the curious branch-work of the lash.

The Duchess fed her eyes on him unconscious; then she said,
'So Casimir; poor Casimir!' The prisoner raised his head,

And ceased his work, but looked not round. She whispered to her lord,
'The breathing corpse that swelters here and lives this death abhorred,   30

78

'Dared think of me, the noblest blood and highest heart there is!
Five years ago a youthful god he seemed; now is he – this!'

And then aloud: 'Aha! my foster-brother, Casimir!
Know then at last that it was I who had you buried here.

'You looked to me! – and yet you come of better-blooded curs
Than he who tramples on the necks of kings and emperors.

'You looked to me, you peasant's son! So on my wedding-morn
You here were set, the enduring mark of my forgetful scorn.

'From then till now your memory has been a bauble thrust
In some disused old cupboard and there left to gather dust.   40

'To-day my suffering soul recalled the vengeance I had wrought
On one who hurt my pride by silent look and secret thought.

'Under the lash you toil and sweat and know nor day nor night,
Rotted with steaming mercury and blanched for lack of light.

'In you I came to see what I would make of that false knave,
The giant-burglar, Bonaparte, the puddle-blooded slave!

'Do you remember Bonaparte who conquered Italy?
He is now the master of the world; while you – why, you are he –

'With fortunes cast like Bonaparte's, a match perhaps for him –
Who here lie buried quick to please an idle woman's whim.'   50

When she had done he raised his eyes – wide, hollow orbs. She shook
With instant dread, beholding awful meanings in his look.

As feeble as a child's his dwindled flesh and palsied frame,
But manhood lightened round him from his glance of purest flame.

'Agnes,' he sighed; and that was all he uttered of rebuke.
He paused, and then melodiously said, though low, 'You took

'God's way when here you buried me; nothing can touch my soul
To discord with the universe. I understand the whole

'Great wonder of creation: every atom in the earth
Aches to be man unconsciously, and every living birth –   60

'The lowest struggling motion and the fiercest blood on fire,
The tree, the flower, are pressing towards a future ever higher,

'To reach that mood august wherein we know we suffer pain.
Napoleon! I am greater by this woe and by this chain;

'Because where all blaspheme and die, slaves of their agony,
I still am master of my thought, friend of my enemy.

'I reverence the force that was before the world began,
And which in me obtained the signal grace to be a man.

'Millions of men there are who happy live and happy die:
But what of that? I, too, am born a man, I, even I!'   70

He shone on her serenely like a solitary star,
Then turned and toiled in anguish at the poisonous cinnabar.

The Duchess gnawed her nether lip, but found no word to say.
'The man is mad,' the Duke declared, and led his wife away.

Glory to those who conquer Fate and peace to those who fail!
But who would be the Duchess, who, her victor-victim pale?

54. A LOAFER

I hang about the streets all day,
    All night I hang about;
I sleep a little when I may,
    But rise betimes the morning's scout;
For through the year I always hear
    Afar, aloft, a ghostly shout.

My clothes are worn to threads and loops;
    My skin shows here and there;
About my face like seaweed droops
    My tangled beard, my tangled hair;   10
From cavernous and shaggy brows
    My stony eyes untroubled stare.

I move from eastern wretchedness
    Through Fleet Street and the Strand;
And as the pleasant people press
    I touch them softly with my hand,
Perhaps to know that still I go
    Alive about a living land.

For, far in front the clouds are riven;
    I hear the ghostly cry,   20
As if a still voice fell from heaven
    To where sea-whelmed the drowned folks lie
In sepulchres no tempest stirs
    And only eyeless things pass by.

In Piccadilly spirits pass:
    Oh, eyes and cheeks that glow!
Oh, strength and comeliness! Alas,
    The lustrous health is earth I know
From shrinking eyes that recognise
    No brother in my rags and woe.   30

I know no handicraft, no art,
　　But I have conquered fate;
For I have chosen the better part,
　　And neither hope, nor fear, nor hate.
With placid breath on pain and death,
　　My certain alms, alone I wait.

And daily, nightly comes the call,
　　The pale, unechoing note,
The faint 'Aha!' sent from the wall
　　Of heaven, but from no ruddy throat　　　　40
Of human breed or seraph's seed,
　　A phantom voice that cries by rote.

55. SUMMER

I

The poets' May is dead and done
　　That warm and soft came shoulder-high
On Leda's twins; for now the sun
　　Scarce breaks the cold and cloudy sky.

But still by fields of grass and corn
　　With mantling green like blushes spread,
The milk-maid in the early morn
　　Trips with her milkpail on her head.

And still through mists that droop and float,
　　Beside the river lingering white,　　　　10
Dew on his wings and in his note,
　　The lark goes singing out of sight.

And still the hawthorn blossoms blow;
　　The belted bee on nectar sups;
And still the dazzling daisies grow
　　Beside the golden buttercups.

II

　　Glow-worm-like the daisies peer;
　　　　Roses in the thickets fade
　　Grudging every petal dear;
　　　　Swinging incense in the shade
　　The honeysuckle's chandelier
　　　　Twinkles down a shadowy glade.

　　Now is Nature's restful mood:
　　　　Death-still stands the sombre fir;
　　Hardly where the rushes brood
　　　　Something crawling makes a stir;　　　　10
　　Hardly in the underwood
　　　　Russet pinions softly whirr.

81

Above the shimmering square
Swallows climb the air;
Like crystal trees the fountain's shower,
A-bloom with many a rainbow flower.

Where the lake is deep
Water-lilies sleep,
Dreaming dreams with open eyes
Enchanted by the dragon-flies –

Azure dragon-flies,
Slivered from the skies,   10
Chased and burnished, joints and rings,
Elfin magic wands on wings.

Like an army dressed
In diamond mail and crest,
The silent light o'er park and town
In burning phalanxes comes down;

And lustrous ambuscades
In glittering streets and glades,
Where daisies crowd or people throng,
Keep watch and ward the whole day long.   20

56. WINTER

Darkness turned on her pillow white;
  A star serenely shone;
Deeply, deeply into the night
  Cut the sword of dawn.

Over the snow the pale east threw
  Abroach where daylight broke,
Crimson stains on the abbey panes
  Above the hamlet smoke.

All night the sad world dreamed;
  The sad world wakes all day,
And casts on the snow a ruddy glow
  From its heart that bleeds for aye.   10

57. THE HAPPIEST WAY

What will my father say
  To a poor man's son?
I will think of a way;
  My father must be won.

82

Love, I know, is strong,
   And breaks the barriers down,
Fighting with sword and song,
   A champion of renown.

But oh, for the lover's art
   That finds the happiest way!   10
Best to strike at his heart,
   And tell him all to-day?

Or after harvest-home
   When the leaves begin to fall,
Hand in hand we'll come,
   And he shall tell him all?

But now while sweet birds sing
   We can roam in the woods all day,
And swing on the orchard swing:
   That is the happiest way.   20

58. A BALLAD OF EUTHANASIA

In magic books she read at night,
   And found all things to be
A spectral pageant brought to light
   By nameless sorcery.

'Bethink you, now, my daughter dear,'
   The King of Norway cried,
' 'Tis summer, and your twentieth year –
   High time you were a bride!

'The sunlight lingers o'er the wold
   By night; the stars above   10
With passion throb like hearts of gold;
   The whole world is in love.'

The scornful princess laughed and said,
   'This love you praise, I hate.
Oh, I shall never, never wed;
   For men degenerate.

'The sun grows dim on heaven's brow;
   The world's worn blood runs cold;
Time staggers in his dotage now;
   Nature is growing old.   20

'Deluded by the summertime,
   Must I with wanton breath
Whisper and sigh? I trow not! – I
   Shall be the bride of Death.'

18 worn *om.* Sp.

Fair princes came with gems of price,
   And kings from lands afar.
'Jewels!' she said. 'I may not wed
   Till Death comes with a star.'

At midnight when she ceased to read,
   She pushed her lattice wide,   30
And saw the crested rollers lead
   The vanguard of the tide.

The mighty host of waters swayed,
   Commanded by the moon;
The wind a marching music made;
   The surges chimed in tune.

But she with sudden-startled ears
   O'erheard a ghostly sound –
Or drums that beat, or trampling feet,
   Above or underground.   40

The mountain-side was girt about
   With forests dark and deep.
'What meteor flashes in and out
   Thridding the darksome steep?'

Soon light and sound reached level ground,
   And lo, in blackest mail,
Along the shore a warrior
   Rode on a war-horse pale!

And from his helm as on he came
   A crescent lustre gleamed;
The charger's hoofs were shod with flame: 50
   The wet sand hissed and steamed.

'He leaves me! Nay; he turns this way
   From elfin lands afar.
' 'Tis Death,' she said. 'He comes to wed
   His true love with a star!

'No ring for me, no blushing groom,
   No love with all its ills,
No long-drawn life! I am the wife
   Of Death, whose first kiss kills.'   60

The rider reached the city wall;
   Over the gate he dashed;
Across the roofs the fire-shod hoofs
   Like summer-lightning flashed.

Before her bower the pale horse pawed
   The air, unused to rest;
The sable groom, he whispered 'Come!'
   And stooped his shining crest.

41–4 *See Notes.*

She sprang behind him; on her brow
    He placed his glowing star.   70
Back o'er the roofs the fire-shod hoofs
    Like lightning flashed afar.

Through hissing sand and shrivelled grass
    And flowers singed and dead,
By wood and lea, by stream and sea,
    The pale horse panting sped.

At last as they beheld the morn
    His sovereignty resume,
Deep in an ancient land forlorn
    They reached a marble tomb.   80

They lighted down and entered in:
    The tears, they brimmed her eyes;
She turned and took a lingering look,
    A last look at the skies;

Then went with Death. Her lambent star
    The sullen darkness lit
In avenues of sombre yews,
    Where ghosts did peer and flit.

But soon the way grew light as day;
    With wonderment and awe,   90
A golden land, a silver strand,
    And grass-green hills she saw.

In gown and smock good country folk
    In fields and meadows worked;
The salt seas wet the ruddy net
    Where glistering fishes lurked.

The meads were strewn with purple flowers,
    With every flower that blows;
And singing loud o'er cliff and cloud
    The larks, the larks arose!   100

'The sun is bright on heaven's brow,
    The world's fresh blood runs fleet;
Time is as young as ever now,
    Nature as fresh and sweet,'

Her champion said; then through the wood
    He led her to a bower;
He doffed his sable casque and stood
    A young man in his flower!

85 lambent star) star illumed Sp.   86 The blackness umber blotched Sp.
87 In) By Sp.   88 Where stealthy creatures watched. Sp.   97 strown Sp.
102 fresh *om*. Sp.   105 Oh! thus her champion whispered low, Sp.
106 He) And Sp.   107 casque and stood) helm, and lo! Sp.

'Lo! I am Life, your lover true!'
    He kissed her o'er and o'er.   110
And still she wist not what to do,
    And still she wondered more.

And they were wed. The swift years sped
    Till children's children laughed;
And joy and pain and joy again
    Mixed in the cup they quaffed.

Upon their golden wedding day,
    He said, 'How now, dear wife?'
Then she: 'I find the sweetest kind
    Of Death is Love and Life.'   120

109 He held her in his arms two; Sp.   115 While happiness and sore distress Sp.
116–17 See Notes.

59. ROBERT LOUIS STEVENSON

Why need we mourn his loss?
His name is with the great;
Close to the Southern Cross
He sleeps in matchless state.

Softly the stars shall shower
Their dewy brilliancies;
And many a Southern flower
Shall climb his grave to kiss.

Far down the murmuring river
Shall join the murmuring surge;   10
The haunted winds for ever
Shall chant his mountain-dirge.

In darkness and in light,
Until the Crack of Doom,
The morning and the night
Shall watch about his tomb.

High over field and fountain,
Far in a place apart,
He sleeps on Pala Mountain:
He lives in every heart.   20

60. SONGS FROM 'THE INTERREGNUM IN FAIRYLAND'

I

Where shall my little one play in his childhood?
Swing him a cradle deep in the wildwood,
    Where the timid squirrel abides,
    And the frightened roe-deer hides,
    Where the bronzy slow-worm crawls,
    And the mousing owlet calls

The world spins round, and the moon;
   And the sun spins round itself;
And this is my distaff tune,
   As I twirl the shining pelf.

The spider spins in the furze,
   And the dew begems his net;
Fate's unseen spindle whirrs,
   And the thread with blood is wet.

But tears nor blood shall stain,
   Nor rust of death or sin,   10
The thread of golden grain
   I spin, I spin.

61. PROEM TO *THE WONDERFUL MISSION OF EARL LAVENDER*

Though our eyes turn ever waveward,
   Where our sun is well-nigh set;
Though our Century totters graveward,
   We may laugh a little yet.

Oh! our age-end style perplexes
   All our elders' time has tamed;
On our sleeves we wear our sexes,
   Our diseases, unashamed.

Have we lost the mood romantic
   That was once our right by birth?   10
Lo! the greenest girl is frantic
   With the woe of all the earth!

But we know a British rumour,
   And we think it whispers well:
'We would ventilate our humour
   In the very jaws of Hell.'

Though our thoughts turn ever Doomwards,
   Though our sun is well-nigh set,
Though our Century totters tombwards,
   We may laugh a little yet.   20

6 elders YB.

62. A BALLAD OF AN ARTIST'S WIFE

'Sweet wife, this heavy-hearted age
   Is nought to us; we two shall look
To Art, and fill a perfect page
   In Life's ill-written doomsday book.'

2 naught MS.

He wrought in colour; blood and brain
   Gave fire and might; and beauty grew
And flowered with every magic stain
   His passion on the canvas threw.

They shunned the world and worldly ways:
   He laboured with a constant will;   10
But few would look, and none would praise,
   Because of something lacking still.

After a time her days with sighs
   And tears o'erflowed; for blighting need
Bedimmed the lustre of her eyes,
   And there were little mouths to feed.

'My bride shall ne'er be common-place.'
   He thought, and glanced; and glanced again:
At length he looked her in the face;
   And lo, a woman old and plain!   20

About this time the world's heart failed –
   The lusty heart no fear could rend;
In every land wild voices wailed,
   And prophets prophesied the end.

'To-morrow or to-day,' he thought,
   'May be Eternity; and I
Have neither felt nor fashioned aught
   That makes me unconcerned to die.

'With care and counting of the cost
   My life a sterile waste has grown,   30
Wherein my better dreams are lost
   Like chaff in the Sahara sown.

'I must escape this living tomb!
   My life shall yet be rich and free,
And on the very stroke of Doom
   My soul at last begin to be.

'Wife, children, duty, household fires
   For victims of the good and true!
For me my infinite desires,
   Freedom and things untried and new!   40

'I would encounter all the press
   Of thought and feeling life can show,
The sweet embrace, the aching stress
   Of every earthly joy and woe;

13 time *corr. from* while MS.   22 The heart we thought no fear could rend; M.S
33 A sterile waste, a living tomb! MS.   41 press) throng PM.   42 thoughts
and feelings PM.   43 The tidal wave, the storm and stress *corr. from* The
swelling tide, the storm and stress MS.; The sweet embrace, the stinging throng PM.

88

'And from the world's impending wreck
      And out of pain and pleasure weave
Beauty undreamt of, to bedeck
      The Festival of Doomsday Eve.'

He fled, and joined a motley throng
      That held carousal day and night;   50
With love and wit, with dance and song,
      They snatched a last intense delight.

Passion to mould an age's art,
      Enough to keep a century sweet,
Was in an hour consumed; each heart
      Lavished a life in every beat.

Amazing beauty filled the looks
      Of sleepless women; music bore
New wonder on its wings; and books
      Throbbed with a thought unknown before.   60

The sun began to smoke and flare
      Like a spent lamp about to die;
The dusky moon tarnished the air;
      The planets withered in the sky.

Earth reeled and lurched upon her road;
      Tigers were cowed, and wolves grew tame;
Seas shrank, and rivers backward flowed,
      And mountain-ranges burst in flame.

The artist's wife, a soul devout,
      To all these things gave little heed;   70
For though the sun was going out,
      There still were little mouths to feed.

And there were also shrouds to stitch,
      And chares to do; with all her might,
To feed her babes, she served the rich
      And kept her useless tears till night.

But by-and-by her sight grew dim;
      Her strength gave way; in desperate mood
She laid her down to die. 'Tell him,'
      She sighed, 'I fed them while I could.'   80

The children met a wretched fate;
      Self-love was all the vogue and vaunt,
And charity gone out of date;
      Wherefore they pined and died of want.

48 Doomsday-Eve *corr. from* Judgement-Eve MS.   64 planets) stars, they MS.
78 in desperate mood) her courage fled: MS.   80 I fed them while I could,'
she said. MS.   82 all *corr. from* now MS.

Aghast he heard the story: 'Dead!
   All dead in hunger and despair!
I courted misery,' he said;
   'But here is more than I can bear.'

Then, as he wrought, the stress of woe
   Appeared in many a magic stain;   90
And all adored his work, for lo,
   Tears mingled now with blood and brain!

'Look, look!' they cried; 'this man can weave
   Beauty from anguish that appals;'
And at the feast of Doomsday Eve
   They hung his pictures in their halls,

And gazed; and came again between
   The faltering dances eagerly;
They said, 'The loveliest we have seen,
   The last, of man's work, we shall see!'   100

Then was there neither death nor birth;
   Time ceased; and through the ether fell
The smoky sun, the leprous earth –
   A cinder and an icicle.

No wrathful vials were unsealed;
   Silent, the first things passed away:
No terror reigned; no trumpet pealed
   The dawn of Everlasting Day.

The bitter draught of sorrow's cup
   Passed with the seasons and the years;   110
And Wisdom dried for ever up
   The deep, old fountainhead of tears.

Out of the grave and ocean's bed
   The artist saw the people rise;
And all the living and the dead
   Were borne aloft to Paradise.

He came where on a silver throne
   A spirit sat for ever young;
Before her Seraphs worshipped prone,
   And Cherubs silver censers swung.   120

He asked, 'Who may this martyr be?
   What votaress of saintly rule?'
A Cherub said, 'No martyr; she
   Had one gift; she was beautiful.'

85 Dead? MS.   85-8 om. MS. 1st reading.   89 Then, as he wrought, the stress
of woe; corr. from Then did he feel the stress of woe MS.   90 Appeared corr.
from It gleamed MS.   94 appalls! MS.   96 in their halls; corr. from on their
walls; MS.

90

Then came he to another bower
   Where one sat on a golden seat,
Adored by many a heavenly Power
   With golden censers smoking sweet.

'This was some gallant wench who led
   Faint-hearted folk and set them free?'
'Oh, no! a simple maid,' they said,   130
   'Who spent her life in charity.'

At last he reached a mansion blest
   Where on a diamond throne, endued
With nameless beauty, one possessed
   Ineffable beatitude.

The praises of this matchless soul
   The sons of God proclaimed aloud;
From diamond censers odours stole;
   And Hierarchs before her bowed.   140

'Who was she?' God himself replied:
   'In misery her lot was cast;
She lived a woman's life, and died
   Working My work until the last.'

It was his wife. He said, 'I pray
   Thee, Lord, despatch me now to Hell.'
But God said, 'No; here shall you stay,
   And in her peace for ever dwell.'

144 Working my will into the last. *corr. from* Doing her duty to the last. MS.

63. A FROSTY MORNING

From heaven's high embrasure
   The sun with tufted rays
Illum'd the wandering azure
   And all the world's wide ways.

Usurping in its olden
   Abode the fog's demesne,
In watchet weeds and golden
   The still air sparkled keen.

On window-sill and door-post,
   On rail and tramway rust,   10
Embroidery of hoar-frost
   Was sewn like diamond dust.

Unthronged, or crowded densely
   By people business-led,
The pavements, tuned intensely,
   Rang hollow to the tread.

The traffic hurled and hammered
  Down every ringing street;
Like gongs the causeys clamoured,
  Like drums the asphalt beat.   20

While ruling o'er the olden
  Abode of fog unclean,
In watchet weeds and golden
  The still air sparkled keen.

18 ringing) vibrant Sp.

64. THE YORKSHIRE MORRIS-DANCERS

We heard the red-deer belling
  Far in the billowy wold,
While the North wind, proudly swelling
  His diapason rolled.

As we came downward striding
  Against the setting sun,
Across the rocky Riding
  We saw the moorland run –

An earthy tide, forsaking
  Its windy wilderness;   10
Dark waves of heather, breaking
  Among the furnaces.

Who can his sorrow measure
  Whom smoky toil confines?
Or what may thrill with pleasure
  The furnaces and mines?

But Time was primed with answers,
  And years a thousand leapt,
When up the Morris-Dancers
  In white and scarlet stept.   20

In fustian piped and braided,
  And armed with naked swords –
Oh, who can dance as they did,
  Chanting outlandish words?

Jig, hornpipe, double-shuffle –
  'Methinks there's music here!'
And not a slip or scuffle,
  For 'some bold captain's near.'

8 moorland *corr. from* heather MS.   13 Who *corr. from* What MS.

92

With toe and heel, and roll and reel
  They flashed their faultless feet;   30
Their hearts were stout, their swords were out;
  The drums Tantiro beat!

Gymnastical, fantastical,
  The rhythmic movements surged;
They sprang and pranced and counter-danced
  In devious mazes merged.

With clashing swords and trumpet words,
  Grand chain and ladies' chain,
They leapt and flang and played and sang,
  And danced it o'er again.   40

Oh, who can tell its history,
  Or when the dance began!
What art was this, what mystery?
  What rite of Christ or Pan?

For these Time has no answers;
  But by the moorland ways
You'll find the Morris-Dancers,
  Dancing for thirty days;

And hear the red-deer belling
  Among the heathery knolls,   50
While the North wind, proudly swelling
  His diapason rolls.

31 were *corr. from* are MS.

65. WINTER RAIN

Motionless, leaden cloud
  The region roofed and walled;
Beneath, a tempest shrieked aloud,
  And the forest beckoned and called.

The blackthorn coppice was all ablaze,
  And shot and garlanded,
With bronzed and wreathing bramble sprays,
  And bright leaves green and red.

The dripping pollards their shock-heads hung,
  And in the glistening shaws,   10
Lustres and glories of rubies, swung
  The dark wet crimson haws.

The dead leaves pattered and stole about
  Like elves in the sheltered glades,
And rushed down the broad green rides and out
  O'er the fields in windy raids.

93

The motionless, leaden sky,
    Emptied itself amain,
And the angry east with hue and cry
    Dashed at the pouring rain.   20

The forest rocked and sang:
    Behind the passing blast
Far off the new blast faintly rang
    Arrived and roared, and passed,
In the liberty of the open sea
    To find a home at last.

66. A BALLAD OF A POET BORN

Upon a ruddy ember eve
    They feasted in the hall;
By custom bound they handed round
    The harp to each and all.

While still the smoky rafters rang
    With burdens loud and long,
There rose a blushing youth and sang
    A wonderful new song.

For he had lounged among the flowers,
    Beside the mountain streams,   10
Deep-dyeing all the rosy hours
    With rosier waking dreams.

And lurked at night in seaside caves,
    Or rowed o'er harbour-bars,
Companion of the winds and waves
    Companion of the stars.

Therefore as searching sweet as musk
    The words were and the tune,
The while he sang of dawn and dusk,
    Of midnight and of noon.   20

'No longer shall more gifted lands
    Cast hither words of scorn.
Behold!' they said, and clapped their hands,
    'We have a poet born!

'Go forth with harp and scrip,' they cried,
    'And sing by land and sea,
In lanes and streets; the world is wide
    For errant minstrelsy.

'Accept their lot in every clime
    Who win the poet's name,   30
Homeless and poor, but rich in rhyme,
    And glittering with fame.'

'Forth would I go without all fear,
    Gladly to meet my fate;
But in the house my mother dear
    And my three sisters wait.

'My father's dead; my mother's eyes
    Are overcast with woe;
I hear my sisters' hungry cries;
    I dare not rise and go.'   40

They jeered him for a craven lout:
    'What care is this of thine?
Thou speakest now, without a doubt,
    Like some false Philistine!

'No poet can to others give:
    Leave folk to starve alone.'
He said, 'I dare not while I live;
    She has no other son.'

His sweetheart whispered in his ear
    'And me, love! what of me?'   50
He shook her off. 'Of you, enough,'
    He sighed; 'I set you free.'

He herded sheep, he herded kine;
    He rose before the day;
He ploughed and sowed and reaped and mowed,
    To keep the wolf at bay.

His harp, it rusted on the wall;
    His hands, his heart, grew hard;
The wine of life was turned to gall
    Because the song was marred.   60

So stubborn the accursed soil,
    So poor his pastoral lore,
With all his weary task and toil
    The wolf still pawed the door.

His mother died uncomforted;
    His sisters, one by one,
By beggars born were wooed and wed,
    And all his hopes undone.

Haggard and worn he took his harp;
    The sun shone broad and low: 70
'At dawn of night there shall be light;
    I now may rise and go.'

As he went o'er the plain he met
    The sweetheart of his youth:
'Whither away at close of day?
    Now answer me in sooth.'

'My kin have left me; it is time
     To win the poet's name;
Homeless and poor, but rich in rhyme,
     I go to conquer fame.'   80

'Oh, once you throned me in your heart
     All other maids above;
Sing to me here, before we part,
     Your sweetest song of love.'

He said, 'I'll play and sing a lay
     The sweetest ever sung.'
Then fumbled with his knotted hands
     The rusty strings among.

His quivering lips gave forth no song,
     His harp no silver sound;   90
Deep like a boy he blushed, and long
     He looked upon the ground.

He gnashed his teeth: 'Hell has begun,'
     He thought; 'I feel its blaze.'
With that he faced the setting sun,
     And then the woman's gaze.

'We two,' she said, 'must never part
     Till one shall reach death's goal.'
Her burning tears blistered his heart;
     Her pity flayed his soul.   100

'Sweetheart,' she pled, 'we can unite
     Life's torn and ravelled weft;
We yet may know love's deep delight:
     I have some beauty left.'

'But I am old – half dead; alack!
     I know the double loss
Of song and love!' He warned her back,
     And broke his harp across.

She stretched her arms: her pleading eyes,
     Her pleading blush were vain;   110
He fled towards the sunset skies
     Across the shadowed plain.

For years he wandered far and near,
     And begged in silence sad;
The children shrank from him in fear;
     The people called him mad.

81 Once thou did'st throne me in thy heart CM.

96

Upon a ruddy ember eve
  They feasted in the hall:
The old broken man, with no one's leave,
  Sat down among them all. 120

And while the swarthy rafters rang
  With antique praise of wine,
There rose a conscious youth and sang
  A ditty new and fine.

Of Fate's mills, and the human grist
  They grind at, was his song;
He cursed the canting moralist
  Who measures right and wrong.

'The earth, a flying tumour, wends
  Through space all blotched and blown 130
With suns and worlds, with odds and ends
  Of systems seamed and sewn;

'Beneath the sun it froths like yeast;
  Its fiery essence flares;
It festers into man and beast;
  It throbs with flowers and tares.

'Behold! 'tis but a heap of dust,
  Kneaded by fire and flood;
While hunger fierce, and fiercer lust,
  Drench it with tears and blood. 140

'Yet why seek after some new birth?
  For surely, late or soon,
This ague-fit we call the earth
  Shall be a corpse-cold moon.

'Why need we, lacking help and hope,
  By fears and fancies tossed,
Vainly debate with ruthless Fate,
  Fighting a battle lost?

'Fill high the bowl! We are the scum
  Of matter; fill the bowl; 150
Drink scathe to him, and death to him,
  Who dreams he has a soul.'

They clinked their cans and roared applause;
  The singer swelled with pride.
'You sneer and carp! Give me the harp,'
  The old man, trembling, cried.

They laughed and wondered, and grew still,
  To see one so aghast
Smiting the chords; but all his skill
  Came back to him at last. 160

And lo, as searching-sweet as musk
    The words were and the tune,
The while he sang of dawn and dusk,
    Of midnight and of noon;

Of heaven and hell, of times and tides;
    Of wintry winds that blow,
Of spring that haunts the world and hides
    Her flowers among the snow;

Of summer, rustling green and glad,
    With blossoms purfled fair;   170
Of autumn's wine-stained mouth and sad,
    Wan eyes, and golden hair;

Of Love, of Love, the wild sweet scent
    Of flowers, and words, and lives,
And loyal Nature's urgent bent
    Whereby the world survives;

Of magic Love that opes the ports
    Of sense and soul, that saith
The moonlight's meaning, and extorts
    The fealty of Death.   180

He sang of peace and work that bless
    The simple and the sage;
He sang of hope and happiness,
    He sang the Golden Age.

And the shamed listeners knew the spell
    That still enchants the years,
When the world's commonplaces fell
    In music on their ears.

'Go, bring a wreath of glossy bay
    To place upon his head!   190
A poet born!' Woe worth the day,
    They crowned a poet dead!

Dead, while upon the pulsing string
    Still beat his early rhyme –
The song the poet born shall sing
    Until the end of Time!

67. A HIGHWAY PIMPERNEL

Blossoms and buds, purple or pale,
    In saffron kerchiefs or watchet snoods,
Linger in ditches, crowd in the dale,
    In passionate tempers, or languorous moods,
High on the hill, deep in the vale,
    Over the fences and into the woods!

2 saffron kerchiefs) golden helmets PMM.

Richer and sweeter far than the rest,
   On the edge of the rut the cart-wheels chafe,
Like a fairy-buoy on a billow's crest,
   Hangs a wonderful little waif: 10
A pimpernel, clutching the earth's warm breast,
   Rocked by the traffic and sleeping safe.

All the morning in crimson state
   It flashed and glowed with zeal entire.
All the morning, steady as fate,
   Aflame with courage and high desire,
It watched the sun, its skyey mate,
   Lighting the world with golden fire.

But not a petal now will budge –
   Fast asleep since the stroke of noon!   20
And weary beggar and hawker trudge
   Grazing its leaves with their mouldy shoon,
And wheels and hoofs go by with a grudge
   To think that a flower should rest so soon!

17 skiey PMM.

68. SUNSET

By down and shore the South-west bore
   The scent of hay, an airy load:
As if at fault it seemed to halt,
   Then, softly whispering, took the road,
To haunt the evening like a ghost,
   Or some belated pilgrim lost.

High overhead the slow clouds sped;
   Beside the moon they furled their sails;
Soon in the skies their merchandise
   Of vapour, built in toppling bales,   10
Fulfilled a visionary pier
   That spanned the eastern atmosphere.

Low in the west the sun addressed
   His courtship to the dark-browed night;
While images of molten seas,
   Of snowy slope and crimson height,
Of valleys dim and gulfs profound
   Aloft a dazzling pageant wound.

Where shadows fell in glade and dell
   Uncovered shoulders nestled deep,   20
And here and there the braided hair
   Of rosy goddesses asleep;
For in a moment clouds may be
   Dead, and instinct with deity.

7 slow) swift SR.   19 shadow SR.

Oh when, and where, and how sirs?
  Down at Hindhead all the way
I wore Grant Allen's trousers
  Half a rainy summer day.

In silk as green as leeks
  One lady left her bower;
And I wore Grant Allen's breeks
  Till the witching midnight hour.

In brown like copper breeches
  A lady-bird came out;   10
And I wore Grant Allen's breeches
  While the rain poured like a spout.

Green velvet had Narceeches,
  And Allen stalked in grey,
And I wore his long-legged breeches
  Half the night and half the day.

I must leave the moorland reaches,
  Leave heather, broom and leave ling;
But I wore Grant Allen's breeches
  All an afternoon and evening.   20

15 his long-legged *corr. from* Grant Allen's MS.

70. THE LAST ROSE

'Oh, which is the last rose?
A blossom of no name.
At midnight the snow came;
At daybreak a vast rose,
In darkness unfurled,
O'er-petaled the world.

Its odourless pallor,
Blossomed forlorn,
Till radiant valour
Established the morn –   10
Till the night
Was undone
In her fight
With the sun.

The brave orb in state rose
And crimson he shone first;
While from the high vine
Of heaven the dawn burst,
Staining the great rose
From sky-line to sky-line.   20

The red rose of morn
A white rose at noon turned;
But at sunset reborn,
All red again soon burned.
Then the pale rose of noonday
Re-bloomed in the night,
And spectrally white
In the light
Of the moon lay.

But the vast rose   30
Was scentless,
And this is the reason:
When the blast rose
Relentless,
And brought in due season
The snow-rose, the last rose
Congealed in its breath,
There came with it treason;
The traitor was Death.

In lee-valleys crowded,   40
The sheep and the birds
Were frozen and shrouded
In flights and in herds.
In highways
And byways
The young and the old
Were tortured and maddened
And killed by the cold.
But many were gladdened
By the beautiful last rose,   50
The blossom of no name
That came when the snow came,
In darkness unfurled –
The wonderful vast rose
That filled all the world.

71. SERENADE (1250 A.D.)

With stars, with trailing galaxies,
   Like a white-rose bower in bloom,
Darkness garlands the vaulted skies,
   Day's ethereal tomb;
A whisper without from the briny west
   Thrills and sweetens the gloom;
Within, Miranda seeks her rest
   High in her turret-room.

4 ethereal) adorn'd CB., WS., NB.

Armies upon her walls encamp
    In silk and silver thread;   10
Chased and fretted, her silver lamp
    Dimly lights her bed;
And now the silken screen is drawn,
    The velvet coverlet spread;
And the pillow of down and snowy lawn
    Mantles about her head.

With violet-scented rain
    Sprinkle the rushy floor;
Let the tapestry hide the tinted pane,
    And cover the chamber door;   20
But leave a glimmering beam,
    Miranda belamour,
To touch and gild my waking dream,
    For I am your troubadour.

I sound my throbbing lyre,
    And sing to myself below;
Her damsel sits beside the fire
    Crooning a song I know;
The tapestry shakes on the wall,
    The shadows hurry and go,   30
The silent flames leap up and fall,
    And the muttering birch-logs glow.

Deep and sweet she sleeps,
    Because of her love for me;
And deep and sweet the peace that keeps
    My happy heart in fee!
Peace on the heights, in the deeps,
    Peace over hill and lea,
Peace through the star-lit steeps,
    Peace on the starlit sea,   40
Because a simple maiden sleeps
    Dreaming a dream of me!

14 coverlets CB.

72. PIPER, PLAY!

Now the furnaces are out,
    And the aching anvils sleep;
Down the road the grimy rout
    Tramples homeward twenty deep.
        Piper, play! Piper, play!
            Though we be o'erlaboured men,
        Ripe for rest, pipe your best!
            Let us foot it once again!

Bridled looms delay their din;
  All the humming wheels are spent;   10
Busy spindles cease to spin;
  Warp and woof must rest content.
    Piper, play! Piper, play!
      For a little we are free!
      Foot it girls and shake your curls,
        Haggard creatures though we be!

Racked and soiled the faded air
  Freshens in our holiday;
Clouds and tides our respite share;
  Breezes linger by the way.   20
    Piper, rest! Piper, rest!
      Now, a carol of the moon!
    Piper, piper, play your best!
      Melt the sun into your tune!

We are of the humblest grade;
  Yet we dare to dance our fill:
Male and female were we made –
  Fathers, mothers, lovers still!
    Piper – softly; soft and low
      Pipe of love in mellow notes,   30
    Till the tears begin to flow,
      And our hearts are in our throats!

Nameless as the stars of night
  Far in galaxies unfurled,
Yet we wield unrivalled might,
  Joints and hinges of the world!
    Night and day! night and day!
      Sound the song the hours rehearse!
    Work and play! work and play!
      The order of the universe!   40

Now the furnaces are out,
  And the aching anvils sleep;
Down the road a merry rout
  Dances homeward, twenty deep.
    Piper, play! Piper, play!
      Wearied people though we be,
    Ripe for rest, pipe your best!
      For a little we are free!

30 Pipe) Play DC.

73. A BALLAD OF A WORKMAN

All day beneath polluted skies
  He laboured in a clanging town;
At night he read with bloodshot eyes
  And fondly dreamt of high renown.

'My time is filched by toil and sleep;
    My heart,' he thought, 'is clogged with dust;
My soul that flashed from out the deep,
    A magic blade, begins to rust.

'For me the lamps of heaven shine;
    For me the cunning seasons care;   10
The old undaunted sea is mine,
    The stable earth, the ample air.

'Yet a dark street – at either end,
    A bed, an anvil – prisons me,
Until my desperate state shall mend,
    And Death, the Saviour, set me free.

'Better a hundred times to die,
    And sink at once into the mould,
Than like a stagnant puddle lie
    With arabesques of scum enscrolled.   20

'I must go forth and view the sphere
    I own. What can my courage daunt?
Instead of dying daily here,
    The worst is dying once of want.

'I drop the dream of high renown;
    I ask but to possess my soul.'
At dawn he left the silent town,
    And quaking toward the forest stole.

He feared that he might want the wit
    To light on Nature's hidden hearth,   30
And deemed his rusty soul unfit
    To win the beauty of the earth.

But when he came among the trees,
    So slowly built, so many-ring'd,
His doubting thought could soar at ease
    In colour steep'd, with passion wing'd.

Occult remembrances awoke
    Of outlaws in the good greenwood,
And antique times of woaded folk
    Began to haunt his brain and blood.   40

No longer hope appeared a crime:
    He sang; his very heart and flesh
Aspired to join the ends of time,
    And forge and mould the world afresh.

'I dare not choose to run in vain;
    I must continue toward the goal.'
The pulse of life beat strong again,
    And in a flash he found his soul.

'The worker never knows defeat,
　Though unvictorious he may die:
The anvil and the grimy street,
　My destined throne and Calvary!'

Back to the town he hastened, bent –
　So swiftly did his passion change –
On selfless plans. 'I shall invent
　A means to amplify the range

'Of human power: find the soul wings,
　If not the body! Let me give
Mankind more mastery over things,
　More thought, more joy, more will to live.'

He overtook upon the way
　A tottering ancient travel-worn:
'Lend me your arm, good youth, I pray;
　I scarce shall see another morn.'

Dread thought had carved his pallid face,
　And bowed his form, and blanched his hair;
In every part he bore some trace,
　Or some deep dint of uncouth care.

The workman led him to his room,
　And would have nursed him. 'No,' he said;
'It is my self-appointed doom
　To die upon a borrowed bed;

'But hear and note my slightest word.
　I am a man without a name.
I saw the Bastille fall; I heard
　The giant Mirabeau declaim.

'I saw the stormy dawn look pale
　Across the sea-bound battle-field,
When through the hissing sleet and hail
　The clarions of Cromwell pealed:

'I watched the deep-souled Puritan
　Grow greater with the desperate strife:
The cannon waked; the shouting van
　Charged home; and victory leapt to life.

'At Seville in the Royal square
　I saw Columbus as he passed
Laurelled to greet the Catholic pair
　Who had believed in him at last:

'I saw the Andalusians fill
　Windows, and roofs, and balconies –
A firmament of faces still,
　A galaxy of wondering eyes:

50

60

70

80

90

'For he had found the unknown shore,
    And made the world's great dream come true:
I think that men shall never more
    Know anything so strange and new.

'By meteor light when day had set
    I looked across Angora's plain,
And watched the fall of Bajazet,
    The victory of Tamerlane.   100

'In that old city where the vine
    Dislodged the seaweed, once I saw
The inexorable Florentine:
    He looked my way; I bent with awe

'Before his glance, for this was he
    Who drained the dregs of sorrow's cup
In fierce disdain; it seemed to me
    A spirit passed, my hair stood up.

Draw nearer: breath and sight begin
    To fail me: nearer, ere I die. –   110
I saw the brilliant Saladin,
    Who taught the Christians courtesy;

'And Charlemagne, whose dreaded name,
    I first in far Bokhara heard;
Mohammed, with the eyes of flame,
    The lightning-blow, the thunder-word.

'I saw Him nailed upon a tree,
    Whom once beside an inland lake
I had beheld in Galilee
    Speaking as no man ever spake.   120

'I saw imperial Cæsar fall;
    I saw the star of Macedon;
I saw from Troy's enchanted wall
    The death of Priam's mighty son.

'I heard in streets of Troy at night
    Cassandra prophesying fire. . . .
A flamelit face upon my sight
    Flashes: I see the World's Desire!

'My life ebbs fast: nearer! I sought
    A means to overmaster fate: 130
Me, the Egyptian Hermes taught
    In old Hermopolis the Great:

123 enchanted) magic SR.   125 streets of Troy) Troy's streets SR.

'I pierced to Nature's inmost hearth,
    And wrung from her with toil untold
The soul and substance of the earth,
    The Seed of life, the Seed of gold.

'Until the end I meant to stay;
    But thought has here so small a range;
And I am tired of night and day,
    And tired of men who never change.   140

'All earthly hope ceased long ago;
    Yet, like a mother young and fond
Whose child is dead, I ache to know
    If there be anything beyond.

'Dark – all is darkness! Are you there?
    Give me your hand. – I choose to die.
This holds my secret – should you dare;
    And this, to bury me. . . . Good-bye.

Amazement held the workman's soul;
    He took the alchemist's bequest –   150
A light purse and a parchment scroll;
    And watched him slowly sink to rest.

And nothing could he dream or think;
    He went like one bereft of sense,
Till passion overbore the brink
    Of all his wistful continence,

When his strange guest was laid in earth
    And he had read the scroll: 'Behold,
I can procure from Nature's hearth
    The Seed of Life, the Seed of Gold!   160

'For ever young! Now, time and tide
    Must wait for me; my life shall vie
With fate and fortune stride for stride
    Until the sun drops from the sky.

'Gold at a touch! Nations and kings
    Shall come and go at my command;
I shall control the secret springs
    Of enterprise in every land;

'And hasten on the Perfect Day:
    Great men may break the galling chains;   170
Sweet looks light up the toilsome way;
    But I alone shall hold the reins!

'All fragrance, all delightfulness,
    And all the glory, all the power,
That sound and colour can express,
    Shall be my ever-growing dower.

'And I shall know, and I shall love
    In every age, in every clime
All beauty. . . . I, enthroned above
    Humanity, the peer of Time!   180

'Nay – selfish! I shall give to men
    The Seed of Life, the Seed of Gold;
Restore the Golden Age again
    At once, and let no soul grow old.

'But gold were then of no avail,
    And death would cease – unhallowed doom!
The heady wine of life grow stale,
    And earth become a living tomb!

'And youth would end, and truth decline,
    And only pale illusion rule;   190
For it is death makes love divine,
    Men human, life so sweet and full!'

He burnt the scroll. 'I shall not cheat
    My destiny. Life, death for me!
The anvil and the grimy street,
    My unknown throne and Calvary!

'Only obedience can be great;
    It brings the Golden Age again:
Even to be still, abiding fate,
    Is kingly ministry to men!   200

'I drop the dream of high renown:
    A nameless private in the strife,
Life, take me; take me, clanging town;
    And death, the eager zest of life.

'The hammered anvils reel and chime;
    The breathless, belted wheels ring true;
The workmen join the ends of time,
    And forge and mould the world anew.'

74. SPRING SONG

About the flowerless land adventurous bees
    Pickeering hum; the rooks debate, divide,
    With many a hoarse aside,
In solemn conclave on the budding trees;
Larks in the skies and ploughboys o'er the leas
Carol as if the winter ne'er had been;
    The very owl comes out to greet the sun;
    Rivers high-hearted run;
And hedges mantle with a flush of green.

The curlew calls me where the salt winds blow; 10
   His troubled note dwells mournfully and dies;
   Then the long echo cries
Deep in my heart. Ah, surely I must go!
For there the tides, moon-haunted, ebb and flow
And there the seaboard murmurs resonant;
   The waves their interwoven fugue repeat
   And brooding surges beat
A slow, melodious, continual chant.

75. A NORTHERN SUBURB

Nature selects the longest way,
   And winds about in tortuous grooves;
A thousand years the oaks decay;
   The wrinkled glacier hardly moves.

But here the whetted fangs of change
   Daily devour the old demesne –
The busy farm, the quiet grange,
   The wayside inn, the village green.

In gaudy yellow brick and red,
   With rooting pipes, like creepers rank,   10
The shoddy terraces o'erspread
   Meadow, and garth, and daisied bank.

With shelves for rooms the houses crowd,
   Like draughty cupboards in a row –
Ice-chests when wintry winds are loud,
   Ovens when summer breezes blow.

Roused by the fee'd policeman's knock,
   And sad that day should come again,
Under the stars the workmen flock
   In haste to reach the workmen's train.   20

For here dwell those who must fulfil
   Dull tasks in uncongenial spheres,
Who toil through dread of coming ill,
   And not with hope of happier years –

The lowly folk who scarcely dare
   Conceive themselves perhaps misplaced,
Whose prize for unremitting care
   Is only not to be disgraced.

76. A BALLAD OF TANNHÄUSER

'What hardy, tattered wretch is that
   Who on our Synod dares intrude?'
Pope Urban with his council sat,
   And near the door Tannhäuser stood.

His eye with light unearthly gleamed;
   His yellow hair hung round his head
In elf locks lusterless: he seemed
   Like one new-risen from the dead.

'Hear me, most Holy Father, tell
   The tale that burns my soul within.   10
I stagger on the brink of hell;
   No voice but yours can shrive my sin.'

'Speak, sinner.' 'From my father's house
   Lightly I stepped in haste for fame;
And hoped by deeds adventurous
   High on the world to carve my name.

'At early dawn I took my way;
   My heart with peals of gladness rang;
Nor could I leave the woods all day,
   Because the birds so sweetly sang.   20

'But when the happy birds had gone
   To rest, and night with panic fears
And blushes deep came stealing on,
   Another music thrilled my ears.

'I heard the evening wind serene,
   And all the wandering waters sing
The deep delight the day had been,
   The deep delight the night would bring.

'I heard the wayward earth express
   In one long-drawn melodious sigh   30
The rapture of the sun's caress,
   The passion of the brooding sky.

'The air, a harp of myriad chords,
   Intently murmured overhead;
My heart grew great with unsung words:
   I followed where the music led.

'It led me to a mountain-chain,
   Wherein athwart the deepening gloom,
High-hung above the wooded plain,
   Appeared a summit like a tomb.   40

'Aloft a giddy pathway wound
   That brough. me to a darksome cave:
I heard, undaunted, underground
   Wild winds and wilder voices rave,

33–5 *See Notes.*

110

'And plunged into that stormy world.
   Cold hands assailed me impotent
In the gross darkness; serpents curled
   About my limbs; but on I went.

'The wild winds buffeted my face;
   The wilder voices shrieked despair;   50
A stealthy step with mine kept pace,
   And subtle terror steeped the air.

'But the sweet sound that throbbed on high
   Had left the upper world; and still
A cry rang in my heart – a cry!
   For lo, far in the hollow hill,

'The dulcet melody withdrawn
   Kept welling through the fierce uproar.
As I have seen the molten dawn
   Across a swarthy tempest pour,   60

'So suddenly the magic note,
   Transformed to light, a glittering brand,
Out of the storm and darkness smote
   A peaceful sky, a dewy land.

'I scarce could breathe, I might not stir,
   The while there came across the lea,
With singing maidens after her,
   A woman wonderful to see.

'Her face – her face was strong and sweet;
   Her looks were loving prophecies;   70
She kissed my brow: I kissed her feet –
   A woman wonderful to kiss.

'She took me to a place apart
   Where eglantine and roses wove
A bower, and gave me all her heart –
   A woman wonderful to love.

'As I lay worshipping my bride,
   While rose leaves in her bosom fell,
And dreams came sailing on a tide
   Of sleep, I heard a matin bell.   80

'It beat my soul as with a rod
   Tingling with horror of my sin;
I thought of Christ, I thought of God,
   And of the fame I meant to win.

55 heart) blood SR.

III

'I rose; I ran; nor looked behind;
    The doleful voices shrieked despair
In tones that pierced the crashing wind;
    And subtle terror warped the air.

'About my limbs the serpents curled;
    The stealthy step with mine kept pace;   90
But soon I reached the upper world:
    I sought a priest; I prayed for grace.

'He said, "Sad sinner, do you know
    What fiend this is, the baleful cause
Of your dismay?" I loved her so
    I never asked her what she was.

He said, "Perhaps not God above
    Can pardon such unheard-of ill:
It was the pagan Queen of Love
    Who lured you to her haunted hill!   100

' "Each hour you spent with her was more
    Than a full year! Only the Pope
Can tell what heaven may have in store
    For one who seems past help and hope."

'Forthwith I took the way to Rome:
    I scarcely slept; I scarcely ate:
And hither quaking am I come,
    But resolute to know my fate.

'Most Holy Father, save my soul! . . .
    Ah God! again I hear the chime,   110
Sweeter than liquid bells that toll
    Across a lake at vesper time . . .

'Her eyelids droop . . . I hear her sigh . . .
    The roseleaves fall . . . She falls asleep . . .
The cry rings in my blood – the cry
    That surges from the deepest deep.

'No man was ever tempted so! –
    I say not this in my defence . . .
Help, Father, help! or I must go!
    The dulcet music draws me hence!'   120

He knelt – he fell upon his face.
    Pope Urban said, 'The eternal cost
Of guilt like yours eternal grace
    Dare not remit: your soul is lost.

'When this dead staff I carry grows
    Again and blossoms, heavenly light
May shine on you.' Tannhäuser rose;
    And all at once his face grew bright.

He saw the emerald leaves unfold,
   The emerald blossoms break and glance;   130
They watched him, wondering to behold
   The rapture of his countenance.

The undivined, eternal God
   Looked on him from the highest heaven,
And showed him by the budding rod
   There was no need to be forgiven.

He heard melodious voices call
   Across the world, an elfin shout;
And when he left the council-hall,
   It seemed a great light had gone out.   140

With anxious heart, with troubled brow,
   The Synod turned upon the Pope.
They saw; they cried, 'A living bough,
   A miracle, a pledge of hope!'

And Urban trembling saw: 'God's way
   Is not as man's,' he said. 'Alack!
Forgive me, gracious heaven, this day
   My sin of pride. Go, bring him back.'

But swift as thought Tannhäuser fled,
   And was not found. He scarcely slept;   150
He scarcely ate; for overhead
   The ceaseless, dulcet music kept

Wafting him on. And evermore
   The foliate staff he saw at Rome
Pointed the way; and the winds bore
   Sweet voices whispering him to come.

The air, a world-enfolding flood
   Of liquid music poured along;
And the wild cry within his blood
   Became at last a golden song.   160

'All day,' he sang – 'I feel all day
   The earth dilate beneath my feet;
I hear in fancy far away
   The tidal heart of ocean beat.

'My heart amasses as I run
   The depth of heaven's sapphire flower;
The resolute, enduring sun
   Fulfils my soul with splendid power.

'I quiver with divine desire;
   I clasp the stars; my thoughts immerse   170
Themselves in space; like fire in fire
   I melt into the universe.

'For I am running to my love:
    The eager roses burn below;
Orion wheels his sword above,
    To guard the way God bids me go.'

At dusk he reached the mountain chain,
    Wherein athwart the deepening gloom,
High hung above the wooded plain
    The Hörselberg rose like a tomb.   180

He plunged into the under-world;
    Cold hands assailed him impotent
In the gross darkness; serpents curled
    About his limbs; but on he went.

The wild winds buffeted his face;
    The wilder voices shrieked despair;
A stealthy step with his kept pace;
    And subtle terror steeped the air.

But once again the magic note,
    Transformed to light, a glittering brand,   190
Out of the storm and darkness smote
    A peaceful sky, a dewy land.

And once again he might not stir,
    The while there came across the lea
With singing maidens after her
    The Queen of Love so fair to see.

Her happy face was strong and sweet;
    Her looks were loving prophecies;
She kissed his brow; he kissed her feet –
    He kissed the ground her feet did kiss.   200

She took him to a place apart
    Where eglantine and roses wove
A bower, and gave him all her heart –
    The Queen of Love, the Queen of Love.

As he lay worshipping his bride
    While rose-leaves in her bosom fell,
And dreams came sailing on a tide
    Of sleep, he heard a matin-bell.

'Hark! Let us leave the magic hill,'
    He said, 'And live on earth with men.'   210
'No; here,' she said, 'we stay, until
    The Golden Age shall come again.'

And so they wait, while empires sprung
    Of hatred thunder past above,
Deep in the earth for ever young
    Tannhäuser and the Queen of Love.

77. 'SOME SAID HE WAS STRONG'

Some said, 'He was strong.' He was weak;
For he never could sing or speak
Of the things beneath or the things above,
Till his soul was touched by death or love.

Some said, 'He was weak.' They were wrong;
For the soul must be strong
That can break into song
Of the things beneath and the things above,
At the stroke of death, at the touch of love.

78. 'HIS HEART WAS WORN AND SORE'

His heart was worn and sore;
He was old before his time;
He had wasted half his life.

Night – it was always night,
And never a star above:
But the ring of a manly stroke,
The flash of a gentle look,
The touch of a comrade's hand
Groping for his on the march,
Were more to him than the day.   10

At the thought of his youth,
At the pulse of love,
At the swoop of death,
He sang aloud in the dark,
And touched the heart of the world.

79. A SONG OF THE ROAD

Among the hills he woke;
  A star, low-hung and late,
Dwindled as the morning broke
  The sable-silvered state
Wherein night braves the ruddy stroke
  That daily seals her fate.

He went by bank and brae
  Where fern and heather spread;
Azure bells beset the way,
  And blossoms gold and red;   10
Below, the burn sang all the day;
  The larks sang overhead.

He left the hills and came
  Among the woods and dells;
Golden helmets flashed like flame;
  The witches wove their spells;
In moss-green silk the elfin dame
  Rode by with silver bells.

He came where four roads met;
  He chose a narrow one;   20
Spiny thorns the way beset;
  But at the end there shone
The bright reward that pilgrims get,
  And Heaven's unsetting sun.

He went with heavy mind,
  For sharp the thorns did sting.
Far and fitfully behind
  He heard sweet laughter ring –
Delighted voices on the wind,
  And freshness of the spring.   30

He paused in sore dismay,
  And, pondering right and wrong,
Turned and left the narrow way
  To join the pleasant throng,
That wandered happily astray
  The primrose path along.

Alas! he fled once more;
  For at the end a cloud,
Streaked with flame, and stained with gore,
  And torn with curses loud,   40
O'er hung a melancholy shore
  And veiled a hopeless crowd.

He followed then the road
  Wherein at first he hied;
Soon he came where men abode
  And loved, and wrought, and died;
And straight the Broad and Narrow ways,
  Heaven fair and Hell obscene,
For ever vanished out of space,
  Spectres that ne'er had been.   50

80. A BALLAD OF A COWARD

The trumpets pealed; the echoes sang
  A tossing fugue; before it died,
Again the rending trumpets rang,
  Again the phantom notes replied.

116

In galleries, on straining roofs,
    At once ten thousand tongues were hushed,
When down the lists a storm of hoofs
    From either border thundering rushed.

A knight whose arms were chased and set
    With gold and gems, in fear withdrew   10
Before the fronts of tourney met,
    Before the spears in splinters flew.

He reached the wilds. He cast away
    His lance and shield and arms of price;
He turned his charger loose, and lay
    Face-downwards in his cowardice.

His wife had seen the recreant fly:
    She followed, found, and called his name.
'Sweetheart, I will not have you die:
    My love,' she said, 'can heal your shame.'   20

Not long his vanity withstood
    Her gentleness. He left his soul
To her; and her solicitude,
    He being a coward, made him whole.

Yet was he blessed in heart and head;
    Forgiving; of his riches free;
Wise was he too, and deeply read,
    And ruled his earldom righteously.

A war broke out. With fateful speed
    The foe, eluding watch and ward,   30
Conquered; and none was left to lead
    The land, save this faint-hearted lord.

'Here is no shallow tournament,
    No soulless, artificial fight.
Courageously, in deep content,
    I go to combat for the right.'

The hosts encountered: trumpets spoke;
    Drums called aloud; the air was torn
With cannon, light by stifling smoke
    Estopped, and shrieking battle born.   40

But he? – he was not in the van!
    The vision of his child and wife?
Even that deserted him. He ran –
    The coward ran to save his life.

The lowliest men would sooner face
    A thousand dreadful deaths, than come
Before their loved ones in disgrace;
    Yet this sad coward hurried home:

117

For, as he fled, his cunning heart
    Declared he might be happy yet   50
In some retreat where Love and Art
    Should swathe his soul against regret.

'My wife! my son! For their dear sakes.'
    He thought, 'I save myself by flight.' –
He reached his place. 'What comet shakes
    Its baleful tresses on the night

'Above my towers?' Alas, the foe
    Had been before with sword and fire!
His loved ones in their blood lay low:
    Their dwelling was their funeral pyre.   60

Then he betook him to a hill
    Which in his happy times had been
His silent friend, meaning to kill
    Himself upon its bosom green.

But an old mood at every tread
    Returned; and with assured device
The wretched coward's cunning head
    Distilled it into cowardice.

'A snowy owl on silent wings
    Sweeps by; and, ah! I know the tune   70
The wayward night-wind sweetly sings
    And dreaming birds in coverts croon.

'The cocks their muffled catches crow;
    The river ripples dark and bright;
I hear the pastured oxen low,
    And the whole rumour of the night.

'The moon comes from the wind-swept hearth
    Of heaven; the stars beside her soar;
The seas and harvests of the earth
    About her shadowy footsteps pour.   80

'But though remembrances, all wet
    With happy tears, their tendrils coil
Close round my heart; though I be set
    And rooted in the ruddy soil,

'My pulses with the planets leap;
    The veil is rent before my face;
My aching nerves are mortised deep
    In furthest cavities of space;

66 Returned) Awoke B.

'Through the pervading ether speed
　My thoughts that now the stars rehearse;　　　　90
And should I take my life, the deed
　Would disarray the universe.'

Gross cowardice! Hope, while we breathe,
　Can make the meanest prize his breath,
And still with starry garlands wreathe
　The nakedness of life and death.

He wandered vaguely for a while;
　Then thought at last to hide his shame
And self-contempt far in an isle
　Among the outer deeps; but came,　　　　100

Even there, upon a seaboard dim,
　Where like the slowly ebbing tide
That weltered on the ocean's rim
　With sanguine hues of sunset dyed,

The war still lingered. Suddenly,
　Ere he could run, the bloody foam
Of battle burst about him; he,
　Scarce knowing what he did, struck home,

As those he helped began to fly,
　Bidding him follow. 'Nay,' he said;　　　　110
'Nay; I die fighting – even I!'
　And happy and amazed fell dead.

106 bloody) ruddy B.

81. WAITING

Within unfriendly walls
　We starve – or starve by stealth.
Oxen fatten in their stalls;
　You guard the harrier's health:
They never can be criminals,
　And can't compete for wealth.
　　From the mansion and the palace
　　　Is there any help or hail
　　For the tenants of the alleys,
　　　Of the workhouse and the jail?　　　　10

Though lands await our toil,
　And earth half-empty rolls,
Cumberers of English soil,
　We cringe for orts and doles –
Prosperity's accustomed foil,
　Millions of useless souls.

119

In the gutters and the ditches
　　Human vermin festering lurk –
We, the rust upon your riches;
　　We, the flaw in all your work.　　　　　　20

Come down from where you sit;
　　We look to you for aid.
Take us from the miry pit,
　　And lead us undismayed:
Say, 'Even you, outcast, unfit,
　　Forward with sword and spade!'
　　　　And myriads of us idle
　　　　　　Would thank you through our tears,
　　　　Though you drove us with a bridle,
　　　　　　And a whip about our ears!　　　30

From cloudy cape to cape
　　The teeming waters seethe;
Golden grain and purple grape
　　The regions overwreathe.
Will no one help us to escape?
　　We scarce have room to breathe.
　　　　You might try to understand us:
　　　　　　We are waiting night and day
　　　　For a captain to command us,
　　　　　　And the word we must obey.　　　40

27 myriads) millions CB.　　　35–6 *See Notes*.　　　37 You might) Will you CB.

82. A NEW SONG OF ORPHEUS

I wandered where the surges rang
　　Tolling a pæan heavily,
And heard the voice that once outsang
　　The Sirens sing across the sea.

Not now beneath the Argo's sails,
　　Nor racked with hope and fear before
Dread Dis; but in the Cretan vales,
　　Where first he learnt his magic lore.

Hoarsely he sang and struck his lyre: –
　　'Once in eight years seven maids seven men　　10
Glutted the Minotaur's desire,
　　Till Theseus slew him in his den.

'But fiercer than the foully-charmed
　　Pasiphæ's son, upon our shore
An Argus-eyed, Briareus-armed,
　　And Hydra-headed Minotaur

120

'Would wallow in the blood of those
    He would defend. Shall Ida watch
What Ararat beheld – her snows
    Turn paler at the fell debauch   20

'Of slaughter, lust, and fire? Behold!' –
    The song grew liquid – 'Who is he
Coming from Athens as of old
    A saviour came across the sea?

'A second Theseus bringing peace!
    What power shall place him under ban?
Who dare forbid the Prince of Greece
    To aid the land where Greece began?

'For Berecynthian Cybele,
    Mother of Gods, here taught the use   30
Of towns and tilth and husbandry;
    Here Almathea suckled Zeus.

'The equal laws Lycurgus gave
    To Sparta first in Crete were known.
Bid us again be free and brave!
    Come, Prince of Greece, and help your own!'

83. COMING

In every noble name
    What are we waiting for?
We pray, and we declaim!
    Are we afraid of war?
        Drummer, beat the drum!
            Trumpets, blow!
        Anguished voices bid us come!
            At last we go!

Shall Europe cry 'God speed!'
    To some less famous land?   10
Nay; who shall take the lead,
    If England holds her hand?
        Proud? We should be proud!
            Drummer, beat the drum!
        Anguished voices call aloud,
            'England, come!'

Upon the blood-stained sod
    A helpless people bow;
We still have stood for God,
    And shall we falter now?   20
        The sword is in our hand;
            Our step is on the sea;
        We are coming, sister land,
            To set you free!

121

Whene'er Thy mosque I trod
    I heard my sabre sigh,
'There is no God but God;
    Believe in Him or die!

'Abdul the Bless'd! You must
    Pursue the Prophet's path!
Up! slake the eager lust
    Of God's avenging wrath!'

Islam! a dreadful call!
    Long, long I made delay.   10
'My back is at the wall:
    Look, Lord; I stand at bay!

'The eagles throng,' I cried,
    'Expecting me to die:
The Powers my throne deride;
    I am the Sick Man, I!'

But there my troops were ranked,
    A weapon to my hand;
And still my sabre clanked,
    'Go forth and purge the land!'   20

At last Mohammed's sword,
    The Key of Heaven and Hell,
I drew; and at my word
    A hundred thousand fell,

God-hated: in their day,
    Foul cumberers of the earth;
Now theirs is ours; and they,
    Fuel for Shetan's hearth.

Though journalists proclaimed
    That things were at the worst;   30
Though Ministers were blamed;
    Though poets sang and cursed;

Though priests in every church
    Prayed God to shield the right,
God left them in the lurch:
    They were afraid to fight!

Words, words they slung; while we,
    Indifferent to the cost,
Fulfilled God's high decree
    In slaughtering the lost.   40

The Powers blasphemed beneath;
    Above Heaven smiled delight;
Ho! Europe gnashed her teeth;
    And Greece began to bite.

They fell into the pit
    They dug for our dismay;
The biter soon was bit;
    The spoilers are our prey!

The Sick Man? No; the Strong!
    Prestige is ours again!   50
God gives us a new song
    Like sunshine after rain.

Grasping a shadow, lo,
    The Dog has lost his bone –
The Christian Dog! Even so!
    Allah is God alone!

85. THE BADGE OF MEN

'In shuttered rooms let others grieve,
    And coffin thought in speech of lead;
I'll tie my heart upon my sleeve:
    It is the Badge of Men,' he said.

His friends forsook him: 'Who was he!'
    Even beggars passed him with a grin:
Physicians called it lunacy;
    And priests, the unpardonable sin.

He strove, he struck for standing-ground:
    They beat him humbled from the field;   10
For though his sword was keen, he found
    His mangled heart a feeble shield.

He slunk away, and sadly sought
    The wilderness – false friend of woe.
'Man is The Enemy,' he thought;
    But Nature proved a fiercer foe:

The vampire sucked, the vulture tore,
    And the old dragon left its den,
Agape to taste the thing he wore –
    The ragged, bleeding Badge of Men.   20

'Against the Fates there steads no charm,
    For every force takes its own part:
I'll wear a buckler on my arm,
    And in my bosom hide my heart!'

But in his bosom prisoned fast
   It pained him more than when it beat
Upon his sleeve; and so he cast
   His trouble to the ghouls to eat.

Back to the city, there and then
   He ran; and saw, through all disguise,   30
On every sleeve the Badge of Men:
   For truth appears to cruel eyes.

Straight with his sword he laid about,
   And hacked and pierced their hearts, until
The beaten terror-stricken rout
   Begged on their knees to know his will.

He said, 'I neither love nor hate;
   I would command in everything.'
They answered him, 'Heartless and great!
   Your slaves we are: be you our King!'   40

86. EARTH TO EARTH

Where the region grows without a lord,
   Between the thickets emerald-stoled,
In the woodland bottom the virgin sward,
   The cream of the earth, through depths of mold
      O'erflowing wells from secret cells,
While the moon and the sun keep watch and ward,
   And the ancient world is never old.

Here, alone, by the grass-green hearth
   Tarry a little: the mood will come!
Feel your body a part of earth;   10
   Rest and quicken your thought at home;
      Take your ease with the brooding trees;
Join in their deep-down silent mirth
   The crumbling rock and the fertile loam.

Listen and watch! The wind will sing;
   And the day go out by the western gate;
The night come up on her darkling wing;
   And the stars with flaming torches wait.
      Listen and see! And love and be
The day and the night and the world-wide thing   20
   Of strength and hope you contemplate.

No lofty Patron of Nature! No;
   Nor a callous devotee of Art!
But the friend and the mate of the high and the low,

23 callous devotee) smirking Pharisee Sp.

And the pal to take the vermin's part,
   Your inmost thought divinely wrought,
In the grey earth of your brain aglow
   With the red earth burning in your heart.

87. THE PIONEER

Why, he never can tell;
   But, without a doubt,
He knows very well
   He must trample out
Through forest and fell
   The world about
A way for himself,
A way for himself.

By sun and star,
   Forlorn and lank,   10
O'er cliff and scar,
   O'er bog and bank,
He hears afar
   The expresses clank,
'You'll never get there,
You'll never get there!'

His bones and bread
   Poor Turlygod
From his wallet spread
   On the grass-green sod,   20
And stared and said
   With a mow and a nod,
'Whither away, sir,
Whither away?'

'I'm going alone,
   Though Hell forfend,
By a way of my own
   To the bitter end.'
He gnawed a bone
   And snarled, 'My friend,   30
You'll soon get there,
You'll soon get there.'

But whether or no,
   The world is round;
And he still must go
   Though depths profound,
O'er heights of snow,
   On virgin ground
To find a grave,
To find a grave.   40

For he knows very well
He must trample out
Through Heaven and Hell,
With never a doubt,
A way of his own
The world about.

88. ROMANCE

The Markethaunters: Now, while our money is piping hot
From the mint of our toil that coins the sheaves,
Merchantman, merchantman, what have you got
In your tabernacle hung with leaves?
What have you got?
The sun rides high;
Our money is hot;
We must buy, buy, buy!

The Merchantman: I come from the elfin king's demesne
With chrysolite, hyacinth, tourmaline;   10
I have emeralds here of living green;
I have rubies, each like a cup of wine;
And diamonds, diamonds that never have been
Outshone by eyes the most divine

The Markethaunters: Jewellery? – Baubles; bad for the soul;
Desire of the heart and lust of the eye!
Diamonds, indeed! We wanted coal.
What else do you sell? Come, sound your cry!
Our money is hot;
The night draws nigh;   20
What have you got
That we want to buy?

The Merchantman: I have here enshrined the soul of the rose
Exhaled in the land of the daystar's birth;
I have casks whose golden staves enclose
Eternal youth, eternal mirth;
And cordials that bring repose,
And the tranquil night, and the end of the earth.

The Markethaunters: Rapture of wine? But it never pays:
We must keep our common-sense alert.   30
Raisins are healthier, medicine says –
Raisins and almonds for dessert.
But we want to buy;
For our money is hot,
And age draws nigh:
What else have you got?

The Merchantman: I have lamps that gild the lustre of noon;
Shadowy arrows that pierce the brain;

Dulcimers strung with beams of the moon;
   Psalteries fashioned of pleasure and pain;   40
A song and a sword and a haunting tune
   That may never be offered the world again.

The Markethaunters: Dulcimers! psalteries! Whom do you mock?
   Arrows and songs? We have axes to grind!
Shut up your booth and your mouldering stock,
   For we never shall deal. – Come away; let us find
             What the others have got
             We must buy, buy, buy;
             For our money is hot,
             And death draws nigh.   50

89. WAR-SONG

In anguish we uplift
   A new unhallowed song:
The race is to the swift;
   The battle to the strong.

Of old it was ordained
   That we, in packs like curs,
Some thirty million trained
   And licensed murderers,

In crime should live and act,
   If cunning folk say sooth   10
Who flay the naked fact
   And carve the heart of truth.

The rulers cry aloud,
   'We cannot cancel war,
The end and bloody shroud
   Of wrongs the worst abhor,
And order's swaddling band:
   Know that relentless strife
Remains by sea and land
   The holiest law of life.   20
From fear in every guise,
   From sloth, from lust of pelf,
By war's great sacrifice
   The world redeems itself.
War is the source, the theme
   Of art; the goal, the bent
And brilliant academe
   Of noble sentiment;
The augury, the dawn
   Of golden times of grace;   30
The true catholicon,
   And blood-bath of the race.'

We thirty million trained
   And licensed murderers,
Like zanies rigged, and chained
   By drill and scourge and curse
In shackles of despair
   We know not how to break –
What do we victims care
   For art, what interest take   40
In things unseen, unheard?
   Some diplomat no doubt
Will launch a heedless word,
   And lurking war leap out!

We spell-bound armies then,
   Huge brutes in dumb distress,
Machines compact of men
   Who once had consciences,
Must trample harvests down –
   Vineyard, and corn and oil;   50
Dismantle town by town,
   Hamlet and homestead spoil
On each appointed path,
   Till lust of havoc light
A blood-red blaze of wrath
   In every frenzied sight.

In many a mountain-pass,
   Or meadow green and fresh,
Mass shall encounter mass
   Of shuddering human flesh;   60
Opposing ordnance roar
   Across the swaths of slain,
And blood in torrents pour
   In vain – always in vain,
For war breeds war again!

The shameful dream is past,
   The subtle maze untrod:
We recognize at last
   That war is not of God.
Wherefore we now uplift   70
   Our new unhallowed song:
The race is to the swift,
   The battle to the strong.

52 And every hamlet spoil SR.

90. SUMMER RAIN

The flowers with dust disgraced
   Droop in garth and plain;
But the summer tempests haste
   With lustral rain.

The banded vapour rolls,
   Shadowing hill and town;
Anon the thunder tolls,
   The showers come down.

Margents where the salt winds pass,
   The freshened sea-pinks fret;   10
The roses change to hippocras
   The heaven's pearly sweat;

And the flowers all shine and all the grass
   Like jewels newly set,
Sapphire bright and chrysolite,
   And emeralds dripping wet.

Like smoke from a happy hearth,
   Out of the meads and the bowers,
The spicy dust of the moistened earth
   And the rainy scent of the flowers   20
Translate to silence sweet the mirth
   Of the silvery ringing showers.

91. INSOMNIA

He wakened quivering on a golden rack
   Inlaid with gems: no sign of change, no fear
   Or hope of death came near;
Only the empty ether hovered black
   And about him stretched upon his living bier,
Of old by Merlin's Master deftly wrought:
   Two Seraphim of Gabriel's helpful race
   In that far nook of space
With iron levers wrenched and held him taut.

The Seraph at his head was Agony;   10
   Delight, more terrible, stood at his feet:
   Their sixfold pinions beat
The darkness, or were spread immovably
   Poising the rack, whose jewelled fabric meet
To strain a god, did fitfully unmask
   With olive light of chrysoprases dim
   The smiling Seraphim
Implacably intent upon their task.

92. MATINÉES

I

Night went down; the twilight ceased;
   The moon withdrew her phantom flame;
In pearl and silver out of the east,
   Pallid and vigilant, morning came:
By heath and hill with trumpets shrill
   The orient wind declared his name: –

'Morning! Morning! Mighty, alone,
    Light, the light, whose titles are
Courage and hope, ascends his throne
    Over the head of every star: 10
Terror and pain are chained and slain,
    And mournful shadows flee afar.'

                    II

From the night-haunt where vapours crowd
    The airy outskirts of the earth
A winding caravan of cloud
    Rose when the morning's punctual hearth
Began to charm the winds and skies
With odours fresh and golden dyes.

It made a conquest of the sun,
    And tied his beams; but, in the game
Of hoodman-blind, the rack, outdone,
    Beheld the brilliant captive claim   10
Forfeit on forfeit, as he pressed
The mountains to his burning breast.

Above the path by vapours trod
    A ringing causey seemed to be,
Whereby the orient, silver-shod,
    Rode out across the Atlantic sea,
An embassy of valour sent
Under the echoing firmament.

But while the hearkener divined
    A clanging cavalcade on high,   20
This rush and trample of the wind
    Arose among the tree-tops nigh,
For mystery is the craft profound,
The sign, and ancient trade of sound.

An unseen roadman breaking flint,
    If echo and the winds conspire
To dedicate his morning's stint,
    May beat a tune out, dew and fire
So wrought that heaven might lend an ear,
And Ariel hush his harp to hear.   30

                93. THE HERO

            My thought sublimes
                A common deed;
            In evil times
                In utmost need,
            My spirit climbs
                Where dragons breed.

                    130

Nor will I trip
　　Even at the hiss
On the drawn lip
　　Of the abyss:　　　　　　　　　　　　　　　　10
My footsteps grip
　　The precipice.

Applause and blame
　　Let prophets share:
My secret aim
　　The deed I dare,
My own acclaim
　　Comprise my care.

Above the laws,
　　Against the light　　　　　　　　　　　　　20
That overawes
　　The world I fight
And win, because
　　I have the might.

94. AFTERNOON

The hostess of the sky, the moon,
　　Already stoops to entertain
The golden light of afternoon,
　　And the wan earthshine from the plain.

No rustling wings, no voices warp
　　The ripened stillness of the day;
Behind the Downs the sheltered thorpe
　　Expectant overhangs the way.

What laughter, whisper, sigh or groan,
　　A hazardous, a destined sound,　　　　　　10
Shall first usurp the airy throne
　　Where silence rules with twilight crowned?

Hark! hark! an antique noise! Across
　　The road the bellows fires anew
With jar and sough the hissing dross,
　　Close-raked about the half-wrought shoe.

From the swart chimney lilac smoke,
　　The blacksmith's prayer, to heaven ascends;
The hammers double stroke on stroke;
　　The stubborn iron sparkling bends.　　　　　20

Then voices near and far break out;
　　The starlings in the tree-tops scold;
The larks against each other shout;
　　The blackbirds scatter pearl and gold;

The jackdaws prate; the cuckoos call;
   And shrill enough to reach the spheres
Resounds the brazen madrigal
   Of half a hundred chanticleers.

95. HOLIDAY AT HAMPTON COURT

Scales of pearly cloud inlay
   North and south the turquoise sky,
While the diamond lamp of day
   Quenchless burns, and time on high
A moment halts upon his way
   Bidding noon again good-bye.

Gaffers, gammers, huzzies, louts,
   Couples, gangs, and families
Sprawling, shake, with Babel-shouts
   Bluff King Hal's funereal trees;   10
And eddying groups of stare-abouts
   Quiz the sandstone Hercules.

When their tongues and tempers tire,
   Harry and his little lot
Condescendingly admire
   Lozenge-bed and crescent-plot,
Aglow with links of azure fire,
   Pansy and forget-me-not.

Where the emerald shadows rest
   In the lofty woodland aisle,   20
Chaffing lovers quaintly dressed
   Chase and double many a mile,
Indifferent exiles in the west
   Making love in cockney style.

Now the echoing palace fills;
   Men and women, girls and boys
Trample past the swords and frills,
   Kings and Queens and trulls and toys;
Or listening loll on window-sills,
   Happy amateurs of noise!   30

That for pictured rooms of state!
   Out they hurry, wench and knave,
Where beyond the palace-gate
   Dusty legions swarm and rave,
With laughter, shriek, inane debate,
   Kentish fire and comic stave.

2 turquoise) violet Sp.   14 Harry) 'Arry Sp.
28 William's Dutchmen, Charles's toys; Sp.

Voices from the river call;
   Organs hammer tune on tune;
Larks triumphant over all
   Herald twilight coming soon,   40
For as the sun begins to fall
   Near the zenith gleams the moon.

96. IN THE ISLE OF DOGS

While the water-wagon's ringing showers
Sweetened the dust with a woodland smell,
'Past noon, past noon, two sultry hours,'
Drowsily fell
From the schoolhouse clock
In the Isle of Dogs by Millwall Dock.

Mirrored in shadowy windows draped
With ragged net or half-drawn blind
Bowsprits, masts, exactly shaped
To woo or fight the wind,   10
Like monitors of guilt
By strength and beauty sent,
Disgraced the shameful houses built
To furnish rent.

From the pavements and the roofs
In shimmering volumes wound
The wrinkled heat;
Distant hammers, wheels and hoofs,
A turbulent pulse of sound,
Southward obscurely beat,   20
The only utterance of the afternoon,
Till on a sudden in the silent street
An organ-man drew up and ground
The Old Hundredth tune.

Forthwith the pillar of cloud that hides the past
Burst into flame,
Whose alchemy transmuted house and mast,
Street, dockyard, pier and pile:
By magic sound the Isle of Dogs became
A northern isle –   30
A green isle like a beryl set
In a wine-coloured sea,
Shadowed by mountains where a river met
The ocean's arm extended royally.

There also in the evening on the shore
An old man ground the Old Hundredth tune,
An old enchanter steeped in human lore,
Sad-eyed, with whitening beard, and visage lank:

35 There) Here Sp.

133

Not since and not before,
Under the sunset or the mellowing moon,   40
Has any hand of man's conveyed
Such meaning in the turning of a crank.

Sometimes he played
As if his box had been
An organ in an abbey richly lit;
For when the dark invaded day's demesne,
And the sun set in crimson and in gold;
When idlers swarmed upon the esplanade,
And a late steamer wheeling towards the quay
Struck founts of silver from the darkling sea,   50
The solemn tune arose and shook and rolled
Above the throng,
Above the hum and tramp and bravely knit
All hearts in common memories of song.

Sometimes he played at speed;
Then the Old Hundredth like a devil's mass
Instinct with evil thought and evil deed,
Rang out in anguish and remorse. Alas!
That men must know both Heaven and Hell!
Sometimes the melody   60
Sang with the murmuring surge;
And with the winds would tell
Of peaceful graves and of the passing bell.
Sometimes it pealed across the bay
A high triumphal dirge,
A dirge
For the departing undefeated day.

A noble tune, a high becoming mate
Of the capped mountains and the deep broad firth;
A simple tune and great,
The fittest utterance of the voice of earth.   70

50 darkling) swarthy Sp.   65 triumphant Sp.   71 voice) heart Sp.

97. THE ARISTOCRAT

They sundered usage like a wedge;
    They swept the ancients from their stools;
By piracy, by sacrilege,
    By war, across the necks of fools
A royal road, the strong men strode.
    But other times have other tools.

The warlord and the churchlord stir
    The pulses of the world no more;
The trader and the usurer
    Have passed the lion-guarded door;   10

134

The praise, the prayer, the incensed air
    Ascend to us from every shore.

A Money-lord, unheralded,
    I issue from a vulger strain
Of churls, who spiced their daily bread
    With hungry toil in sun and rain,
A secret dower of patience, power
    And courage in my blood and brain.

Though Corner, Trust and Company
    Are subtler than the old-time tools,   20
The Sword, the Rack, the Gallowstree,
    I traverse none of Nature's rules;
I lay my yoke on feeble folk,
    And march across the necks of fools.

My friends and foes adventured much;
    But elbowing iron pots the delf
Go down in shards; or some rude touch
    Of fact installs upon the shelf
Souls slimly cast: for me, I last,
    I wiser, braver, more myself.   30

12 *See Notes.*   13 MONEY-LORD, SR.   17 *See Notes.*

98. A BALLAD OF LANCELOT

By coasts where scalding deserts reek,
    The apanages of despair;
In outland wilds, by firth and creek,
    O'er icy bournes of silver air;

In storm or calm delaying not,
    To every noble task addressed,
Year after year, Sir Lancelot
    Fulfilled King Arthur's high behest.

He helped the helpless ones; withstood
    Tyrants and sanctioners of vice;   10
He rooted out the dragon brood,
    And overthrew false deities.

Alone with his own soul, alone
    With life and death, with day and night,
His thought and strength grew great and shone
    A tongue of flame, a sword of light.

And yet not all alone. On high,
    When midnight set the spaces free,
And brimming stars hung from the sky
    Low down, and split their jewellery,   20

135

Behind the nightly squandered fire,
    Through a dark lattice only seen
By love, a look of rapt desire
    Fell from a vision of the Queen.

From heaven she bent when twilight knit
    The dusky air and earth in one;
He saw her like a goddess sit
    Enthroned upon the noonday sun.

In passages of gulfs and sounds,
    When wild winds dug the sailor's grave,   30
When clouds and billows merged their bounds,
    And the keel climbed the slippery wave,

A sweet sigh laced the tempest; nay,
    Low at his ear he heard her speak;
Among the hurtling sheaves of spray
    Her loosened tresses swept his cheek.

And in the revelry of death,
    If human greed of slaughter cast
Remorse aside, a violet breath,
    The incense of her being passed   40

Across his soul, and deeply swayed
    The fount of pity; o'er the strife
He curbed the lightning of his blade,
    And gave the foe his forfeit like.

Low on the heath, or on the deck,
    In bloody mail or wet with brine,
Asleep he saw about her neck
    The wreath of gold and rubies shine;

He saw her brows, her lovelit face,
    And on her cheek one passionate tear;   50
He felt in dreams the rich embrace,
    The beating heart of Guinevere.

'Visions that haunt my couch, my path,
    Although the waste, unfathomed sea
Should rise against me white with wrath
    I must behold her verily,

'Once ere I die,' he said, and turned
    Westward his faded silken sails
From isles where cloudy mountains burned,
    And north to Severn-watered Wales.   60

Beside the Usk King Arthur kept
    His Easter court, a glittering rout.
But Lancelot, because there swept
    A passion of despair throughout

His being, when he saw once more
   The sky that canopied, the tide
That girdled Guinevere, forbore
   His soul's desire, and wandered wide

In unknown seas companionless,
   Eating his heart, until by chance   70
He drifted into Lyonesse,
   The wave-worn kingdom of romance.

He leapt ashore and watched his barque
   Unmastered stagger to its doom;
Then doffed his arms and fled baresark
   Into the forest's beckoning gloom.

The exceeding anguish of his mind
   Had broken him. 'King Arthur's trust,'
He cried; 'ignoble, fateful, blind!
   Her love and my love, noxious lust!   80

'Dupes of our senses! Let us eat
   In caverns fathoms underground,
Alone, ashamed! To sit at meat
   In jocund throngs? – the most profound

'Device of life the mountebank,
   Vendor of gilded ashes! Steal
From every sight to use the rank
   And loathsome needs that men conceal;

'And crush and drain in curtained beds
   The clusters called of love; but feed   90
With garlanded uplifted heads;
   Invite the powers that sanction greed

'To countenance the revel; boast
   Of hunger, thirst; be drunken; claim
Indulgence to the uttermost,
   Replenishing the founts of shame!'

He gathered berries, efts, and snails,
   Sorrel, and new-burst hawthorn leaves;
Uprooted with his savage nails
   Earth-nuts; and under rocky eaves   100

Shamefast devoured them, out of sight
   In darkness, lest the eye of beast,
Or bird, or star, or thing of night
   Uncouth, unknown, should watch him feast.

At noon in twilight depths of pine
   He heard the word Amaimon spoke;
He saw the pallid, evil sign
   The wred-eld lit upon the oak.

The viper loitered in his way;
    The minx looked up with bloodshot leer;   110
Ill-meaning fauns and lamiæ
    With icy laughter flitted near.

But if he came upon a ring
    Of sinless elves, and crept unseen
Beneath the brake to hear them sing,
    And watch them dancing on the green,

They touched earth with their finger-tips;
    They ceased their roundelay; they laid
A seal upon their elfin lips
    And vanished in the purple shade.   120

At times he rent the dappled flank
    Of some fair creature of the chase,
Mumbled its flesh, or growling drank
    From the still-beating heart, his face

And jowl ruddled, and in his hair
    And beard, blood-painted straws and burs,
While eagles barked screening the air,
    And wolves that were his pensioners.

Sometimes at night his mournful cry
    Troubled all waking things; the mole   130
Dived to his deepest gallery;
    The vixen from the moonlit knoll

Passed like a shadow underground,
    And the mad satyr in his lair
Whined bodeful at the world-old sound
    Of inarticulate despair.

Sir Lancelot, beloved of men!
    The ancient earth gat hold of him;
A year was blotted from his ken
    In the enchanted forest dim.   140

At Easter when the thorn beset
    The bronzing wood with silver sprays,
And hyacinth and violet
    Empurpled all the russet ways;

When buttercup and daffodil
    A stainless treasure-trove unrolled,
And cowslips had begun to fill
    Their chalices with sweeter gold,

He heard a sound of summer rush
    By swarthy grove and kindled lawn;   150
He heard, he sighed to hear the thrush
    Singing alone before the dawn.

138

Forward he stalked with eyes on fire
    Like one who keeps in sound and sight
An angel with celestial lyre
    Descanting rapturous delight.

He left behind the spell-bound wood;
    He saw the branchless air unfurled;
He climbed a hill and trembling stood
    Above the prospect of the world.   160

With lustre in its bosom pent
    From many a shining summer day
And harvest moon, the wan sea leant
    Against a heaven of iron-grey.

Inland on the horizon beat
    And flickered, drooping heavily,
A fervid haze, a vaporous heat,
    The dusky eyelid of the sky.

White ways, white gables, russet thatch
    Fretted the green and purple plain;   170
The herd undid his woven latch;
    The bleating flock went forth again;

The skylarks uttered lauds and prime;
    The sheep-bells rang from hill to hill;
The cuckoo pealed his mellow chime;
    The orient bore a burden shrill.

His memory struggled half awake;
    Dimly he groped within to see
What star, what sun, what light should break
    And set his darkened spirit free.   180

But from without deliverance came:
    Afar he saw a horseman speed,
A knight, a spirit clad in flame
    Riding upon a milkwhite steed.

For now the sun had quenched outright
    The clouds and all their working charms,
Marshalled his legionary light,
    And fired the rider's golden arms.

Softly the silver billows flowed;
    Beneath the hill the emerald vale   190
Dipped seaward; on the burnished road
    The milkwhite steed, the dazzling mail

Advanced and flamed against the wind;
    And Lancelot, his body rent
With the fierce trial of his mind
    To know, reeled down the steep descent.

Remembrances of battle plied
　His soul with ruddy beams of day.
'A horse! a lance! to arms!' he cried,
　And stood there weeping in the way.　　　　　200

'Speak!' said the knight. 'What man are you?'
　'I know not yet. Surely of old
I rode in arms, and fought and slew
　In jousts and battles manifold.'

Oh, wistfully he drew anear,
　Fingered the reins, the jewelled sheath;
With rigid hand he grasped the spear,
　And shuddering whispered, 'Life and death,

'Love, lofty deeds, renown – did these
　Attend me once in days unknown?'　　　　　210
With courtesy, with comely ease,
　And brows that like his armour shone,

The golden knight dismounting took
　Sir Lancelot by the hand and said,
'Your voice of woe, your lonely look
　As of a dead man whom the dead

'Themselves cast out – whence are they, friend?'
　Sir Lancelot a moment hung
In doubt, then knelt and made an end
　Of all his madness, tensely strung　　　　　220

In one last effort to be free
　Of evil things that wait for men
In secret, strangle memory,
　And shut the soul up in their den.

'Spirit,' he said, 'I know your eyes:
　They bridge with light the heavy drift
Of years . . . A woman said, "Arise;
　And if you love the Queen, be swift!"

'The token was an emerald chased
　In gold, once mine. Wherefore I rode　　　　　230
At dead of night in proudest haste
　To Payarne where the Queen abode.

'A crafty witch gave me to drink:
　Almost till undern of the morn
Silent, in darkness . . . When I think
　It was not Guinevere, self-scorn

'Cuts to the marrow of my bones,
　A blade of fire. Can wisdom yield
No mood, no counsel, that atones
　For wasted love! . . . Heaven had revealed　　　　　240

'That she should bear a child to me
    My bed-mate said . . . Yet am I mad?
The offspring of that treachery!
    The maiden knight! You – Galahad,

'My son, who make my trespass dear!'
    His look released his father's thought –
The darkling orbs of Guinevere;
    For so had Lancelot's passion wrought.

With tenderer tears than women shed
    Sir Galahad held his father fast.   250
'Now I shall be your squire,' he said.
    But Lancelot fought him long. At last

The maiden gently overpowered
    The man. Upon his milkwhite steed
He brought him where a castle towered
    Midmost a green enamelled mead;

And clothed his body, clothed his heart
    In human garniture once more.
'My father, bid me now depart.
    I hear beside the clanging shore,   260

'Above the storm, or in the wind,
    Outland, or on the old Roman street,
A chord of music intertwined
    From wandering tones deep-hued and sweet.

'Afar or near, at noon, at night,
    The braided sound attends and fills
My soul with peace, as heaven with light
    O'erflows when morning crowns the hills.

'And with the music, seen or hid,
    A blood-rose on the palace lawn,   270
A fount of crimson, dark amid
    The stains and glories of the dawn;

'Above the city's earthly hell
    A token ominous of doom,
A cup on fire and terrible
    With thunders in its ruddy womb;

'But o'er the hamlet's fragrant smoke,
    The dance and song at eventide,
A beating heart, the gentle yoke
    Of life the bridegroom gives the bride;   280

'A ruby shadow on the snow;
    A flower, a lamp – through every veil
And mutable device I know,
    And follow still the Holy Grail

'Until God gives me my new name
    Empyreal, and the quest be done.'
Then like a spirit clad in flame,
    He kissed his father and was gone.

Long gazed Sir Lancelot on the ground
    Tormented till benign repose
Enveloped him in depths profound
    Of sweet oblivion. When he rose

The bitterest was past. 'And I
    Shall follow now the Holy Grail,
Seen, or unseen, until I die:
    My very purpose shall avail

'My soul,' he said. By day, by night
    He rode abroad, his vizor up;
With sun and moon his vehement sight
    Fought for a vision of the cup –

In vain. For evermore on high
    When darkness set the spaces free,
And brimming stars hung from the sky
    Low down, and split their jewellery,

Behind the nightly squandered fire,
    Through a dim lattice only seen
By love, a look of rapt desire
    Fell from a vision of the Queen.

From heaven she bent when twilight knit
    The dusky air and earth in one;
He saw her like a goddess sit
    Enthroned upon the noonday sun.

Wherefore he girt himself again:
    In lawless towns and savage lands,
He overthrew unrighteous men,
    Accomplishing the King's commands.

In passages of gulfs and sounds
    When wild winds dug the sailor's grave,
When clouds and billows merged their bounds,
    And the keel climbed the slippery wave,

A sweet sigh laced the tempest; nay,
    Low at his ear he heard her speak;
Among the hurtling sheaves of spray
    Her loosened tresses swept his cheek.

And in the revelry of death,
    If human greed of slaughter cast
Remorse aside, A violet breath,
    The incense of her being passed

290

300

310

320

142

Across his soul, and deeply swayed
   The fount of pity; o'er the strife 330
He curbed the lightning of his blade,
   And gave the foe his forfeit life.

His love, in utter woe annealed,
   Escaped the furnace, sweet and clear –
His love that on the world had sealed
   The look, the soul of Guinevere.

99. BATTLE

The war of words is done;
   The red-lipped cannon speak;
The battle has begun.

The web your speeches spun
   Tears and blood shall streak;
The war of words is done.

Smoke enshrouds the sun;
   Earth staggers at the shriek
Of battle new begun.

Poltroons and braggarts run: 10
   Woe to the poor, the meek!
The war of words is done.

'And hope not now to shun
   The doom that dogs the weak,'
Thunders every gun;

'Victory must be won.'
   When the red-lipped cannon speak,
The war of words is done,
The slaughter has begun.

100. THE GIFT

Solacing tears,
   The suppliant's sigh,
Repentant years
   The fates deny;
But tortured breath
   Has one ally,
The gift of death,
   The power to die.

101. THE PRINCE OF THE FAIRIES

Over the mountains, happy and bold,
   The Prince of the Fairies a-wooing came
With a ring and a brooch and a crown of gold,
   And a heart of the same, a heart of the same!
And each of them, all of them, every one
     He would lay at her feet
     If he only could meet
The loveliest maiden under the sun.

They hated him heartily, burghers and peers;
   For the merchants' daughters were ready to die
And the queens of the earth would have given their ears   10
   For a touch of his hand or a glance of his eye:
But he laughed and he said to them every one,
     'Now, by yea and by nay,
     I have nothing to say
Except to the loveliest under the sun.'

Back o'er the mountians, hardly so bold,
   The Prince of the Fairies lamenting came,
Till he met in the way with her curls of gold
   And her heart of the same, her heart of the same,   20
A damsel a-watching her geese every one:
     'Lo,' he shouted, 'my queen!
     For at last I have seen
The loveliest maiden under the sun!'

102. THE UNRESIGNED MOURNER

Unwilling tears on silken lashes,
   Sighs and lamentations deep!
Why do you sit in dust and ashes,
   Lady, lady, why do you weep?

'Because, although my soul that hastened
   To welcome love is now bereft
Of happiness, I live unchastened,
   And curse the bitter anguish left.'

103. MY LILY

I must sing you a song,
   Or my heart will break,
For all the night long
   I lie awake,

And all the day through
I am sorry like you
    For nobody's sake,
    For nobody's sake,
My lily, my lily
You and I,
My lily, sad lily!

Since the day has the sun,
    And the night the moon,
Though love we have none,
    How soon, how soon
Our hearts may awake
For somebody's sake,
    And our lives be in tune,
    Our lives be in tune,
My lily, my lily
You and I,
My lily, sweet lily!

104. THE STOOP OF RHENISH

When dogs in office frown you down,
And malice smirches your renown;
When fools and knaves your blunders twit,
And melancholy dries your wit;
        Be no more dull
            But polish and plenish
        Your empty skull
            With a stoop of Rhenish.
        Drink by the card,
            Drink by the score,
        Drink by the yard,
            Drink evermore.

When seamy sides begin to show,
And dimples into wrinkles grow;
When care comes in by hook or crook
And settles at your ingle-nook,
        Never disdain
            To polish and plenish
        Your rusty brain
            With a stoop of Rhenish.
        Drink by the card,
            Drink by the score,
        Drink by the yard,
            Drink evermore!

When hope gets up before the dawn,
And every goose appears a swan;
When time and tide, and chance and fate
Like lackeys on your wishes wait;

Then fill the bowl,
    And polish and plenish
Your happy soul
    With a stoop of Rhenish.
Drink by the card,
    Drink by the score,
Drink by the yard,
    Drink evermore!

30

105. THE PRICE

Terrible is the price
    Of beginning anew, of birth;
For Death has loaded dice.

Men hurry and hide like mice;
    But they cannot evade the Earth,
And Life, Death's fancy price.

A blossom once or twice,
    Love lights on Summer's hearth;
But Winter loads the dice.

In jangling shackles of ice,
    Ragged and bleeding, Mirth
Pays the Piper's price.

10

The dance is done in a trice:
    Death belts his bony girth;
And struts, and rattles his dice.

Let Virtue play or Vice,
    Beside his sombre firth
Life is the lowest price
Death wins with loaded dice.

106. THE UNKNOWN

To brave and to know the unknown
    Is the high world's motive and mark,
Though the way with snares be strewn.

The Earth itself alone
    Wheels through the light and the dark
Onward to meet the unknown.

Each soul, upright or prone,
    While the owl sings or the lark,
Must pass where the bones are strewn.

146

Power on the loftiest throne
　　Can fashion no certain ark
That shall stem and outride the unknown.

Beauty must doff her zone,
　　Strength trudge unarmed and stark,
Though the way with eyes be strewn.

This only can atone,
　　The high world's motive and mark,
To brave and to know the unknown
Though the way with fire be strewn.

107. THE OUTCAST

Soul, be your own
　　Pleasance and mart,
A land unknown,
　　A state apart.

Scowl, and be rude
　　Should love entice;
Call gratitude
　　The costliest vice.

Deride the ill
　　By fortune sent;
Be scornful still
　　If foes repent.

When curse and stone
　　Are hissed and hurled,
Aloof, alone
　　Disdain the world.

Soul, disregard
　　The bad, the good;
Be haughty, hard,
　　Misunderstood.

Be neutral; spare
　　No humblest lie,
And overbear
　　Authority.

Laugh wisdom down;
　　Abandon fate;
Shame the renown
　　Of all the great.

Dethrone the past;
    Deed, vision – naught
Avails at last
    Save your own thought.   30

Though on all hands
    The powers unsheathe
Their lightning-brands
    And from beneath,

And from above
    One curse be hurled
With scorn, with love
    Affront the world.   40

108. VILLANELLE

The power we would amass
    Escapes our faint desire;
The hours like coursers pass.

The world's a magic glass,
    Wherein while we admire
The power we would amass,

And trim our hopes, alas,
    Wild-eyed and shod with fire
The hours like coursers pass!

Though arms of beaten brass   10
    Match not the soul's attire
Of power we should amass,

With Pegasus at grass,
    We saunter in the mire,
While the hours like coursers pass.

Leave mead and hippocras:
    With Hippocrene aspire
To power we must amass.

Relinquish creed and class;
    Pursue through brake and briar   20
The power we shall amass,
On the swift hours as they pass!

109. A NEW SONG OF EMPIRE

A thousand years of war
    Behind our banners throng:
Empire Britain battled for
    Against heroic wrong,

148

Unconscious of her fate, exalts
  Our new imperial song;
    And still we make our ancient boast
      At home, or by the battle's hearth –
    'We venture furthest, dare the most,
      The chosen valour of the earth.'   10

Our doom is written thus,
  So may our souls find grace!
Empire is the gift of us,
  The genius of the race –
An Empire winning for the world
  A nobler power and place;
    Establishing our ancient boast
      That Freedom lights their genial hearth
    Who venture furthest, dare the most,
      And are the valour of the earth.   20

Who fall in Britain's wars,
  How fortunate are they,
Sepulchred as conquerors
  In Britain's memory!
And those who mourn, how sweet their tears,
  How proud their grief shall be,
    When of their glorious dead they boast
      Who shone upon the battle's hearth,
    Who ventured furthest, dared the most,
      And were the valour of the earth.   30

No sacrifice shall tame,
  No terror daunt our will:
Destiny's immortal aim
  Our conquering arms fulfil,
Redeem the earth for man and make
  Our boast a surety still!
    While women dry their tears and run
      To feed the battle's glowing hearth
    With husband, brother, lover, son,
      The chosen valour of the earth.   40

A thousand years of war
  In front of Britain throng:
Empire Britain battled for
  Against heroic wrong,
The sword that won must guard and beat
  The measure of her song;
    While Britons make their ancient boast
      By every battle's glowing hearth –
    'We venture furthest, dare the most,
      The chosen valour of the earth.'   50

110. ODE ON THE CORONATION OF EDWARD VII., OF BRITAIN AND OF GREATER BRITAIN, KING

We crown our King, the son of her whose fame
Has hallowed monarchy; we crown our race,
Accomplishing a thousand years of war,
Of travail and of triumph greatly borne.
Wherefore in England's lordly measure, tuned
When the long-buried past resurgent sought
Embodiment anew, when recent shores,
Unknown, but dreamt-of, in the night of Time,
Appealed to fate for utterance virginal,
And the profound insatiate soul of man   10
Required a deep-toned, more material song:
In England's lordly measure, armed and winged
When England conquered sea-room for her ships
And first began to mould the modern world,
It well becomes our honour to acclaim
This noble birth of Time, mature at length,
Imperial Britain, risen above the sea,
Enthroned and of her destiny aware.

When every eager pulse of Matter ached
To yield its new idea and be glad,   20
An ancient subtle thought, a loftier hope
Than any mediate life of plant or beast,
Imbued the inmost womb, and urged a way
Throughout the range, of being, climbing up
From lowliest cells to forms uncouth that walk
Abashed and wistful that they are not Man,
The deep primeval aim, so long delayed,
So late accomplished; for the steadfast Earth,
A Spartan mother, passionate as Love,
Patient as Time, implacable as Truth,   30
In travail with her son nine epochs, vowed
Millenniums of remorseless discipline
To shape the hero of eternal dreams.

The steadfast Earth, the parent, treasure, home,
Pleasance and sepulchre of all her kin,
Assured of her design, by simple craft
And great undid the parasitic cord
That tethered Britain; closed and soldered well
The magic hoop of ocean set with storms,
Wedding this isle for ever to the world.   40
At once from orient valleys, folk on folk,
Horizon-haunting Aryans westward thronged,
Instinctive wanderers borne in nebulous drifts,

1–5 *See Notes.*   8 Time TS.   9 to fate *corr. from* at last TS.
17 risen above the sea, *corr. from* conscious of her doom. Ts.
18 *om.* TS. *first reading*   37 parasitic cord) cord of land that bound TS., DC.
38 That) And TS., DC.   40 Wedding) And wed TS.   43 borne *om.* TS., DC.

150

Till Rome with iron axle wound an orb
Of light far-gleaned and thrice empurpled power –
A sanguine orb high-pitched in heaven awhile,
Whose crimson beams on Britain's argent cliff
In setting splendour lodged and tarried long,
Before mortality asunder burst
The power and light of that luxurious star.   50
Foam-necked forthwith the war-keels plied the deep;
Hengist and Horsa, Cerdic, Ivar, Cnut,
The Conqueror – Jutes, Saxons, Angles, Danes,
Norsemen and Normans into Britain surged,
The fertile, temperate, envied isle of fate.
Confronted there, they wrestled tribe with tribe
Of those who ventured furthest, dared the most,
Through sounding centuries at Brunanburgh,
Senlac and Bannockburn and Flodden-field.
Molten and founded in one cast of men,   60
As in a furnace heated seventy times
With love and hate the fuel and the flame
That feed the roaring blood-red hearth of war;
And yoked with willing or reluctant clans,
Their greater travail seized them when the dawn
Of pure intelligence – discovered shores
And vision whetted to behold with power –
Assailed the mediaeval firmament,
And launched the world-debate of old and new
Whose present rumour shrouds the echoing past.   70

The doom that thundered in their blood – that beat
In every brimming star whose sea-washed lamp
Beckons the sleepless rapt adventurer –
Athwart unhallowed destinies, nor stayed
By falling empires, and the desperate clutch
Of palsied creeds in ruined fanes aghast,
O'er many a smitten field and sanguine sea
Advanced on hazard, terror, and the night
With Liberty and Justice for the World.

Thus they, magnanimous, a guide innate   80
Obeyed unwitting, till a drowsy fire
That smouldered southward flamed to heaven in wild
Belated war as of the Heptarchy –
Tribe against tribe again of that grim folk
Who venture furthest, dare the most, and are
The valour of the earth; not otherwise
Could Boer and Saxon weld enduring peace.
Then was it Britain o'er the tropics flung
Her bridge of ships from England to the Cape;
Then trusty British people, east and west,   90

63 feeds TS.   64 And yoked) Affied TS., DC.   64–5 See Notes.
66 shores) lands TS., DC.   74 nor corr. from not TS.   79 the World corr. from
Mankind TS.   80 om. TS.   81 Obeyed unwitting,) Unconscious always: TS.
85 and are corr. from advance TS.   90 Then) And TS.

Vaulting the Indian and Atlantic main
From blood-bought continents and treasured isles,
In Britain's day of need upheld her hands,
Forbade her foes to doubt one heart and strength
Inspired and armed her sea-linked Ocean-State,
And gave the world to know how great a thing
Had risen at last above the tide of Time,
Imperial Britain, mighty and aware.

So forged, so tempered, like the adamant
In Nature's crucible, our sovereign race   100
Thrust through the earth its way: a breed of men
Concerned alone to be what them behoves;
Forthright regarders, looking not askance
Through doctrine, lifeless vision turned to stone
And lenses warped and flawed, but seers indeed;
Perceivers deeply versed in certainty,
Who challenge light with light of faithful looks,
Within whose souls a lamp self-nourished burns
As on an altar fed with sacred fire;
Doers, endurers, fighters, poets, kings,   110
The genius of the Universe that leaves
Its shadow in the abyss, and unperturbed
By ill-conditioned good or evil blent
With passionate aspiration, every hour
Sloughs off the past to reach a truer truth,
A beauty more divine, a destiny
Still unimagined in the dreams of fate.

We crown our King, we crown our sovereign race,
And garner now the harvest of our blood
Broadcast in battle for a thousand years,   120
The seed, the token, the courageous price
Of Liberty and Justice for the World –
Our blood that with imperial purple dyes
The quartered globe, that stains and turns to wine
The shadowy depths of ocean's jewelled cup,
Making a sacrament of all the earth.

91 Vaulting) Fording TS.   113 or corr. from and TS.
122 the World corr. from Mankind TS.   125 depths corr. from depth TS.

III. THE SOUL

From aimless conflict and the tangled urn
Of asps, decaying flowers and Dead-Sea fruit,
The dross and vapid recrement of life,
The soul of man in golden human cells
Of wrought experience sedulously built,
A sweeter aromatic honey hives
Than reservoirs of carder-bees that drain

4 The immortal Soul of Man in golden cells WG.

The perfumed nectar of the wilderness,
And store it underground in mossy founts.
Unhappy wisdom tastes and learns to laugh   10
With dulcet breath; unhappy folly tastes
And learns its own inherent happiness.

112. THE WASTREL

An eyesore to the tourist on the shoulder of the knock
    Above the green-fledged larches where the squirrel keeps its house,
The pale dissenting chapel, like a pharos on a rock,
    With strong, pathetic preaching that the very dead might rouse,
Was lighted for an hour and twenty minutes by the clock,
    While the cushats moaned and muttered deep among the rustling boughs.

With Conybeare-and-Howson laid on thick for local hue,
    And Meyer's and Lange's comments to elucidate the text,
The minister exhibited a panoramic view
    Of the story of the wastrel and the father that he vext: 10
Of little but his Bible and his creed the preacher knew,
    And dogma like a razor his emotions had unsexed.

Then came the modern instance, and the congregation stirred,
    And scrutinised the pew in which the preacher's family sat.
'I knew it,' thought each member, 'at the very opening word!'
    And felt as perspicacious as a dog that smells a rat:
The preacher's wife and daughters seized their Bibles when they heard;
    And his son, as red as poppies, stooped and glanced at this and that.

'But recently,' the preacher said, 'to London town there went
    A youth from our vicinity against his father's wish;   20
To make a fortune – honestly, if possible – he meant,
    Forgetting quite how God examines both sides of the dish:
Unless a holy life exhale to Heaven a savoury scent,
    We know how very profitless the loaves are and the fish.' . . .

The wife and daughters shrivel up and shut their eyes and cry,
    As the preacher drives the lancet home and lays their heart-strings bare;
But the wastrel, cool and clammy, feels a wind of fate go by,
    And hears his pulses clank above monition, praise and prayer –
'Oho, for London Town again, where folk in peace can die,
    And the thunder-and-lightning devil of a train that takes me there!'

26 heart-strings) feelings PMG.

113. AT THE DOOR

From a clime where the land's fair face
    No manner of usage mars,
And the wind, blowing pure out of space,
    Gathers the scent of the stars,
He came, where the air has a sulphurous breath,
To the turbulent City of Death.

At the end of the world far down,
  Obscure in the dark abyss,
Like a planet of baleful renown,
  Glimmers the City of Dis: 10
As pulses that flicker the dim windows beat,
For the fog overflows every street.

And he heard – as he stood heart-sore,
  But eager to enter in,
All alone, in his shroud, at the door –
  Sadly transcending the din,
A voice which he thought had been singing above
In the peaceable Kingdom of Love.

He had won, he had lost, hard-driven;
  He knew what it is to wait;   20
And he fell at the last out of Heaven
  Laughing aloud at his fate;
But he never knew fear till her wailing came
O'er the walls of the City of Flame.

From a clime where the land's fair face
  No manner of usage mars,
And the wind, blowing pure over space,
  Gathers the scent of the stars,
He came where the voice of his dearest one fell
On his shuddering soul out of Hell.

12 For) And PMG.   20 is) was PMG.   23 But) For PMG.

114. THE WORLD'S FAILURE

Before the mystery and the cult of sin,
Eternal sorrow and eternal toil
In old, unhallowed dens and mouldering streets,
Or model tenements and haunts of woe,
Can any hopeful thing be said or sung?

Somewhere delighted larks, forestalling day,
Ascend and garland heaven with flower and fruit,
Enwreathe and overrun the shining air,
When darkness crumbles from the firmament,
With fresco, fantasy and arabesque   10
Of splendid sound; but here the iron heavens
Ring to the factory-whistle, here the dawn,
All overgrown and quenched in creeping smoke,
Decays unseen. Here each promoter's face,
Employer's, owner's, broker's, merchant's, mean
As any eunuch's and as evil, tells
How souls unsexed by business come to love
Elaborate torture and the sullen joy
Of coining men and women into wealth.
But somewhere trumpets sound and gallant Knights   20
Fight to the death to win a lady's smile;

Somewhere a gentle voice, a tender hand
Console the anguished offal of the world;
Somewhere with breaking heart a poet sings;
Somewhere a woman loves a worthless man.

This the earth, the thing we know and hate,
The torture-chamber of the universe,
Wherein the entangled spirit, torn and shred,
And quickened to endure intenser pangs
With every pulse and interval of time,   30
Expects deliverance only when the sun
Reclaims our mundane fragment, to be purged
Of failure and the memory of men
In tides and tempests of millennial fire.
Yet here the nightingale throughout the night
Will sing enraptured, while the beating stars
Attend; and here a boy and girl will watch
The pallid moon with earnest looks and eyes
Of infinite appeal! Does God somewhere
Behold it all and know it to be good?   40

115. A SONG OF CHANGE

Citizens, noblemen, sinner and saint,
    Merchantmen, labourers, folk of the shires,
Now, is it now that our courage grows faint,
    Is it now that we falter, we sellers and buyers,
        Now that the war's of the market,
        Now that the war's in the shops?

Not on the battlefield, not on the sea,
    Can any, can all of them set us at naught:
Shall we be beaten by traffickers, we
    Who fought till we conquered wherever we fought?   10
        Must we be cast for a doctrine,
        Killed by the letter that kills?

Us, unto us was the victory given,
    Glory and power to the ends of the earth:
Nation of shopkeepers? Wealthy? By heaven,
    There beats the heart of their tragical mirth!
        That's where the world wants to have us,
        That's where the jealousy sticks!

Fight them with tariffs, then, frank as of old
    We fought them and beat them with cannon and steel.   20
Blood we have spent: are we chary of gold?
    Shall duty go dutiless just for a meal?
        Fight them with masterful foresight,
        Fight them with honester work.

155

Empire and rank in our preference lie:
    Hesitate now and decide to be small,
Then will the dead who have died for us die,
    Die, then, indeed, and their monument fall;
        Children unborn will arraign us
        Cowards that feared to be great.   30

Merchantmen, citizens, folk of the shires,
    Gentle and simple attendants on fate,
Labourers, noblemen, sellers and buyers,
    Now, it is now that we *mean* to be great!
        Now for the hope of the future,
        Now for our children to be!

116. MERRY ENGLAND

Island-kingdom, our island-state,
    Merry England, where fancy dwells
In pageant, pilgrimage, high debate,
    And sprightly music of morris-bells;
Tourneys for love and battles for hate;
    Torches, garlands, exultant bells –
    Challenging trumpets and festal bells;
Wars of the Roses, land-locked strife,
    World-wide wars with France and Spain:
The colour and pulse of that gallant life –   10
    Shall we never recover the mood again?

Rhythmic deeds, melodious words: –
    Merry England, the heart of mirth: –
Songs of lovers and songs of birds;
    A bell for death and a bell for birth –
Jubilant fifths and sombre thirds:
    Pessimist? Optimist? – death and birth!
    Englishmen only on English earth!
Confident daring, travail and strife,
    Battle and storm on the Spanish Main –   20
How shall the fancy that donned that life
    Be decked and renewed with such pride again?

England's fancy shall live again –
    Merry England across the seas! –
Jewelled with isles of the Spanish Main,
    Gifts of the opulent destinies:
England's heart and England's brain,
        Throbbing and thinking in many seas
        Belov'd of the opulent destinies.
Bluebird, oriole, bobolink,   30
    Hark to them, hear them how they sing,
Where England's Canadians work and think,
    Woo and wed in the throng of Spring!

Axes ring on the mountain-sides –
　　England's gain from England's loss! –
Lonely at night the ranchman rides,
　　Humming a tune to the Southern Cross;
Argosies on Austral tides,
　　From Charles's Wain to the Southern Cross,
　　Barter the Plough for the Southern Cross!　　　40
Lord! how the English hew their way,
　　Courage and fortune leading the van!
Round the world with the break of day,
　　Room for him, room for the Englishman!

Saxon, Norman, Dansker, Celt –
　　Merry England, mother of mirth! –
Gird the earth with an English belt,
　　Englishmen all to the ends of the earth!
Gold and grain on Rand and Veldt,
　　Orchards, harvests over the earth –　　　50
　　Liners and merchantmen round the earth;
Power from East to Western Ind,
　　Power and pomp on the Indian Main,
And wonder with every whispering wind
　　To dip our dreams in the dew again.

England, decked and dowered by fate –
　　Room for England, so please you room!
Sea-Kings' realm, our Ocean-state,
　　Woven upon the world's wide loom;
Dyed and tried in high debate,　　　60
　　And ever renewed on the world's wide loom,
　　With weaving fleets in a world-wide loom –
　　Warp and woof of the sea's wide loom:
Shall garnish fancy in every land
　　With rhythmic deed and delight again –
Merry England from strand to strand,
　　From the Spanish Main to the Indian Main.

47 earth) world Ou.

117. IN THE CITY

Is it heaven and its city-porch,
Or a ceiling high-hung of old
With lacquer fumed and scrolled
Of many a festal torch?

High heaven it is, and the day
With its London doom of smoke
No storm can quite revoke,
No deluge wash away.

When their march and song grow mute
In the city's labyrinth trapped,   10
The storms themselves are wrapped
In draggled shrouds of soot.

Whirlwinds by lightnings paced
To run their wild career,
With ragged gossamere
Of fine-spun carbon laced,

As soon as they quit the shires
Are lost beyond all hail:
The mightiest tempests quail
In the midst of a million fires.   20

But the heavens are clear today
Though their London doom of smoke,
No storm can quite revoke,
No deluge wash away.

18 hail: *corr. from* hope MS.

118. APPLE-TREES

When autumn stains and dapples
The diverse land,
Thickly studded with apples
The apple-trees stand.

Their mystery none discovers,
So none can tell –
Not the most passionate lovers
Of garth and fell;
For the silent sunlight weaves
The orchard spell,   10
Bough, bole, and root,
Mysterious, hung with leaves,
Embossed with fruit.

Though merle and throstle were loud,
Silent *their* passion in spring,
A blush of blossom wild-scented;
And now when no song-birds sing,
They are heavy with apples and proud
And supremely contented –
All fertile and green and sappy,   20
No wish denied,
Exceedingly quiet and happy
And satisfied!

No jealousy, anger, or fashion
Of strife
Perturbs in their stations
The apple-trees. Life

Is an effortless passion,
Fruit, bough, and stem,
A beautiful patience   30
For them.

Frost of the harvest-moon
Changes their sap to wine;
Ruddy and golden soon
Their clustered orbs will shine,
By favour
Of many a wind,
Of morn and noon and night,
Fulfilled from core to rind
With savour   40
Of all delight.

39 Full-filled PMM.

119. A RUNNABLE STAG

When the pods went pop on the broom, green broom,
    And apples began to be golden-skinned,
We harboured a stag in the Priory coomb,
    And we feathered his trail up-wind, up-wind,
    We feathered his trail up-wind –
        A stag of warrant, a stag, a stag,
        A runnable stag, a kingly crop,
        Brow, bay and tray and three on top,
        A stag, a runnable stag.

Then the huntsman's horn rang yap, yap, yap,   10
    And 'Forwards' we heard the harbourer shout;
But 'twas only a brocket that broke a gap
    In the beechen underwood, driven out,
    From the underwood antlered out
        By warrant and might of the stag, the stag,
        The runnable stag, whose lordly mind
        Was bent on sleep, though beamed and tined
        He stood, a runnable stag.

So we tufted the covert till afternoon
    With Tinkerman's Pup and Bell-of-the-North;   20
And hunters were sulky and hounds out of tune
    Before we tufted the right stag forth,
    Before we tufted him forth,
        The stag of warrant, the wily stag,
        The runnable stag with his kingly crop,
        Brow, bay and tray and three on top,
        The royal and runnable stag.

4 we *om.* PMM.

It was Bell-of-the-North and Tinkerman's Pup
  That stuck to the scent till the copse was drawn.
'Tally ho! tally ho!' and the hunt was up,   30
  The tufters whipped and the pack laid on,
  The resolute pack laid on,
    And the stag of warrant away at last,
    The runnable stag, the same, the same,
    His hoofs on fire, his horns like flame,
    A stag, a runnable stag.

'Let your gelding be: if you check or chide
  He stumbles at once and you're out of the hunt;
For three hundred gentlemen, able to ride,
  On hunters accustomed to bear the brunt,   40
  Accustomed to bear the brunt,
    Are after the runnable stag, the stag,
    The runnable stag with his kingly crop,
    Brow, bay and tray and three on top,
    The right, the runnable stag.'

By perilous path in coomb and dell,
  The heather, the rocks, and the river-bed,
The pace grew hot, for the scent lay well,
  And a runnable stag goes right ahead,
  The quarry went right ahead –   50
    Ahead, ahead, and fast and far;
    His antlered crest, his cloven hoof,
    Brow, bay and tray and three aloof,
    The stag, the runnable stag.

For a matter of twenty miles and more,
  By the densest hedge and the highest wall,
Through herds of bullocks he baffled the lore
  Of harbourer, huntsman, hounds and all,
  Of harbourer hounds and all –
    The stag of warrant, the wily stag,   60
    For twenty miles, and five and five,
    He ran, and he never was caught alive,
    This stag, this runnable stag.

When he turned at bay in the leafy gloom,
  In the emerald gloom where the brook ran deep,
He heard in the distance the rollers boom,
  And he saw in a vision of peaceful sleep,
  In a wonderful vision of sleep,
    A stag of warrant, a stag, a stag,
    A runnable stag in a jewelled bed,   70
    Under the sheltering ocean dead,
    A stag, a runnable stag.

55 a) the PMM.

So a fateful hope lit up his eye,
   And he opened his nostrils wide again,
And he tossed his branching antlers high
    As he headed the hunt down the Charlock glen,
   As he raced down the echoing glen
      For five miles more, the stag, the stag,
      For twenty miles, and five and five,
      Not to be caught now, dead or alive,   80
      The stag, the runnable stag.

Three hundred gentlemen, able to ride,
   Three hundred horses as gallant and free,
Beheld him escape on the evening tide,
    Far out till he sank in the Severn Sea,
   Till he sank in the depths of the sea –
      The stag, the buoyant stag, the stag
      That slept at last in a jewelled bed
      Under the sheltering ocean spread,
      The stag, the runnable stag.   90

120. YULETIDE

   Now wheel and hoof and horn
   In every street
   Stunned to its chimney-tops,
   In every murky street –
   Each lamp-lit gorge by traffic rent
   Asunder,
   Ravines of serried shops
   By business tempests torn –
   In every echoing street,
   From early morn   10
   Till jaded night falls dead,
   Wheel, hoof, and horn
   Tumultuous thunder
   Beat
   Under
   A noteless firmament
   Of lead.

   When the winds list
   A fallen cloud
   Where yellow dregs of light   20
   Befouled remain,
   The woven gloom
   Of smoke and mist,
   The soot-entangled rain
   That jumbles day and night
   In city and town,
   An umber-emerald shroud
   Rehearsing doom,
   The London fog comes down.

1 Then PMM.

But sometimes silken beams,   30
As bright
As adamant on fire,
Of the uplifted sun's august attire,
With frosty fibrous light
Magnetic shine
On happier dreams
That abrogate despair,
When all the sparkling air
Of smoke and sulphur shriven,
Like an iced wine   40
Fills the high cup
Of heaven;
For urban park and lawn,
The city's scenery,
Heaths, commons, dells
That compass London rich
In greenery,
With diamond-dust of rime
Empowdered, flash
At dawn;   50
And tossing bells
Of stealthy hansome chime
With silvery crash
In radiant ways
Attuned and frozen up
To concert pitch –
In resonant ways,
Where wheels and hoofs inwrought,
Cars, omnibuses, wains,
Beat, boom, and clash   60
Discordant fugal strains
Of cymbals, trumpets, drums;
While careless to arrive,
The nerved pedestrian comes
Exulting in the splendour overhead,
And in the live
Elastic ground,
The pavement, tense and taut,
That yields a twangling sound
At every tread.   70

121. HOLIDAY

Lithe and listen, gentlemen:
Other knight of sword or pen
Shall not, while the pleants shine,
Spend a holiday like mine: –

Fate and I, we played at dice:
    Thrice I won and lost the main;
Thrice I died the death, and thrice
    By my will I lived again.

First, a woman broke my heart,
  As a careless woman can, 10
Ere the aureoles depart
  From the woman and the man.

Dead of love, I found a tomb
  Anywhere: beneath, above,
Worms nor stars transpierced the gloom
  Of the sepulchre of love.

Wine-cups were the charnel-lights;
  Festal songs, the funeral dole;
Joyful ladies, gallant knights,
  Comrades of my buried soul. 20

Tired to death of lying dead
  In a common sepulchre,
On an Easter morn I sped
  Upward where the world's astir.

Soon I gathered wealth and friends;
  Donned the livery of the hour;
And atoning diverse ends
  Bridged the gulf to place and power.

All the brilliances of Hell
  Crushed by me, with honeyed breath 30
Fawned upon me till I fell,
  By pretenders done to death.

Buried in an outland tract,
  Long I rotted in the mould,
Though the virgin woodland lacked
  Nothing of the age of gold.

Roses spiced the dews and damps
  Nightly falling of decay;
Dawn and sunset lit the lamps
  Where entombed I deeply lay. 40

My Companions of the Grave
  Were the flowers, the growing grass;
Larks intoned a morning stave;
  Nightingales, a midnight mass.

But at me, effete and dead,
  Did my spirit gibe and scoff:
Then the gravecloth from my head,
  And my shroud – I shook them off!

Drawing strength and subtle craft
  Out of ruin's husk and core, 50
Through the earth I ran a shaft
  Upward to the light once more.

Soon I made me wealth and friends;
  Donned the livery of the age;
And atoning many ends
  Reigned as sovereign, priest, and mage.

But my pomp and towering state,
  Puissance and supreme device
Crumbled on the cast of Fate –
  Fate, that plays with loaded dice.   60

I whose arms had harried Hell
  Naked faced a heavenly host:
Carved with countless wounds I fell,
  Sadly yielding up the ghost.

In a burning mountain thrown
  (Titans such a tomb attain)
Many a grisly age had flown
  Ere I rose and lived again.

Parched and charred I lay; my cries
  Shook and rent the mountain-side;   70
Lustres, decades, centuries
  Fled while daily there I died.

But my essence and intent
  Ripened in the smelting fire:
Flame became my element;
  Agony, my soul's desire.

Twenty centuries of Pain,
  Mightier than Love or Art,
Woke the meaning in my brain
  And the purpose of my heart.   80

Straightway then aloft I swam
  Through the mountain's sulphurous sty:
Not eternal death could damn
  Such a hardy soul as I.

From the mountain's burning crest
  Like a god I come again,
And with an immortal zest
  Challenge Fate to throw the main.

122. L'ENVOI

Born, enamoured, built of fact,
  Daily on destruction's brink
Venture all to put in act
  Truth we trust and thought we think.

Nothing has been said or done:
    Free from the forbidding past,
Knowledge only now begun
    Makes an actual world at last.

Powers of Earth, of Heaven, of Hell,
    Blent in us and tried and true,   10
By dynamic deed and spell
    Forge and mould the world anew.

123. NOVEMBER

I. *Regent's Park.*

Poplars, ashes, flaunting wreaths of June
    Green among the tarnished oaks, outstayed
Lindens, plane-trees, chestnuts, elms so soon
    Ragged, draggle-tailed, or stripped and flayed.

Somnolent canal and urban wold,
    Lawn and lake with saffron leaves and red,
Crimson leaves and olive, brown and gold,
    Bronze and topaz leaves engarlanded,

Underneath the feet of winter flung –
    Cloth of Bagdad richer than the stuff   10
Woven in Tyrian looms, by poets sung
    Barbarous when the world was young enough

Frankly to adore a purple stain –
    Graced the season mantled in its breath
Glittering pale, or draped in swarthy rain,
    Victor in decay and peer of death.

1 *Lionel*: Ou.   11 in) on Ou.

II. *The Enfield Road.*

Capitalled and coped with massive cloud,
    Lofty elms, a wayside colonnade,
Shaft or bole erect and interboughed,
    Forestward, a beckoning passage made.

Like a golden haze, a misty veil
    Diapered with sequins, foliage lined
All the vista, yellow discs and frail
    Stalks that snapped against the chariest wind.

Flapping rooks alit on blighted sheaves;
    Ruddy haws in ragged hedges glowed;   10
Elfin companies of withered leaves
    Pattered nowhere down the sodden road.

1 *Vivian*: Ou.   4–5 *See Notes.*

Sullen in the west across the floor
  Swept and garnished of the wintry plain,
Sunset smouldered like a furnace-door
  Black and shot with cramoisie in grain.

III. *Epping Forest.*

Woods and coppices by tempest lashed;
  Pollard shockheads glaring in the rain;
Jet-black underwood with crimson splashed –
  Rich November, one wet crimson stain!

Turf that whispered moistly to the tread;
  Bursts of laughter from the shuffled leaves;
Pools of light in distant arbours spread;
  Depths of darkness under forest eaves.

High above the wind the clouds at rest
  Emptied every vat and steeply hurled   10
Reservoirs and floods; the wild nor'west
  Raked the downpour ere it reached the world;

Part in wanton sport and part in ire,
  Flights of rain on ruddy foliage rang:
Woven showers like sheets of silver fire
  Streamed; and all the forest rocked and sang.

1 *Vivian*: Change – a change! The woods by tempest lashed: Ou.

IV. *Box Hill*

Brilliant month by legend slandered so!
  Down in Surrey in the shining air
Mid-November saw the woodland grow
  Green as summer still, and still as fair:

Elms perhaps, and fragrant limes forlorn
  Drooped a branch, yet half I thought to hear
Men and swift machines among the corn,
  Voices and the ringing harvest-gear.

Sunset saw I from the sinuous height
  Box Hill rears on sombre Mulla's bank: 10
Darker and more dark the ruby light
  Over Polsdon Arbour dying sank;

But or ever Time's nocturnal seal
  Fixed the doom of day, the mid-moon's power
Did in star-attended state repeal
  Darkness and the sentence of the hour.

1 *Ninian*: Ou.

166

v. *London, W.*

Deep delight in volume, sound, and mass,
    Shadow, colour, movement, multitudes,
Murmurs, cries, the traffic's rolling bass –
    Subtle city of a thousand moods!

Distance, rumour, mystery, things that count,
    Bravely in the memory scored and limned!
Sunset, welling like a crimson fount
    Underneath the Marble Arch, o'erbrimm'd

All the smoky west. In Oxford Street
    Lamps, like jewels fallen by the way   10
While the sun upon his urban beat
    Bore the lofty burden of the day,

Magnified their offices and grew
    Vital and a rosary of light,
Wreathing life that gathered heart anew
    Hungry for the pleasure of the night.

Trees of winter's nakedness aware
    Gleamed and disappeared like things afraid,
Dryads of the terrace and the square,
    Silvery in the shadow and the shade.   20

Swarthy-purple creepers draped the high
    Houses; leaves in elm-tree tops astir
Blurred like flakes of soot the darkling sky,
    Lit with faded light of lavender.

1–4 *See Notes.*   5 *Basil*: Colour, distance, noises – things that count, Ou.
7 *Lionel*: Ou.   14 Vital) Golden Ou.

VI. *The Chilterns.*

I remember once a glorious thing
    Crowned the season in my wandering time.
Through the year I went from earliest Spring
    Hither, thither, weaving prose and rhyme,

Like a gleeman of the former age.
    Sound and colour were my pensioners;
Constant on my passionate pilgrimage
    Love attended me, and friends of hers,

Life and Death besides. But one day, late
    Roaming in the Chilterns, want of will   10
Irked me, and the impotence of Fate –
    Something lacking in the World, until

1 *Basil*: Ou.

167

Bluff November in the coppice near
  Loud on orient horns an onset wound,
While the larks that through the golden year
  Garlanded the air with dazzling sound,

Surged upon the tempest's deafening cry –
  Crests of foam about the ocean driven,
Lightning scribbled on a thund'rous sky,
  Tongues of flame upon the top of heaven!   20

124. LABURNAM AND LILAC

Where the New River strays,
Eddying in olive green
And chrysophrase,
And briefly seen
In traffic-troubled ways,
Laburnum showers
Its verdant gold,
Its clustered flowers
Instilled and scrolled
With emerald sap: 10
Green-tinted gold
In April's lap
Unpursed, unrolled;
A mint of flowers,
A hoard untold,
Laburnine showers
Of greenish gold.

Like ostrich plumes
The jolly donahs wear,
Light-tressed or dark,   20
The lilac blooms
In every park and square
And blooms in Finsbury Park;
Or heliotrope or mauve,
Snowy or dark,
The lilac blooms
In white and purple plumes.

'What? Russel Square!'
There's lilac there!
And Torrington   30
And Woburn Square
Intrepid don
The season's wear.
In Gordon Square and Euston Square –
There's lilac, there's laburnum there!
In green and gold and lavender
Queen Square and Bedford Square,

All Bloomsbury and all Soho
With every sunbeam gayer grow,
Greener grow and gayer.   40

The lindens in the Mall
Resound with bees;
The plane-trees shed their bark –
The eager trees
That promptly grow so tall;
And in St. James's Park
Full-throated chant
The song-thrush and the merle
Till dusk forbids,
And dim-eyed night encamps   50
Where now the chestnuts vaunt
Their leafy pyramids
And lustrous lamps
Of ruby, gold, and pearl;
But in St. James's shade
Of elms antique,
The mystic porch
Of Nature's bridal-room
That coupled songsters seek,
The lilac swings a censer   60
Of ravishing perfume,
And rich laburnums braid
The green-gilt gloom
With flame intenser
Than the chestnut's torch.

125. THE LAST SONG

'Songster' – say you? – 'sing!'
    Not a note have I!
Effort cannot bring
    Fancy from the sky:
Hark! – the rusty string!
    Leave me here to die.
        'Songster, songster, sing!
            Tune your harp and try.
        Sing! we bid you sing
            Once before you die!'   10

Withered, angry, mad,
    Who would list to me,
Since my singing sad
    Troubled earth and sea
When my heart was glad
    And my fancy free?
        'Sad or joyful, sing!
            Look about, above!
        Trust the world and sing
            Once again of love!'   20

169

Love? I know the word:
  Love is of the rose.
Have you seen or heard
  Love among the snows?
Yet my heart is stirred!
  Nay, my fancy glows!
    'Summon all your powers;
      Sing of joy or woe –
    Love among the flowers,
      Love amidst the snow.'   30

Death is but a trance:
  Life, but now begun!
Welcome change and chance:
  Though my days are done,
Let the planets dance
  Lightly round the sun!
    Morn and evening clasp
      Earth with loving hands –
    In a ruddy grasp
      All the pleasant lands!   40

Now I hear the deep
  Bourdon of the bee,
Like a sound asleep
  Wandering o'er the lea;
While the song-birds keep
  Urging nature's plea.
    Hark! the violets pray
      Swooning in the sun!
    Hush! the roses say
      Love and death are one!   50

Loud my dying rhyme
  Like a trumpet rings;
Love in death sublime
  Soars on sovran wings,
While the world and time
  Fade like shadowy things.
    'Love upon his lip
      Hovers loath to part;
    Death's benignant grip
      Fastens on his heart.'   60

Look, a victor hies
  Bloody from the fight,
And a woman's eyes
  Greet him in the night –
Softly from the skies
  Like sidereal light!
    'Love is all in all,
      Life and death are great.
    Bring a purple pall;
      Bury him in state.'   70

126. A SONG OF TRIUMPH

On faction, clique and sect
    We take our stand for good;
And let who will protect
    Your lives and livelihood.

With reverent fear and awe
    We worship to the last
The letter of the law
    Our careful fathers passed.

We count him but a fool
    Who for your weal would strain   10
The self-denying rule
    Whereby your rivals gain.

Both knave and fool, we say,
    And evermore accursed!
What! Change a doctrine? Nay,
    Let England perish first!

Defend your trade? Fie! We,
    Magnanimously made,
Keeping your imports free,
    Defend all other trade.   20

We mean to make you rue
    Your warfare; to forbid
Your triumph; to undo
    The splendid thing you did.

Our aim shall be, our strife,
    To hear you yet complain
That all the wealth and life
    You spent were spent in vain.

What! keep your honour bright,
    Your sceptre and your crown?   30
Have done with power and might!
    Have done with high renown!

Who cares for England's trust,
    Her scattered kith and kin?
Let fleets and armies rust
    Since we at last are in!

127. MARIA SPIRIDONOVA

'From one until eleven
They tortured her . . .'
Is the sun still in Heaven?

You doubt
If anyone
Could think or bid it?
How could it come about?
Where was it done?
Who did it?

Not men! Not here!   10
Oh, not beneath the sun!
But, for this thing of fear
No tongue can tell,
By devil's bastards done
In some unheard-of,
Some profounder Hell,
There shall be word of
Vengeance yet,
When to that ancient tryanny is set
The torch that smouldered till the cup o'er-ran, –   20
The wrath of God which is the wrath of Man.

128. THE CAKE OF MITHRIDATES

Quenched is the fire on Autumn's hearth,
    The ingle vacant, hushed the song;
But the resolved, consistent earth,
    And nature, tolerant and strong,

Serenely wait the ordered change
    Of times and tides. Ten thousand years
Of day and night, the scope and range
    Of liberal seasons; smiles and tears

Of June and April; brumal storm,
    Autumnal calm, and flower and fruit: 10
These are the rich content, the form
    Of nature's mind; these constitute

The academe and discipline,
    The joust and knightly exercise,
The culture of the earth wherein
    The earth's profound composure lies.

The wisdom of the earth excels
    The craft and skill of every age.
Witness the tale the Persian tells
    Of Mithridates, King and mage: –   20

The whole divan extolled his powers:
    They said the soil revered him so,
That, if he planted sawdust, flowers
    Of every hue would promptly grow.

19 Witness) Hear now Bl.

'So be it!' quoth the King of kings:
　'Bring hither sweepings of the street,
Chaff, sawdust, money, jewels, rings,
　And fifty grains of summer wheat.'

He sowed them in a fertile bed,
　And set a guard about the plot　　　　　　　　　　30
Both day and night: 'Although,' he said,
　'The earth is honest, men are not.'

The wheat betimes began to grow:
　In shame as in a mordant steeped,
The viziers, sulking in a row,
　Beheld at length the harvest reaped.

Said then the King, 'A sheaf! Proceed:
　Thresh, winnow, grind it, bolt and bake,
And bring with all convenient speed
　Of leavened bread a goodly cake.　　　　　　　　　40

'For you, my worthy viziers – come!
　The marvellous crops you promised me?'
The whole perturbed divan, as dumb
　As oysters, felt indeed at sea.

'Ha!' cried the King, 'when shall we laugh
　At prodigies great nature grants
Almighty monarchs? Fruit of chaff,
　Where is it? Where, my sawdust-plants?

'The vine and vintage of my gold?
　My silver-bushes where are they?　　　　　　　　50
My coin should yield a hundredfold
　By nature's lavish usury!

'My fragrant banks of posied rings
　Where diamonds blossom, show me; show
In arbours where the bulbul sings
　A branch of budding rubies glow.

'My jewel-orchards, money-shrubs?
　Perhaps they're sprouting underground?
My cash, at least, among the grubs –
　My cash and gems! Let them be found!　　　　　　60

'Dig, viziers, dig!' The viziers dug:
　Among the deep roots of the grain,
With here an earthworm, there a slug
　They found the treasure, sowed in vain.

And all the sweepings of the street,
　The chaff, the rubbish? Like a jest
Forgiven, forgotten! So discreet
　Is nature's kindly alkahest.

173

Then every vizier lost his nerve,
   Expecting death, a prompt despatch.   70
But Mithridates said, 'Observe
   How great the soil is: bulbuls hatch

'The cuckoo's eggs, whereas the earth
   Ignores the costliest stone to feed
With chosen fare and bring to birth
   The soul of any honest seed.

'The earth is true and harbours not
   Imposture: all your flattering lies
Are buried in this garden-plot;
   Be genuine if you would be wise.'   80

With that the baker, breathing spice,
   Produced the cake hot from the fire,
And every vizier ate a slice
   Resolving to be less a liar.

80 genuine *corr. from* truthful MS.

129. SONG

Closes and courts and lanes,
   Devious, clustered thick,
The thoroughfare, mains and drains,
   People and mortar and brick,
Wood, metal, machinery, brains,
Pen and composing-stick:
      Fleet Street now, but exquisite flame
        In the nebula once ere day and night
      Began their travail, or earth became,
      And all was passionate light.   10

Networks of wire overland,
   Conduits under the sea,
Aerial message from strand to strand
   By lightning that travels free,
Hither in haste to hand
   Tidings of destiny
      These tingling nerves of the world's affairs
        Deliver remorseless, rendering still
      The fall of empires, the price of shares,
      The record of good and ill.   20

Tidal the traffic goes
   Citywards out of the town;
Townwards the evening ebb o'erflows
   This highway of old renown,

5 *See Notes.*   7 *See Notes.*

When the fog-woven curtains close,
　　And the urban night comes down,
　　　　Where souls are split and intellects spent
　　　　　　O'er news vociferant near and far,
　　　　From Hesperus hard to the Orient,
　　　　　　From dawn to the evening star.　　　　　　　　　30

This the royal refrain
　　That burdens the boom and the thud
Of omnibus, mobus, wain,
　　And the hoofs on the beaten mud,
From the Griffen at Chancery Lane
　　To the portal of old King Lud –
　　　　Fleet Street, diligent night and day,
　　　　　　Of news the mart and the burnished hearth,
　　　　Seven hundred paces of narrow way,
　　　　　　A notable bit of the earth.　　　　　　　　　40

130. THE CITY OF DOVES

Veranda and portal, piazza and square
　　(Oh the birds of the city, their lives and loves!)
Are winnowed with wings and of rumour aware,
　　For the city of fogs is the city of doves.

Withdraw from the traffic, come out of the ranks,
　　(But the business of us and our final cause!)
The street and its tide and its turbulent banks,
　　And pause to consider, pedestrian, pause!

Wherever you tarry your ears will report,
　　(Now the birds of the city, their lives and loves!)　　　10
In alley or faubourg, quadrangle or court,
　　A sweet din of cooing, the cooing of doves.

Monotonous music – but oh, such delight! –
　　(Now cornice and copestone for what were made?)
Both winter and summer from morning till night,
　　Transcends the tumultuous discord of trade.

Elastic and fresh as a morning in May,
　　(Now the genius of us and our atmosphere!)
There dawned over London the ultimate day,
　　A notable day, of a notable year,　　　　　　　　　20

When murmuring voices broke out in mid-air,
　　(Oh the birds of the city, their lives and loves!)
As spellbound I stood of a sudden aware
　　That the city of fogs is the city of doves.

175

Two dogs on Bournemouth beach: a mongrel, one,
With spaniel plainest on the palimpsest,
The blur of muddled stock; the other, bred,
With tapering muzzle, rising brow, strong jaw –
A terrier to the tail's expressive tip,
Magnetic, nimble, endlessly alert.

The mongrel, wet and shivering, at my feet
Deposited a wedge of half-inch board,
A foot in length and splintered at the butt;
Withdrew a yard and crouched in act to spring,   10
While to and fro between his wedge and me
The glancing shuttle of his eager look
A purpose wove. The terrier, ears a-cock,
And neck one curve of sheer intelligence,
Stood sentinel: no sound, no movement, save
The mongrel's telegraphic eyes, bespoke
The object of the canine pantomine.

I stooped to grasp the wedge, knowing the game;
But like a thing uncoiled the mongrel snapped
It off, and promptly set it out again,   20
The terrier at his quarters, every nerve
Waltzing inside his lithe rigidity.

'More complex than I thought!' Again I made
To seize the wedge; again the mongrel won,
Whipped off the jack, relaid it, crouched and watched,
The terrier at attention all the time.
I won the third bout: ere the mongrel snapped
His toy, I stayed my hand; he halted, half
Across the neutral ground, and in his pause
Of doubt I seized the prize. A vanquished yelp   30
From both; and then intensest vigilance.

Together, when I tossed the wedge, they plunged
Before it reached the sea. The mongrel, out
Among the waves, and standing to them, meant
Heroic business; but the terrier dodged
Behind, adroitly scouting in the surf,
And seized the wedge, rebutted by the tide,
In shallow water, while the mongrel searched
The English Channel on his hind-legs poised.
The terrier laid the trophy at my feet;   40
And neither dog protested when I took
The wedge: the overture of their marine
Diversion had been played out once for all.

29 his) the FSOP.   41 took) picked WG.   42 The wedge:) It up; WG.

A second match the reckless mongrel won,
Vanishing twice under the heavy surf,
Before he found and brought the prize to land.
Then for an hour the aquatic sport went on,
And still the mongrel took the heroic rôle,
The terrier hanging deftly in the rear.
Sometimes the terrier when the mongrel found   50
Betrayed a jealous scorn, as who should say,
'Your hero's always a vulgarian! Pah!'
But when the mongrel missed, after a fight
With such a sea of troubles, and saw the prize
Grabbed by the terrier in an inch of surf,
He seemed entirely satisfied, and watched
With more pathetic vigilance the cast
That followed.
    'Once a passion, mongrel, this
Retrieving of a stick,' I told the brute,
'Has now become a vice with you. Go home!   60
Wet to the marrow and palsied with the cold,
You won't give in; and, good or bad, you've earned
My admiration. Go home now and get warm,
And the best bone in the pantry.' As I talked
I stripped the water from his hybrid coat,
Laughed and made much of him – which mortified
The funking terrier.
    'I'm despised, it seems!'
The terrier thought. 'My cleverness (my feet
Are barely wet!) beside the mongrel's zeal
Appears timidity. This biped's mad   70
To pet the stupid brute. Yap! Yah!' He seized
The wedge and went; and at his heels at once,
Without a thought of me, the mongrel trudged.

Along the beach, smokers of cigarettes,
All sixpenny-novel-readers to a man,
Attracted Master Terrier. Again the wedge,
Passed to the loyal mongrel, was teed with care;
Again the fateful overture began.
Upon the fourth attempt, and not before,
And by a feint at that, the challenged youth   80
(Most equable, be sure, of all the group:
Allow the veriest dog to measure men!)
Secured the soaked and splintered scrap of deal.
Thereafter, as with me, the game progressed,
The breathless, shivering mongrel, rushing out
Into the heavy surf, there to be tossed
And tumbled like a floating bunch of kelp,
While gingerly the terrior picked his steps
Strategic in the rear, and snapped the prize
Oftener than his more adventurous, more   90
Romantic, more devoted rival did.

46 prize) wedge WG.

The uncomfortable moral glares at one!
And, further, in the mongrel's wistful mind
A primitive idea darkly wrought:
Having once lost the prize in the overture
With his bipedal rival, he felt himself
In honour and in conscience bound to plunge
For ever after it at the winner's will.
But the smart terrier was an Overdog,
And knew a trick worth two of that. He thought –   100
If canine cerebration works like ours,
And I interpret canine mind aright –
'Let men and mongrels worry and wet their coats!
I use my brains and choose the better part.
Quick-witted ease and self-approval lift
Me miles above this anxious cur, absorbed,
Body and soul, in playing a game I win
Without an effort. And yet the mongrel seems
The happier dog. How's that? Belike, the old
Compensatory principle again: 110
I have pre-eminence and conscious worth;
And he his power to fling himself away
For anything or nothing. Men and dogs,
What an unfathomable world it is!'

112 his) has FSOP.

132. THE WASP

Once as I went by rail to Epping Street,
Both windows being open, a wasp flew in;
Through the compartment swung and almost out
Scarce seen, scarce heard; but dead against the pane
Entitled 'Smoking,' did the train's career
Arrest her passage. Such a wonderful
Impervious transparency, before
That palpitating moment, had never yet
Her airy voyage thwarted. Undismayed,
With diligence incomparable, she sought   10
An exit, till the letters like a snare
Entangled her; or else the frosted glass
And signature indelible appeared
The key to all the mystery: there she groped,
And flirted petulant wings, and fiercely sang
A counter-spell against the sorcery,
The sheer enchantment that inhibited
Her access to the world – her birthright, there!
So visible, and so beyond her reach!
Baffled and raging like a tragic queen,   20
She left at last the stencilled tablet; roamed
The pane a while to cool her regal ire,

3 swung) flashed At.

178

Then tentatively touched the window-frame:
Sure footing still, though rougher than the glass;
Dissimilar in texture, and so obscure!

Perplexed now by opacity with foot and wing
She coasted up and down the wood, and worked
Her wrath to passion-point again. Then from the frame
She slipped by chance into the open space
Left by the lowered sash – the world once more   30
In sight! She paused; she closed her wings, and felt
The air with learned antennæ for the smooth
Resistance that she knew now must belong
To such mysterious transparences.
No foothold? Down she fell – six inches down!' –
Hovered a second, dazed and dubious still;
Then soared away a captive queen set free.

133. THE THAMES EMBANKMENT

As gray and dank as dust and ashes slaked
With wash of urban tides the morning lowered;
But over Chelsea Bridge the sagging sky
Had colour in it – blots of faintest bronze,
The stains of daybreak. Westward slabs of light
From vapour disentangled, sparsely glazed
The panelled firmament; but vapour held
The morning captive in the smoky east.
At lowest ebb the tide on either bank
Laid bare the fat mud of the Thames, all pinched   10
And scalloped thick with dwarfish surges. Cranes,
Derricks and chimney-stalks of the Surrey-side,
Inverted shadows, in the motionless,
Dull, leaden mirror of the channel hung:
Black flags of smoke broke out, and in the dead
Sheen of the water hovered underneath,
As in the upper region, listlessly.
Across the viaduct trailing plumes of steam,
The trains clanked in and out.

                                    Slowly the sun
Undid the homespun swathing of the clouds,   20
And splashed his image on the northern shore –
A thing extravagantly beautiful:
The glistening, close-grained canvas of the mud
Like hammered copper shone, and all about
The burning centre of the mirror'd orb's
Illimitable depth of silver fire
Harmonious beams, the overtones of light,
Suffused the emboss'd, metallic river bank.

8 morning *corr. from* smoky east MS.   12 chimney-stacks WG.
25 orbs FSOP.   27 *See Notes.*

Woven of rainbows a dewdrop can dissolve
And packed with power a simple lens can wield,   30
The perfect, only source of beauty, light
Reforms uncouthest shapelessness and turns
Decoloured refuse into ornament;
The leafless trees that lined the vacant street
Had all their stems picked out in golden scales,
Their branches carved in ebony; and shed
Around them by the sanction of the morn
In lieu of leaves each wore an aureole.

Barges at anchor, barges stranded, hulks
Ungainly, in the unshorn beams and rich   40
Replenished palette of a winter sun,
Appeared ethereal, and about to glide
On high adventure chartered, swift away
For regions undiscovered.

                              Huddled wharfs
A while, and then once more a reach of Thames
Visibly flowing where the sun and wind
Together caught the current. Quays and piers
To Vauxhall Bridge; and there the Baltic Wharf
Exhibited its wonders: figureheads
Of the old wooden walls on gate and post –   50
Colossal torsos, bulky bosoms thrown
Against the storm, sublime uplifted eyes
Telling the stars. As white as ghosts
They overhung the way, usurping time
With carved memorials of the past. Forlorn
Elysium of the might of England!

                              Gulls,
Riparian scavengers, arose and wheeled
About my head, for morsels begging loud
With savage cries that piercingly reverbed
The tempest's dissonance. Birds in themselves   60
Unmusical and uninventive ape
Impressive things with mockery undesigned:
The eagle's bark mimics the crashing noise
That shakes his eyry when the thunder roars;
And chanticleer's imperious trumpet-call
Re-echoes round the world his ancestor's
Barbaric high-wrought challenge to the dawn.
But birds of homely feather and tuneful throat,
With music in themselves and masterdom,
To beauty turn obsessive sights and sounds: 70
The mounting larks, compact of joyful fire,
Render the coloured sunlight into song;
Adventurous and impassioned nightingales

37 morn) day, WG.   41 See Notes.   51-2 See Notes.
62 mocking FSOP.   70 sight and sound: FSOP.

180

Transmute the stormy equinox they breast
With courage high, for hawthorn thickets bound
When spring arrives, into the melody
That floods the forest aisles; the robin draws
Miraculously from the rippling brook
The red wine of his lay; blackbird and thrush,
Prime-artists of the woodland, proudly take   80
All things sonorous for their province, weave
The gold-veined thunder and the crystal showers,
The winds, the rivers and the choir of birds
In the rich strains of their chromatic score.

By magic mechanism the weltering clouds
Re-grouped themselves in continents and isles
That diapered the azure firmament;
And sombre chains of cumulus, outlined
In ruddy shade along the house-tops loomed,
Phantasmal alp on alp. The sunbeams span   90
Chaotic vapour into cosmic forms,
And juggled in the sky with hoods of cloud
As jesters twirl on sticks their booby-caps –
The potent sunbeams, that had fished the whole
Enormous mass of moisture from the sea,
Kneaded, divided and divided, wrought
And turned it to a thousand fantasies
Upon the ancient potter's wheel, the earth.

134. RAIL AND ROAD

March Many-weathers, bluff and affable,
The usher and the pursuivant of Spring,
Had sent his North wind blaring through the world –
A mundane wind that held the earth, and puffed
The smoke of urban fire and furnace far
Afield. An ashen canopy of cloud,
The dense immobled sky, high-pitched above
The wind's terrestrial office, overhung
The city when the morning train drew out.
Leaping along the land from town to town,   10
Its iron lungs respired its breath of steam,
Its resonant flanges, and its vertebral
Loose-jointed carcase of a centipede
Gigantic, hugged and ground the parallel
Adjusted metals of its destined way
With apathetic fatalism, the mark
Of all machinery. – From Paddington
To Basingstoke the world seemed standing still:
Nothing astir between the firmaments
Except the aimless tumult of the wind,   20
And clanging travail of the ponderous train
In labour with its journey on the smooth,

The ineludible, the shining rails.
    But prompt at Basingstoke an interlude
Began: a reckless youth, possessed with seven
Innocuous devils of self-consciousness
Primeval, bouncing in irruptively,
Lusty-Juventus-wise, annexed the whole
Compartment – as a pendant to the earth,
Already his! Wind-shaven, ruddy; hunched   30
And big; all knees and knuckles; with a mouth
That opened like a portal; fleshy chops
And turned-up nose widespread, the signature
Of jollity; a shapeless, elvish skull;
His little pig's eyes in their sockets soused
But simmering merrily; just twenty years;
One radiation of nervous energy;
A limber tongue and most unquenchable,
Complacent blaze of indiscretion, soft
As a night-light in a nursery. 'Where away?'   40
Quoth he; and 'Hang the weather! I've seen worse,
In my time for the season.' Then: Did we think
The train was doing thirty or forty miles
An hour? Sometimes, by instinct, he could tell
To a mile the rate at which a train went.
This morning, for a wonder, he couldn't trust
His judgement in the matter; – annoying! – still
A man's form varied, and we must excuse
His inability to gauge our speed.
Good golf about here, – very! Did we play?   50
And, by the bye, talking of golf, he did
A brilliant thing just now: – missing the train
At Farnham on the other line, instead
Of waiting for the next, he tramped across
To Basingstoke, – some decent tale of miles;
His destination being Winchester,
Either line suited, – see? The weather, – yes,
The weather; healthy, of course; – your moist cold kills;
Your dry cold cures; – to-day it seemed as cold, –
But that must be the wind; in sheltered roads   60
It smelt like Spring; – to-morrow, – who could tell
To-morrow's weather? – a funny climate, ours!
Was that a cow there, or a – Yes, a cow.
He didn't know how we regarded it,
But he, for his part, took it that the hand
That rocked the cradle ruled the world; to drop
A signature into a ballot-box
Would make no earthly! (Slang, elliptical.)
Although we must remember, all of us,
This rocking of the cradle was out of date;   70
But that he wouldn't canvass; – we were to mind
There must be no mistake: women were women
All the world to nothing; and – mark him – if
They *had* political enfranchisement,

No one could say – no one at all! – what might
And mightn't happen: not a doubt of that.
Getting along more quickly; forty miles,
He thought; or less, perhaps. He meant to lunch
At Winchester; then hire a trap and drive . . .
'Instanter to the devil,' someone sighed.   80
    All this, and further, an infinitude
Of dislocated prattle, with a smile
Indelible, and such a negligent
Absorbition in self that no appeal,
Except a sheer affront, abuse or blow,
Could have revealed remotely any gleam
Or shade, to him apparent, of his own
Insipid and grotesque enormity!
When time, distemper or disaster sap
Such individuals, and they see themselves,   90
In facets of disrupted character,
As others see them, stupid and absurd,
How bad the quarter of an hour must be!
Natheless there are extant a hearty breed,
Incorrigibly cheerful, who behold
Themselves for ever in the best of lights.
And by the pipe and bowl of Old King Cole
They have the best of it! To see ourselves
As others see us may be good enough;
But to love others in their vanities,   100
And to portray the glorious counterfeit –
In sympathetic ink that sympathy
Alone can read aright, – why, that's a gift
Vouchsafed to genius of the rarest strain!
    At Lyndhurst-road the coach for Lyndhurst took
The turnpike at its best commercial pace.
And there the sun burst out with moted beams
In handfuls, clenched like sheaves of thunderbolts.
The riven clouds, of homespun slashed and gored,
Displayed through unhemmed slits the turquoise sky, –   110
As tender as a damsel's bosom-thoughts.
Across the forest's swarthy-purple ridge
A sparse shower twinkled; but the broken bulk
Of vapour, by the sunbeams bundled up,
Slipped o'er the sky-edge and was no more seen.
Like a lithe weapon by gigantic hands
In pastance wielded, keen the brandished wind
Whistled about us all the uphill way
To Lyndhurst, where the lofty church o'erlooks
The forest's metes and bounds, its modish spire   120
A landmark far and wide. But in the glebes
And garden-closes ancient houses – thatched,
Of post-and-panel, and with arching eaves
Above their high and deep-set windows – peer
Occultly out of many centuries.

124 Above) About FSOP.

An old-world use and wont, the neighbourhood
And venue of the place are everywhere
Presumptive, – in the High-street, new and raw,
As in the sylvan faubourgs; for a gust
Of burning log and faggot importunes   130
The passer-by – the forest's bitter-sweet
Aroma, as it turns to genial warmth
And toothsome savour for the villager.

135. SONG FOR THE TWENTY-FOURTH OF MAY

The character and strength of us
    Who conquer everywhere,
We sing the English of it thus,
    And bid the world beware: –
    We bid the world beware
The perfect heart and will,
    That dare the utmost men may dare
And follow freedom still.
        Sea-room, land-room, ours, my masters, ours,
        Hand in hand with destiny, and first among the Powers!   10
        Our boasted Ocean Empire, sirs, we boast of it again,
        Our Monarch, and our Rulers, and our Women, and our Men!

The pillars of our Empire stand
    In unforgotten graves;
We built dominion on the land,
    And greatness on the waves: –
    Our Empire on the waves,
Established firm and sure,
    And founded deep in ocean's caves
While honour shall endure.   20
        Sea-room, land-room, honourably ours,
        Hand in hand with destiny and first among the Powers!
        Our boasted Ocean Empire, sirs, we boast of it again,
        Our ancient Isles, our lands afar, and all our loyal Men!

Our flag, on every wind unfurled,
    Proclaims from sea to sea
A future and a nobler world
    Where men and thoughts are free: –
    Our men, our thoughts are free;
Our wars are waged for peace;   30
    We stand in arms for liberty
Till bonds and bondage cease.
        Sea-room, land-room, ours, appointed ours,
        Conscious of our calling and the first among the Powers!
        Our boasted Ocean Sovereignty, again and yet again!
        Our Counsel, and our Conduct, and our Armaments and Men!

136. SNOW

I

'Who affirms that crystals are alive?'
   I affirm it, let who will deny: –
Crystals are engendered, wax and thrive,
   Wane and wither; I have seen them die.

Trust me, masters, crystals have their day,
   Eager to attain the perfect norm,
Lit with purpose, potent to display
   Facet, angle, colour, beauty, form.

II

Water-crystals need for flower and root
   Sixty clear degrees, no less, no more;   10
Snow, so fickle, still in this acute
   Angle thinks, and learns no other lore:

Such its life, and such its pleasure is,
   Such its art and traffic, such its gain,
Evermore in new conjunctions this
   Admirable angle to maintain.

Crystalcraft in every flower and flake
   Snow exhibits, of the welkin free:
Crystalline are crystals for the sake,
   All and singular, of crystalry.   20

Yet does every crystal of the snow
   Individualize, a seedling sown
Broadcast, but instinct with power to grow
   Beautiful in beauty of its own.

Every flake with all its prongs and dints
   Burns ecstatic as a new-lit star:
Men are not more diverse, finger-prints
   More dissimilar than snow-flakes are.

Worlds of men and snow endure, increase,
   Woven of power and passion to defy   30
Time and travail: only races cease,
   Individual men and crystals die.

III

Jewelled shapes of snow whose feathery showers,
   Fallen or falling wither at a breath,
All afraid are they, and loth as flowers
   Beasts and men to tread the way to death.

Once I saw upon an object-glass,
  Martyred underneath a microscope,
One elaborate snow-flake slowly pass,
  Dying hard, beyond the reach of hope.   40

Still from shape to shape the crystal changed,
  Writhing in its agony; and still,
Less and less elaborate, arranged
  Potently the angle of its will.

Tortured to a simple final form,
  Angles six and six divergent beams,
Lo, in death it touched the perfect norm
  Verifying all its crystal dreams!

IV

Such the noble tragedy of one
  Martyred snow-flake. Who can tell the fate   50
Heinous and uncouth of showers undone,
  Fallen in cities! – showers that expiate

Errant lives from polar worlds adrift
  Where the great millennial snows abide;
Castaways from mountain-chains that lift
  Snowy summits in perennial pride;

Nomad snows, or snows in evil day
  Born to urban ruin, to be tossed,
Trampled, shovelled, ploughed and swept away
  Down the seething sewers: all the frost   60

Flowers of heaven melted up with lees,
  Offal, recrement, but every flake
Showing to the last in fixed degrees
  Perfect crystals for the crystal's sake.

V

Usefulness of snow is but a chance
  Here in temperate climes with winter sent,
Sheltering earth's prolonged hibernal trance:
  All utility is accident.

Sixty clear degrees the joyful snow,
  Practising economy of means,   70
Fashions endless beauty in, and so
  Glorifies the universe with scenes

Arctic and antarctic: stainless shrouds,
  Ermine woven in silvery frost, attire
Peaks in every land among the clouds
  Crowned with snows to catch the morning's fire.

The harvests of purple and gold
   Are garnered and trodden; dead leaves
Tomorrow will carpet the wold;
   And the arbours and sylvan eaves
Dismantled, no welcome extend;
   The bowers and the sheltering eaves
Will witness tomorrow the end
   Of their stained, of their sumptuous leaves,
While tempests apparel the wold
In their cast-off crimson and gold.   10

But I of abundance to be
   Think only, the corn and the wine,
The manifold wealth of the sea
   And the harvest-home of the mine.
Decay and the fall of leaf,
   Lost lives in the tenebrous mine,
Disaster, disconsolate grief
   Molest not the corn and the wine,
The infinite wealth of the sea
And the bountiful harvests to be.   20

For beneath are the heavens and above,
   And time is a silken yoke;
My lute is my friend; and I love
   A beautiful maid of my folk –
A marvel to see and adore,
   Astounding her foes and her folk
With silence and exquisite lore
   Of youth and its delicate yoke,
With wonderful wisdom in love,
And the music beneath and above.   30

I think how her beauty would kill
   A lover less ardent than I;
I faint and my heart stands still
   In the street when she passes by;
My lute, I bid to be dumb: –
   'Hush, for my love goes by!
Oh hush, or she may not come!
   A lover less ardent than I
Her beauty might palsy, might kill!
Lute-strings, heart-strings, be still!'   40

But when she has passed a spell
   Delivers my voice and my lute;
My songs and my melodies well
   Like fountains; like clusters of fruit

My fantasy ripens; my rhymes,
  With savour of wayside fruit
And sweet as aërial chimes
  Of flower-bells, ring to my lute;
Like fountains my melodies well
When the thought of her works like a spell.   50

She walks and the emerald lawn
  Is jewelled at every tread;
Like the burning tresses of dawn
  The virgin gold of her head
Illumines the land and the sea;
  From her glittering feet to her head
Is the essence of being – is she
  Who walks with a magical tread
As she dazzles the eyes of dawn,
And jewels the grass-green lawn.   60

Though the harvests of purple and gold
  Are garnered, and fallen leaves
Tomorrow will carpet the wold,
  I think how the sylvan eaves
A welcome in summer extend,
  How the bowers and the sheltering eaves
Will mantle in summer and bend
  With their bloom and their burden of leaves,
And autumn apparel the wold
In harvests of purple and gold.   70

138. ST MICHAEL'S MOUNT

St Michael's Mount, the tidal isle,
  In May with daffodils and lilies
Is kirtled gorgeously a while
  As ne'er another English hill is:
About the precipices cling
The rich renascence robes of Spring.

Her gold and silver, nature's gifts,
  The prodigal with both hands showers:
O not in patches, not in drifts
  But round and round, a mount of flowers –   10
Of lilies and of daffodils,
The envy of all other hills.

And on the lofty summit looms
  The castle: none could build or plan it.
The foursquare foliage springs and blooms,
  The piled elaborate flower of granite,
That not the sun can wither; no,
Nor any tempest overthrow.

More than one way of walking? Verily;
But, for the art of walking, only one.
Beginners in the ambulative art,
As in all art, are immethodical:
Your want of method, rightly understood,
Is faculty, and not its absence; style
Adventurous of genius; say, a gift;
Immethod, necessary handicap
Upon originality, that loses
Matches many on time or weight, but beats   10
The winner virtually. The crammer's wiles,
And royal roads to knowledge, short-cuts, keys,
And time-and-labour-saving mechanism
Beset the ambulative acolyte;
But true originality in art
Would not at first, even if it could, possess
Impeccable technique; and your foredoomed
Pedestrian errs designedly (if one
Whose privilege it is to deviate
Can ever be arraigned for trespass) bent   20
On quitting, jeopardy or none, the old
Immediately seductive methods blazed
By trained precursors in pedestrial art.

At first then the prospective walker, rash
As any hero, dedicates himself
To chance. A vagabond upon the earth
He leads a life uncertain: art and craft
Pedalian suffer secret chrysalid
Probations and adventures ere they gain
The ultimate imago of complete   30
Pedestrianism. Through gross suburban miles
And over leagues of undistinguished ground
He plods, he tramps. Utilitarian thoughts
Of exercise and health extenuate
The dullness of the duty; he persuades
Himself he likes it; finds, where none exist,
Amazing qualities; and tires his limbs,
His thought, his fancy, o'er and o'er again.
But in the dismal watches of the night
He knows it all delusion; beauty, none,   40
Nor pleasure in it; ennui only – eased
By speculation on the wayside-inn,
Or country-town hotel where lunch permits
An hour's oblivion of his self-imposed,
His thriftless drudgery. Despair! – And life?
Worth picking from the gutter? No; not worth
The stooping for! Natheless, a walker born,
He takes the road next day; steps out once more,
As if the world were just begun, and he,

Sole monarch; plods the suburb, tramps the waste –   50
Again returning baffled and dismayed.

He tries a comrade. Worse and worse! – for that,
In high pedestrianism, turns out to be
A double misery, a manacled
Contingence with vexation. Walking-tours?
Belletrists crack them up. He takes one: – lo,
A sheer atrocity! A man may like
To drink; but who would quench next morning's drouth,
Unholy though it be, with torture *forte*
Ed dure in gallon draughts when by his bed   60
A hair gleams of the dog that bit him! Tours
Pedestrious? Madness, like the poet's who thought
To write a thousand sonnets at the rate
Of three a day! And this the tale of years!

Forth from his travail and despair at last,
Crash through his plodding apparatus, breaks
The dawn of art. He recollects a mile,
Or half a mile that pleased him; a furlong here,
And there a hundred yards; or an hour's march
Over some curve of the world when everything   70
Above him and about him from the zenith
To the sky-edge, and radiant from his feet
Toward every cardinal point, put off the veil,
Becoming evident as guilt or love, as things
That cannot hide: – becoming him,
And he becoming them; and all his past
And all his future wholly what they are,
The very form and meaning of the earth
Itself. And at these times he recollects,
And in these places, how his thoughts were clear   80
As crystal, deeper than the sea, as swift
As light – the pulse, the bosom and the zone
Of beauty infinite. And then and there
Whatever he imagined took at once
A bodily shape; and nought conceived or done
Since life began appeared irrational,
Wanton or needless. Time, the world and fate,
Material functions of each other, apt
As syllables of power and magic mind
In some self-reading riddle, as fracted bits   90
In self-adjusting instruments that play
Unheard ethereal music of the spheres,
Assumed their places equably; all things
Fell duly into line and dressed their ranks.

Thus art begins, as sudden as a star
In some unconstellated tract of space,
Where two extinct long-wandering orbs collide

75 That) They FSOP.   87 Time) Since FSOP.

And smite into each other and become
A lamp of glory, no crepuscular
Uncertainty, no interval between   100
The old misfortune and the new delight.
And thus at once the plodder of the waste
Attains utility and finds himself
Aristocrat and patron of the road;
The artisan, an artist – aristocrat
And artist being ever synonymes.
All vagabondage, all bohemianism,
All errantry, the unlicked, chrysalid
Condition of aristocracy and art,
Cut off for ever, the proud pedestrian free   110
Of the world, walks only now in picket resorts,
And can without a chart, without a guide,
Discover lands richer than El Dorado,
Sweeter than Beulah, and with ease
Ascend secluded mountains more delectable
Than heights in ancient pilgrimages famed,
Or myth-clad hills, or summits of romance.
Old traversed roads he traverses again,
Untroubled; nothing new he sees
Except the stretch of pleasure-ground, like one   120
Who turns the leaves o'er of a tedious book,
Careless of verbiage to reperuse
The single page inspired; in regions new
He goes directly to his own like beasts
That never miss the way; and having marked
A province with the beauties of his choice,
In them alone he walks, lord of the world.

106 ever) over FSOP.

140. RAIN IN THE NEW FOREST

By Emery Down to Minstead
In the rain on a lenten day –
About the Forest to Minstead,
And back by the Cadnam Way.

It was afternoon when the rain came down,
Compact, precipitate, icy cold, –
None of your showers that drain them dry
Before the hurricane clears the sky, –
Lean showers, themselves afraid of the wet,
That sprinkle the forest and spray the town,
But only harden the shrivelled mould,
And leave the dust-clouds waltzing yet!
In the afternoon real rain began, –
Vaporous phalanxes enrolled,   10

5 *om*. MS. *first reading.*   5 Lean) Such *corr. from* Your MS.   9 real) the MS.
10 Vaporous) Such vaporous MS.

A pluvial ban and arrière ban
Arrayed, deployed, ordained and set
To drench and saturate garth and wold,
And liquidate nature's vernal debt;
For when the herbage begins to grow
The rain is due though the dust may blow.
   But the birds considered it nothing at all:
In nest and nest a clutch of hopes
Would soon be hungry and musical;
So sparrow and starling, finch and wren   20
In thicket and clump and sprouting copse
Chuckled and chirmed and whistled again:
No bird considers the heaviest rain
When nests are warm and a mystery broods
In the heart of the world and the heart of the woods.
And as for the merle,
'Twas a thing to be heard,
How he sang at his peril –
So valiant a bird! –
The whole of his song from beginning to end,   30
Expending his passion as prodigals spend;
While the throstle laughed in his olive wing,
And turned an astonishing phrase or two
Of the matchless music he means to sing
When the woods are green and the heavens are blue; –
The song-thrush laughed in his feathered sleeve
At the sound of the blackbird's squandered song,
And the triumph his melody must achieve
When the nights grow short and the days grow long,
When cherries redden and berries swell,   40
And songs should be sweeter than song can tell.
But the larks were the miracles, – they, the larks,
Climbing the sky in the teeth of the rain, –
A navy of gallant aerial barques
(Your bird is your pristine aeroplane),
All primely rated,
With passion stored,
With music freighted,
And love on board.
   The timbered gables, the umber thatch   50
In thorpe and village and farm, or nooked
In glade and valley and lonely lane,
The wicket door on the clinking latch,
The darkling eaves and the gleaming pane
Of sheltered foresters' dwellings looked
Antiquely through the fringe of the rain,
And tenderly out of the centuries: –
So homelike, so habitable these,
So mellow and so entirely grown
Partakers of fate with the forest-trees,   60
That time has fashioned them nature's own;

24 nests) the nests MS.

While households of forest-folk unknown,
And living and dying and change and chance
Have steeped their chambers in sanctity,
And storied them all with an untold tale
More poignant than any high romance
Of frowning donjon, enchanted vale,
Pilgrimage, battle or stormy sea.
   In open woodland and fenced demesne
The swarthy thickets with stripes and studs   70
And knops and clusters of evergreen
Were brindled and pied; the unburst buds
With a blushing promise of summer glowed
On the crimson birch; and the garnered rain
Emptied in torrents its glistening load
On the purple background and sanguine stain
Of the birch-lit forest, – a wash of rain
Like glistening, silvery lacquer flowed
On the purple woods where the birch-buds glowed
On the swarthy ground like a crimson stain.   80
   Rooks fell on a ruddy field with a rush
And gobbled the worms like dainty sops.
Against the music of blackbird and thrush
Amorous doves in the fir-trees tops, –
To the flute and oboe of blackbird and thrush,
And the eager larks like a soaring flush
Of newly embodied chromatic scales,
Doves in the lofty fir-tree tops
Rumbled their drums at intervals.
A nut-brown brook in love with the rain,   90
Telling its chaplet of pebbles, turned
Under a bridge with a hushed refrain,
The muted murmur of earth's desire
For the falling, bounteous rain.
Lamps of gold on the dark gorse burned,
Golden blossoms all spiced with fire, –
Tawny gold and honey and fire;
Shade and shine their tissue wove,
Pearl and umber and snowy white,
Silver and olive-green and gray, –   100
Shadow and shine their draperies wove
And hung the forest with changing light;
Drift of moorland and gloomy grove
Haunted the open winding way,
And falling heavy and dense the rain
Enriched and freshened the world again.

62–3 *See Notes.*   79 On the purple forest where birch-buds glowed MS.
80 In the swarthy woods MS.   81–2 *See Notes.*   87 Of violins ringing
chromatic scales, MS   101 Shadow and shine) Gleam and shadow MS.
105 dense) thick MS.

II

ECLOGUES

141. NEW YEAR'S DAY

Brian: This trade that we ply with the pen,
Unworthy of heroes or men,
Assorts ever less with my humour:
Mere tongues in the raiment of rumour,
We review and report and invent:
In drivel our virtue is spent.

Basil: From the muted tread of the feet,
And the slackening wheels, I know
The air is hung with snow,
And carpeted the street.   10

Brian: Ambition, and passion, and power
Come out of the north and the west,
Every year, every day, every hour,
Into Fleet Street to fashion their best:
They would shape what is noble and wise;
They must live by a traffic in lies.

Basil: Sweet rivers of living blood
Poured into an ocean of mud.

Brian: Newspapers flap o'er the land,
And darken the face of the sky;   20
A covey of dragons, wide-vanned,
Circle-wise clanging, they fly.
No nightingale sings; overhead
The lark never mounts to the sun;
Beauty and truth are dead,
And the end of the world begun.

Basil: Far away in a valley of peace,
Swaddled in emerald,
The snow-happed primroses
Tarry till spring has called.   30

194

Sandy: And here where the Fleet once tripped
In its ditch to the drumlie Thames,
We journalists, haughtly though hipped,
Are calling our calling names.

Brian: But you know, as I know, that our craft
Is the meanest in act and intention;
You know that the Time-spirit laughed
In his sleeve at the Dutchman's invention:
Old Coster of Haarlem, I mean,
Whose print was the first ever seen.   40

Basil: I can hear in that valley of mine,
Loud-voiced on a leafless spray,
How the robin sings, flushed with his holly wine,
Of the moonlight blossoms of May.

Brian: These dragons that hide the sun!
The serpents flying and fiery,
That knotted a nation in one
Writhen mass; the scaley and wirey,
And flame breathing terror the saint
Still slays on our coins; the thing   50
That wandering artists paint
Where creaking sign-boards swing;
Gargouille, famous in France
That the fire at Rouen slew;
The dragon, Petrarca's lance
In Laura's defence overthrew;
The sea-beast Perseus killed;
Proserpine's triple team;
Tarasque whose blood was spilled
In Rhone's empurpled stream;   60
For far-flying strength and ire
And venom might never withstand
The least of the flourishing quire
In Fleet Street stalled and the Strand.

Basil: Through the opening gate of the year
Sunbeams and snowdrops peer.

Brian: Fed by us here and groomed
In this pestilent reeking stye,
These dragons I say have doomed
Religion and poetry.   70

Sandy: They may doom till the moon forsakes
Her dark, star-daisied lawn;
They may doom till doomsday breaks
With angels to trumpet the dawn;

50-2 *See Notes.*   54 That entered Rouen to his sorrow; 1893.
56 Overthrew in defence of his Laura; 1893.

195

While love enchants the young,
And the old have sorrow and care,
No song shall be unsung,
Unprayed no prayer.

Brian: Leaving the dragons alone –
   I say what the prophet says –   80
   The tyrant on the throne
   Is the morning and evening press.
   In all the land his spies,
   A little folk but strong,
   A second plague of flies,
   Buzz of the right and the wrong;
   Swarm in our ears and our eyes –
   News and scandal and lies.
   Men stand upon the brink
   Of a precipice every day;   90
   A drop of printer's ink
   Their poise may overweigh;
   So they think what the papers think,
   And do as the papers say.
   Who reads the daily press,
   His soul's lost here and now;
   Who writes for it is less
   Then the beast that tugs a plough.

Basil: Round happy household fires
   I hear sweet voices sing;   100
   And the lamb's-wool of our sires,
   Spiced ale, is a draught for a king.

Sandy: Now, journalist, perpend.
   You soil your bread and butter:
   Shall guttersnipes pretend
   To satirise the gutter?
   Are parsons ever seen
   To butt against the steeple?
   Brian, I fear you've been
   With very superior people.   110
   We, the valour and brains of the age,
   The brilliant, adventurous souls,
   No longer in berserkir rage –

Brian: Spare us the berserkir rage!

Sandy: Not I; the phrase outrolls
   As freshly to me this hour,
   As when on my boyish sense
   It struck like a trumpet-blare.
   You may cringe and cower
   To critical pretence;   120

If people will go bare
They may count on bloody backs;
Cold are the hearts that care
If a girl be blue-eyed or black-eyed;
Only to souls of hacks
Are phrases hackneyed. –
When the damsel had her bower,
And the lady kept her state,
The splendour and the power
That made adventure great,   130
Were not more strong and splendid
Than the subtle might we wield;
Though chivalry be ended,
There are champions in the field.
Nor are we warriors giftless;
Deep magic's in our stroke;
Ours are the shoes of swiftness:
And ours the darkling cloak;
We fear no golden charmer;
We dread no form of words;   140
We wear enchanted armour;
We wield enchanted swords.
To us the hour belongs;
Our daily victory is
O'er hydras, giant wrongs,
And dwarf iniquities.
We also may behold,
Before our boys are old,
When time shall have unfurled
His heavy hanging mists,   150
How the future of the world
Was shaped by journalists.

Basil: Sing hey for the journalist!
          He is your true soldado;
          Both time and chance he'll lead a dance,
          And find out Eldorado.

Brian: Sing hey for Eldorado!

Basil: A catch, a catch, we'll trowl!

Brian: Sing hey for Eldorado!

Sandy: And bring a mazer-bowl,   160
          With ale a-frothing brimmed.

Brian: We may not rest without it.

Sandy: With dainty ribbons trimmed,
          And love-birds carved about it.

197

Basil:	With roasted apples scented,
	And spiced with cloves and mace.

Brian: Praise him who ale invented!

Sandy: In heaven he has a place!

Basil: Such a camarado
Heaven's hostel never missed! 170

Brian: Sing hey for Eldorado!

Sandy: Sing ho for the journalist!

Basil: We drink them and we sing them
In mighty humming ale.

Brian: May fate together bring them!

Sandy: Amen!

Basil: Wass hael!

Brian: Drinc hael!

142. ST VALENTINE'S EVE

Percy: A-moping always, journalist? For shame!
Though this be Lent no journalist need mope:
    The blazing Candlemas was foul and wet;
    We shall be happy yet:
Sweethearts and crocuses together ope.

Menzies: Assail, console me not in jest or trope:

Give me your golden silence; or if speech
    Must wake a ripple on the stagnant gloom
    Of this lamp-darkened room,
Speak blasphemy, and let the mandrake screech. 10

Percy: Dread words – 'tis Ercles' vein – and fit to teach
The mandrake's self new ecstasies of woe,
    Have passed my lips in blame of God and man.
    Now surely nothing can
Constrain my soul serene to riot so.

Menzies: But you are old; the tide of life is low;
No wind can raise a tempest in a cup:
    Easy it is for withered nerves and veins,
    Parched hearts and barren brains
To be serene and give life's question up. 20

Percy: Although no longer chamber-doors I dup
             For willing maids (that never conquered me);
                 Though unimpassioned be my tranquil mind,
                 And all my force declined,
             My quenchless soul confronts its destiny. –
             But tell me now what ghastly misery

             Peeps from the shadowy cupboards of your eye?
                 This chastened month in white and gold is
                     dressed,
                 Lilies and snowdrops blessed:
             Be shriven by me as you were now to die;   30
             Shrove-tide is come.

Menzies: Confessions purify.
             My skeletons I will uncupboard straight;
                 And if you think me pitiful and weak,
                 I pray you do not speak,
             But go and leave me lonely with my fate. –
             My daily toil has irked me much of late:

             Of books that never will be read I write
                 What, save the anxious authors no one reads,
                 And chronicle the deeds
             Of Fashion, Crime, and Council, day and night.   40
             Once in a quarter when my heart is light

             I write a poem in a weekly sheet,
                 To lie in clubs on tables crowned with baize,
                 Immortal for seven days:
             This is the life my echoing years repeat.

Percy: The very round my aged steps still beat!

Menzies: And brooding thus on my ephemeral flowers
                 That smoulder in the wilderness, I thought,
                 By envy sore distraught,
             Of amaranths that burn in lordly bowers,   50
             Of men divinely blessed with leisured hours,

             And all the savage in my blood was roused.
                 I cursed the father who begot me poor,
                 The patient womb that bore
             Me, last of ten, ill-fed, ill-clad, ill-housed;
             I cursed the barren common where I browsed

             And sickened on the arid mental fare
                 The state has sown broad-cast; I cursed the strain
                 Whence sprang my blood and brain
             Frugal and dry; I cursed myself the heir   60
             Of dreadful things that met me everywhere:

Of uncouth nauseous vennels, smoky skies;
    A chill and watery clime; a thrifty race,
    Using all means of grace
To save their souls and purses; lingering lies,
Remnants of creeds and tags of party cries –

Scarecrows and rattles; then I cursed this flesh,
    Which must be daily served with meat and drink,
    Which will not let me think,
But holds me prisoner in the sexual mesh;   70
I cursed all being, and began afresh –

My education and my geniture,
    Which keep me running always from the goal,
    Or stranded on Time's shoal –
In naked speech, a sixpenny reviewer,
A hungry parasite of literature.

Percy: No reasoning can meet so fierce a mood.
    I'll tell you of a journalist instead,
    These many winters dead,
Who out of evil could distil the good.   80
He found his lot untameable and rude,

And sometimes ate what beggars had disdained
    Left at the donor's door. Once on a time
    A wanton youthful rhyme
I read him with my tears and heart's blood
        stained,
Wherein of Fate I bitterly complained.

He praised my rhymes; then said, 'The Poet's name
    Is overhallowed; and the Statesman's praise
    Unearned; unearned the bays
That crown the Warrior; Beauty, Art, I blame   90
For love alone deserves the meed of fame.'

Menzies: I understand you not.

Percy: Be still and mark.
    'And so,' he said, 'though I am faint and old,
    High in my garret cold –
While on the pane Death's knuckles rattle stark,
And hungry pangs keep sleep off – in the dark,

'I think how brides and bridegrooms, many a pair,
    With human sanction, or all unavouched,
    Together softly couched,
Wonder and throb in rapture; how the care   100
Of ways and means, the thought of whitening hair,

'Of trenchant wrinkles fade when night has set,
    And many a long-wed man and woman find
        The deepest peace of mind,
Sweet and mysterious to each other yet.
I think that I am still in Nature's debt.

'Scorned, disappointed, starving, bankrupt, old,
    Because I loved a lady in my youth,
        And was beloved in sooth.
I think that all the horrors ever told   110
Of tonsured men and women sable-stoled,

'Of long-drawn tortures wrought with subtle zest,
    Of war and massacre and martyrdom,
        Of slaves in Pagan Rome –
In Christian England, who begin to test
The purpose of their state, to strike for rest

'And time to feel alive in: all the blight
    Of pain, age, madness, ravished innocence,
        Despair and impotence,
The lofty anguish that affronts the light,   120
And seems to fill the past with utter night,

'Is but Love's needful shadow: though the poles,
    The spangled zodiac, and the stars that beat
        In heaven's high Watling Street
Their myriad rounds; though every orb that rolls
Lighting or lit, were filled with tortured souls,

'If one man and one woman, heart and brain
    Entranced above all fear, above all doubt
        Might wring their essence out,
The groaning of a universe in pain   130
Were as an undersong in Love's refrain.

'Then in a vision holy Time I see
    As one sweet bridal night, Earth softly spread
        One fragrant bridal bed,
And all my unrest leaves me utterly:
I sometimes feel almost that God may be.'

Menzies: You touch me not. I, stretched upon the rack
        Of consciousness, still curse. Woman and love?
            I would be throned above
    Humanity. Yet were I god, alack!   140
    I think that I should want my manhood back,

    Hating and loving limits –

Percy: Ah! I know
        How ill you are. You shall to-morrow do
        What I now order you.

201

At early dawn through London you must go
Until you come where long black hedgerows grow,

With pink buds pearled, with here and there a tree,
    And gates and stiles; and watch good country folk;
    And scent the spicy smoke
Of withered weeds that burn where gardens be;   150
And in a ditch perhaps a primrose see.

The rooks shall stalk the plough, larks mount the skies,
    Blackbirds and speckled thrushes sing aloud,
    Hid in the warm white cloud
Mantling the thorn, and far away shall rise
The milky low of cows and farmyard cries.

From windy heavens the climbing sun shall shine,
    And February greet you like a maid
    In russet-cloak arrayed;
And you shall take her for your mistress fine,   160
And pluck a crocus for her valentine.

Menzies: In russet-cloak arrayed with homespun smock
            And apple cheeks.

Percy: I pray you do not mock.

Menzies: I mock not, I shall see earth and be glad:
            London's a darksome cell where men go mad.

143. GOOD-FRIDAY

Sandy: Pfff! journalists; the wind blows snell!

Brian: To-day, we freeze, to-morrow fry.

Basil: And yesterday the black rain fell
                In sheets from London's smoky sky,

            Like water through a dirty sieve.

Menzies: March many weathers, as they say,
                In country nooks where proverbs live,
                    And folk distinguish night from day.

Sandy: Well, we shall make a day of night:
                Behold with *gules* and *or* a fire   10
            Emblazoned, and a mellow light;
                And things that journalists require.

            So let us open out our lore,
                And chat as snugly as the dead;
            And damned be those who came before,
                And all our brilliant sayings said.

202

Brian:	I love not brilliance; give me words
	Of meadow-growth and garden plot,
	Of larks and blackcaps; gaudy birds,
	Gay flowers and jewels like me not.

20

Basil:	The age-end journalist it seems
	Can change his spots and turn his dress,
	For you are he whose copy teems
	With paradox and preciousness.

Brian:	Last night I watched the evening star
	Outshine the moon it so excelled;
	And since my thought has been afar
	With deep and simple things of eld.

I heard in Fleet Street all the day,
   While traffic rolled and bells were rung,   30
The sombre, wailing Tenebræ,
   The Sistine Miserere sung.

I saw great people make their Maunds;
   The prelate leave his lofty seat;
A kaiser break imperial bonds
   To serve the poor and wash their feet.

I saw where countless hearts besought
   Pardon, for heaven's sweet peace athirst;
And through my soul the tender thought
   Of Mary, Virgin-mother pierced.   40

I saw a city kneeling down,
   I saw the gonfanon unfurled,
I saw the Pope in triple crown
   Stand up for God and bless the world.

Templars I saw, and monks and nuns,
   I saw frail priests strong kings command;
I thought how great the world was once
   When Heaven and Hell were close at hand.

The gloaming came; I ceased to ache,
   For in my veins the springtime welled,   50
And soothed my fancy to forsake
   The deep and simple things of eld,

And fly away where blackbirds sing,
   To wander free in dale and down.

Basil:	I would that I could see the spring!
Sandy:	Has any one been out of town?
Menzies:	I have for weeks.

Basil: For weeks? By heaven!
   What deeds heroic have you wrought
 That such a foretaste should be given
  Of Paradise?   60

Menzies: I earned it not

 'Twas accident: nor did I know
  Till now, that when they come to die
 Good press-men to the country go.

Brian: I think it's true.

Sandy: And so do I.

 Heaven is to tread unpaven ground,
  And care no more for prose or rhyme.
 Dear Menzies, talk of sight and sound,
  And make us feel the blossom-time.

Menzies: Then let my fancy dive and hale
  Pearls from my wandering memory,   70
 Unstrung, unsorted, else I fail
  To see the spring and make you see.

 Already round the oak at eve
  Good people prate of gain and loss;
 With folded hands some sit and grieve –
  New mounds the green churchyard emboss.

 The osier-peelers – ragged bands –
  In osier-holts their business ply;
 Like strokes of silver willow-wands
  On river banks a-bleaching lie.   80

 The patchwork sunshine nets the lea;
  The flitting shadows halt and pass;
 Forlorn, the mossy humble-bee
  Lounges along the flowerless grass.

 With unseen smoke as pure as dew,
  Sweeter than love or lovers are,
 Wood-violets of watchet hue
  Their secret hearths betray afar.

 The vanguards of the daisies come,
  Summer's crusaders sanguine-stained, 90
 The only flowers that left their home
  When happiness in Eden reigned.

 They strayed abroad, old writers tell,
  Hardy and bold, east, west, south, north:
 Our guilty parents, when they fell,
  And flaming vengeance drove them forth,

Their haggard eyes in vain to God,
    To all the stars of heaven turned;
But when they saw where in the sod,
    The golden-hearted daisies burned,   100

Sweet thoughts that still within them dwelt
    Awoke, and tears embalmed their smart;
On Eden's daisies couched they felt
    They carried Eden in their heart.

Basil: Oh, little flower so sweet and dear!

Sandy: Oh, humanest of flowers that grow!

Brian: Oh, little brave adventurer!
             We human beings love you so!

Menzies: We human beings love it so!
             And when a maiden's dainty shoe   110
             Can cover nine, the gossips know
             The fulness of the Spring is due.

Brian: The gallant flower!

Sandy: Its health! Come, drink!

Menzies: Its health! By heaven, in Highland style!

Basil: The daisy's health! And now, we'll think
             Of Eden silently a while.

144. ST SWITHIN'S DAY

Basil: We four – since Easter-time we have not met.

Brian: And now the Dog Days bake us in our rooms
             Like heretics in Dis's lidded tombs.

Sandy: Oh, for a little wind, a little wet!

Brian: A little wet, but not from heaven, I pray!
             Have you forgotten 'tis St Swithin's Day?

Basil: Cast books aside, strew paper, drop the pen!
             Bring ice, bring lemons, bring St Julien!

Sandy: Bring garlands!

Brian: With the laurel, lest it fade,
             Let Bacchus twist vine-leaf and cabbage blade!   10

205

Basil:	I would I lay beside a brook at morn,
	And watched the shepherd's-clock declare the hours;
	And heard the husky whisper of the corn,
	Legions of bees in leagues of summer flowers.

Brian: Who has been out of London?

Basil: Once, in June
Upstream I went to hear the summer tune
The birds sing at Long Ditton in a vale
Sacred to him who wrote his own heart's tale.
Of singing birds that hollow is the haunt:
Never was such a place for singing in!   20
The valley overflows with song and chaunt,
And brimming echoes spill the pleasant din.
High in the oak-trees where the fresh leaves sprout,
The blackbirds with their oboe voices make
The sweetest broken music all about
The beauty of the day for beauty's sake,
The wanton shadow and the languid cloud,
The grass-green velvet where the daisies crowd;
And all about the air that softly comes
Thridding the hedgerows with its noiseless feet,   30
The purling waves with muffled elfin drums,
That step along their pebble-paven street;
And all about the mates whose love they won,
And all about the sunlight and the sun.
The thrushes into song more bravely launch
Than thrushes do in any other dell;
Warblers and willow-wrens on every branch,
Each hidden by a leaf, their rapture tell;
Green-finches in the elms sweet nothings say,
Busy with love from dawn to dusk are they.   40
A passionate nightingale adown the lane
Shakes with the force and volume of his song
A hawthorn's heaving foliage; such a strain,
Self-caged like him to make his singing strong,
Some poet may have made in days of yore,
Untold, unwritten, lost for evermore.

Sandy: Your holiday was of a rarer mood,
A dedication loftier than mine;
But yet I swear my holiday was good:
I went to Glasgow just for auld lang syne.   50
In Sauchiehall Street in the afternoon
I saw a lady walking all in black,
But on her head a hat shaped like the moon,
Crescent and white and clouded with a veil.
I could not see if she were fair or pale
Because her beauty hid her like a mist:
But well I knew her bosom from her back;

19 that) this Sp.   22–3 See Notes.

And all her delicacy well I wist;
And every boy and man that saw her pass
Adored the beauty of that Scottish lass.   60
I said within: 'Three things are worthiest knowing,
And when I know them nothing else I know.
I know unboundedly, what needs no showing,
That women are most beautiful; and then
I know I love them; and I know again
Herein alone true Science lies, for, lo!
Old Rome's a ruin; Caesar is a name;
The Church? – alas! a lifeboat, warped and sunk;
God, a disputed title: but the fame
Of those who sang of love, fresher than spring,   70
Blossoms for ever with the tree of life,
Whose boughs are generations; and its trunk
Love; and its flowers, lovers.'

Brian: Love we sing,
Towards Love we strive; no other song or strife
We know, or heed. – You, Menzies, what say you?
Dark, in your corner – with a volume too!

Menzies: Now that I hang above the loathesome hell
Of smouldering spite and foul disparagement,
Even as a Christian, singed and basted well
By Christians, hung in dreadful discontent   80
Chained to a beam, and dangling in the fire;
And like an ocean-searching sailor-wight
Whose lonely eyes and clinging fingers tire;
And like a desperate, pallid acolyte
Of giddy Fortune, who with straining clutch
Swings in her wheel's wind from its lower rim,
Doubting of all things, disbelieving much,
I come to him who sang the heavenly hymn.

Brian: To Colin Clout! But whence this desperate thought?

Menzies: Two months ago I published –   90

Brian: (Out! Alack!)

Menzies: A book that held the essence of my life;
Wrong praise and wrong abuse was all I got.

Basil: We all have suffered from the critic's knife.

Sandy: And helpless lain on many a weekly rack.

Menzies: But I am weak.

Basil: No, Menzies; you are strong.
Already you have cast aside the wrong,
And solace found in Spenser's noble song.

When I was in like case it took a year
Before my wounds were whole, my vision clear.

Menzies: What brought you to yourself?   100

Basil: I prayed.

Menzies: Indeed!

Brian: To whom?

Basil: I know not; 'tis the mood I need –
Submissive aspiration.

Menzies: Pray with us:
Here from the city's centre make appeal.

Brian: Where hawkers cry, where roar the cab and 'bus.

Basil: So be it. On your knees, then: Sandy, kneel, –

Sweet powers of righteousness protect us now!
Your adversary, Fate, has driven us down
From that green-crowned, sun-fronting mountain-brow,
Where peace and aspiration (ebb and flow
Of thought that strives to whelm the infinite;   110
And, as the sun for ever fails to drown
More than a little hollow of the night,
Pierces a rush-light's ray's length into it)
Swung our ecstatic spirits to and fro
Between the Heaven and Hades of delight,
Down to that Bedlam of the universe,
That sepulchre of souls for ever yawning,
That jug of asps – God's enemy, Time's hearse,
The world, that blister raised by every dawning.
Help, ere it drive us mad, this devil's din!   120
The clash of iron, and the clink of gold;
The quack's, the beggar's whining manifold;
The harlot's whisper, tempting men to sin;
The voice of priests who damn each other's missions;
The babel-tongues of foolish politicians,
Who shout around a swaying Government;
The groans of beasts of burden, mostly men,
Who toil to please a thankless upper ten;
The knowledge-monger's cry, 'A brand-new fact!'
The dog's hushed howl from whom the fact was
          rent;   130
The still-voice 'Culture'; and the slogan 'Act!'
Save us from madness; keep us night and day,
Sweet powers of righteousness to whom we pray.

208

Herbert: The farmer roasts his stubble goose.

Menzies: The pard and tiger moths are loose.

Sandy: The broom-pods crackle in the sun;
And since the flowers are nearly done,
From thymy slopes and heather hills,
The wearied bee his pocket fills.

Brian: The wearied bee!

Herbert: On ancient walls
The moss turns greener.

Sandy: Hark! St Paul's
Booms midnight.

Brian: Basil is asleep.

Sandy: Boom, iron tongue! boom, slow and deep!   10

Menzies: The berries on the hawthorn tree
Are red as blood.

Brian: The wearied bee!

Herbert: In Devon cider-presses flow,
And lads and lasses nutting go.

Basil: Twelve notes the bell-voiced midnight peeled;
The moon stood still; the wan stars reeled.

Brian: Lord! Basil, are you off your head?

Basil: The opening knell had awakened me;
The twelve rang out a lullaby.

Brian: What passion's this? whose mare is dead?   20

Sandy: Fie, Brian! Let him say his say,
Begin again and fire away.

Basil: I started from uneasy slumber,
And heard night's stately tongue o'er-number
Twelve measured beats. While rang the last
I slept again; but ere it passed
In still-attenuating sound
I wakened from that sudden swound.
A dream begotten by the bell,
Was born within its lingering knell.   30

The deep reverberation clung
About my spirit; anguish wrung
My flesh; the mortal veil was rent;
And from the world's imprisonment,
And out of penitential Time
I soared into a ransomed clime.
The air was balmier than the west
That bends the barley's nodding crest,
When happy folk the greenwood seek,
And summer roasts the apple's cheek. 40
A darkness of another dye
Than earthly night o'erspread the sky
If any heaven were heaved on high:
The only light that guided me
My soul's enkindled radiancy.
The splendour that my spirit threw
Revealed new green, new golden dew
Wherein I saw new flowers encamp:
They glimmered in my silvery lamp
Like gems in an illumined grot: 50
I glided on; my light waned not;
Fresh wonders peered forth as I passed;
Without me brooded darkness vast.
Among the branches of the trees
That trembled to the fingering breeze,
And far more softly sang and sighed
Than soft Æolian harps, I spied
Looks brighter than the liquid gold
That streams before the peal has rolled.
Notes sweeter than the nightingale's, 60
More piercing than the lowly rail's,
And wealthier than the gorgeous chime
The mocking-bird at coupling time
Re-rings again and o'er and o'er
In changes richer than before,
With ruffling throat and spiral motion –
The vortex of a whirling ocean,
Whose floods are seething music waves
Outwelling from his heart's glad caves –
Surged and re-surged about my sense, 70
That revelled in their vehemence.
A blackness then waylaid my soul,
Intense, unfrayed, a perfect whole:
My beams could not irradiate
This ebon front, this cloudy gate.
Far up I saw a shimmer dim,
Like that above a night-cloud's rim,
Left trailing by the long-sunk sun,
When half the summer-time is done:
It coped the high-reared dense black blind: 80
I wondered what might be behind;

But when I pressed no step might be,
And yet between the wall and me,
The strange sward flower-strewn I could see.
Soon sang a voice; and, strange to tell,
It was my own voice singing well
A new song that I cannot mind;
Vanished at once the dense black blind;
Far, wide, a rainbow heaven of light
Clouded a while my silly sight.   90

I saw a sky of purple gloom,
That glowed as from a Tyrian loom,
And blushing hills perfumed with heath,
And flower-decked valleys hung beneath,
Where water purled a signal noise,
Melodious, like an angel's voice.
And there were forests great and old,
The carpet of whose fertile mould
Was woven of ferns and lustrous flowers;
And caves were there and pleasant bowers: 100
And rocks, immortally undressed,
That shone through many a loose green vest.
And in the sky, and on the hills,
And through the woods, and by the rills,
A host of lights of every hue,
And every shape lit up the view.
Some shone with blood-streaked glow of green
Like jasper; the carnation sheen
Of sardonyx beamed bright and pale;
And like a maiden's finger-nail   110
The hue of chalcedony gleamed;
And some pale blue like jacinth seemed;
And there were flames like chrysolites,
And rubies – gems that love delights
Beside the well-loved lips to shame;
And there was many an emerald flame;
And topazes and sapphires came,
And smouldering amethystine hues,
Like purple grapes where lights infuse
A glow of garden violets,   120
Or women's eyes love's sweet dew wets.

The flaming shapes for ever changed
As fixed they hung or widely ranged.
Like meteors some wide heaven spanned;
Like wisps some shot about the land;
And others moved their scrolls and curls,
Like waving skirts where lovely girls
Evolve from mazy minstrelsy
A moving silk-draped melody,
Dancing at the bridal-feast   130
Of some grand monarch of the east.

Transcending in magnificence,
In beauty, and in eloquence
Of movement, and in variance
Of shapely forms, and in the dance
The loftiest height with poise of state
Maintaining easily, elate
Above the others sailing far,
Now beaming like an opal star,
Now like the rainbow's shifting bridge   140
Wheeling from mountain ridge to ridge,
And now expanding like the dawn,
Now like the northern lights, there shone
A glorious flame; and one bright form,
As grand in motion as a storm,
Exceeded symmetry. I knew
What these two were; but memory grew
A jumbled chaos when I hoped
To seize their names. While yet I groped
Within the darkened lumber-room   150
Of memory, a sound did loom
Upon my hearing, which till then
Had been a hollow empty den,
Its sense being stolen into my sight
To give it power to grasp the light.
Eftsoons the looming sound, evolved
Whence I perceived not then, resolved
Its misty volume into dew,
That rose and fell and rose anew,
And showering gently seemed to bear   160
Odours from Cytherea's hair,
Or from the thousand flowers that please
The vigilant Hesperides
Within their bower on Atlas' top,
Whose shoulders huge the heavens prop,
So dulcet was the harmony.
It rained into my memory,
And, freshening that fallow mead,
Awakened many a sleeping seed
That sprang and blossomed into flower,   170
A bell for every happy hour.
But yet my wakening intuition
That longed to execute its mission,
To call those two supremest flames,
Bloomed not in flower of their names.
Oh me! that airy melody!
Its memory distresses me,
Like old men's thoughts of love's first kiss,
Like damned imaginings of bliss.
No thrilling movement with me stays;   180
The shadow of one subtle phrase
Cools not the burning of desire;
Tears cannot quench that ardent fire;

So sweet and low the voices sung,
So deep and high the singing swung,
Or, like the bird of heaven, hung
In joyous swoon, on brooding wing
Intensely, stilly, hovering.
Then far away across the vale
A sapphire sea with ripples pale   190
I saw: the golden, further shore
A group of wan lights wandered o'er
Hueless and shadowy: and I thought
That those the airy music wrought.
Sudden a great globe brimmed my sight,
And all my senses took their flight
To it to make it capable;
I was one eye and it was full,
But can a brazier hold the sun,
Or any cup the ocean?

Menzies: None.   200

Basil: This splendour, now in mist diffused,
Hung like a cloud of diamond-dust;
Contracted to a point anon,
It still so luminously shone
Its dense light could be seen alone.
I was one eye, one questioning gaze:
At once the scintillating haze,
In answer to my inquisition
Appeared as two; and each division
A shadowy human outline carried   210
Less bright divided than when married.
Then straight the black gulf hung between
My aching sight and heaven's scene.

Brian: But this is nonsense triple-piled.

Herbert: Is nonsense then to be reviled?

Menzies: Not so; for fancy where it lists
Breathes like the wind: he who resists
His wanton moods for ever, ends
In being moodless.

Basil: Good, my friends,
Forgive, forget. The dream was long,   220
Too long. – Let some one sing a song.

Menzies: Your bass is rusty, Herbert; come.

Herbert: I'll sing a song of Harvest-home.

222 bass) base 1893.

213

Song.

The frost will bite us soon;
  His tooth is on the leaves:
Beneath the golden moon
  We bear the golden sheaves:
We care not for the winter's spite,
We keep our Harvest-home to-night.
    Hurrah for the English yeoman!   230
      Fill full, fill the cup!
    Hurrah! he yields to no man!
      Drink deep; drink it up!

The pleasure of a king,
  Is tasteless to the mirth
Of peasants when they bring
  The harvest of the earth.
With pipe and tabor hither roam
All ye who love our Harvest-home.
    Hurrah for the English yeoman!   240
      Fill full; fill the cup!
    Hurrah; he yields to no man!
      Drink deep; drink it up!

The thresher with his flail,
  The shepherd with his crook,
The milkmaid with her pail,
  The reaper with his hook –
To-night the dullest blooded clods
Are kings and queens, are demigods.
    Hurrah for the English yeoman!   250
      Fill full; fill the cup!
    Hurrah! he yields to no man!
      Drink deep; drink it up!

146. QUEEN ELIZABETH'S DAY

Basil: A noble fog! Though I
           Were comfortably dead,
           Shrouded and buried deep
           In my last bed,
           Tucked in for my long sleep,
           Where generations lie,
           I scarce were more at ease
           Than now I feel beneath
           This heavy-laden silent atmosphere.

Menzies: A kraken of the skies! Its teeth   10
           Are closing in my throat;
           A lithe arm rummages
           Each aching lung.

Sandy: On your disaster, Menzies. Here,
Like people of Pompeii,
Or like Saharan denizens,
Sitting for centuries
O'erwhelmed with sand or lava, we
Are quite at home in fogs like these.

Basil: And feel as if our tongues and pens   20
Had wagged and scrawled since Arthur's time;
And we had seen the best and worst
Of England's youth and England's prime;
As if this day might be the first
Day of Elizabeth –
Or any day: the dead, like God,
Breathing eternal breath,
Can be in any period.

Menzies: Alas, I cannot but remember
That this is London in November!   30

Basil: Be out of London; off!
Command your soul; away,
Where woods their wardrobes doff
To give the wind free play.
Brocaded oak-trees wait,
Reluctant to undress;
But the woods accept from Fate
Their lusty nakedness,
And with a many-armed caress
Welcome their stormy mate.   40

Sandy: Or where on rivers blacken
Close fleets of hurrying leaves.

Basil: Or where with tawny bracken
A lonely moorland heaves.

Sandy: Where ribbed and spiny hedges
Hold fast the empty ear.

Basil: Or where like summer's pledges
The ruddy hips appear.

Sandy: Where coal-black brambles shimmer.

Basil: Where in the naked copse,   50
Gems in a charnel, glimmer
The nightshade's coral drops.

Sandy: Or where in twilight shaws
The dusky-glowing thorn,
Hides in its hoard of haws
The crimson of the morn.

215

Basil:	Where earth beholds the skies,
	Or heaven looks on the sea,
	Or where great mountains rise
	Command your soul to be. 60
Menzies:	I may not; all my brains
	Are baked and dried; my veins
	shrunk and unflushed.
Basil:	Drink wine.
Menzies:	It steads not; moods like mine
	Must run their courses out;
	Nothing can put to rout
	My gloom when I have swilled
	Life's sadness to the lees;
	Nepenthe may not ease,
	Or nectar, heaven-distilled. 70
Sandy:	Basil, tell us, pray,
	Why you called the day
	After the maiden queen?
Basil:	Three centuries away
	The child of Anne Boleyn
	Came to the English throne
	Upon this very day.
Menzies:	Ah! what a splendid age!
	Then England's hope was high;
	The world was half unknown; 80
	And heaven and hell were nigh.
	On such a glorious stage
	I could have played a part
	With other souls devout:
	But the world is now a mart,
	And all the earth found out.
	Hesperia is no more!
	From Himalayan vales
	Our fathers sought its shore,
	And lit on isles and dales 90
	Of Greece and Arcady;
	But soon they set their sails
	Sadly across the sea,
	And came to Ætna's base;
	Yet by Sicilian ways
	No dragon guarded tree
	With golden apples grew.
	Undauntedly they passed
	The Tyrrhene waters blue,
	And reached the Iberian strand – 100
	Hesperia at last!

Not there the promised land.
Westward that vision old
Fled o'er the Atlantic main
To sink for ever, slain
By Californian gold.

Basil: *This* is the promised land;
God saw that it was good:
You fail to understand
That the world is but a mood,   110
And time ours to command.
This is the hour of doom,
Or this creation's morn
Or Calvary's day of gloom:
We die not; were not born.

Menzies: Ah, you anachronists!
You poets! It is you,
With mellow purple mists
That shade the dreary view
Of life, a naked precipice   120
Overhanging death's deep sea.

Sandy: Anachronists! I rest on this,
Who'er may count it schism:
Mere by-blows are the world and we,
And time within eternity
A sheer anachronism.

Basil: A bull! a thundering bull!

Menzies: But not a blundering one;
For Chance directs the sun,
And Fate is Fortune's fool.   130
The world was scarcely made
Ere Chance began its trade
And changed to frozen poles
And spaces tropic-bound
What Fate created good;
And soulless or with souls
Beasts grew each other's food:
With floods all flesh was drowned;
And foul diseases came;
Earth issued forth in flame,   140
And swallowed cities up;
Peoples and languages,
Kingdoms and hierarchies,
With wars and tortures rose;
Nay, our most bitter cup
For ever overflows
With rich and poor alone:

123 it) a 1893.   147 Rich-and-poor 1893.

Chance has always spurned
Our struggles to atone.
Lo, in the simplest thing   150
The good is overturned,
Fate set aside with scorn!
The air is clear and sweet;
But the fog is in the street;
In June the squares were green,
What dreary places now!
Ere we may greet the spring,
Must winter come again;
And man may not be born
Without a woman's pain.   160

Basil: But God has no machine
            For punching perfect worlds from cakes of chaos.

Sandy: How!

Basil: He works but as He can;
            God is an artist, not an artisan.
            Darkly imagining,
            With ice and fire and storm,
            With floods and earthquake-shocks
            He gave our sphere its form.
            The meaning of His work
            Grew as He wrought.   170
            In creases of the mud, in cooling rocks
            He saw ideas lurk –
            Mountains and streams.
            Of life the passionate thought
            Haunted His dreams.
            At least He tried to do
            The thing He dreamt.
            With plasm in throbbing motes,
            With moss and ferns and giant beasts unkempt
            He laboured long, until at length He seemed   180
            To breathe out being. Flowers and forests grew
            Like magic at His word: mountain and plain,
            Jungle and sea and waste,
            With miracles of strength and beauty teemed:
            In every drop and every grain,
            Each speck and stain,
            Was some new being placed,
            Minute or viewless. Then was He aghast,
            And all His passion to create grew tame;
            For life battened on life. He thought   190
            To shatter all; but in a space
            He loved His work again and sought
            To crown it with a sovereign grace;
            And soon the great idea came.
            'If I could give my work a mind;

218

If I could make it comprehend
How wondrously it is designed;
Enable it with head and heart
To mould itself to some accomplished end –
That were indeed transcendent art.'   200
Trembling with ecstasy He then made man,
To be the world's atonement and its prince.
And in the world God has done nothing since:
He keeps not tinkering at a finished plan;
He is an artist, not an artisan.

Menzies: I've heard it sung, I've heard it said,
I've read if oft in many books,
That truth's as long as it is broad.
I like your dillettante God:
When man His work has perfected,   210
Straight God will blot it out again,
Or change it to a sterile moon,
Upon whose past shall speculate
Star-gazers from some brand-new land-and-sea.
Andy why should mortal man complain
Although no memory shall be
Of all the millions of his race,
Who broke brave hearts still fronting Fate;
Although no rumour of Helen's looks,
Although no Caesar's name of note,   220
No mellow word that Shakespeare wrote,
No echo of Wagner's spheral tune,
Shall sound in any nook of space?
God is an artist, and all art
Is useless, other artists say.

Sandy: If God is art and art is God,
I fear I don't believe in God.

Basil: That matters not since this is true –
Hear me before you go away,
And turn this over in your heart –   230
That God Himself believes in you.

147. CHRISTMAS EVE

Sandy: In holly hedges starving birds
     Silently mourn the setting year.

Basil: Upright like silver-plated swords
     The flags stand in the frozen mere.

Brian: The mistletoe we still adore
     Upon the twisted hawthorn grows.

Menzies: In antique gardens hellebore
    Puts forth its blushing Christmas rose.

Sandy: Shrivelled and purple, cheek by jowl,
    The hips and haws hang drearily.   10

Basil: Rolled in a ball the sulky owl
    Creeps far into his hollow tree.

Brian: In abbeys and cathedrals dim
    The birth of Christ is acted o'er;
The kings of Cologne worship Him,
    Balthazar, Jasper, Melchior.

Menzies: And while our midnight talk is made
    Of this and that and now and then,
The old earth-stopper with his spade
    And lantern seeks the fox's den.   20

Sandy: Oh, for a northern blast to blow
    These depths of air that cream and curdle!

Basil: Now are the halcyon days, you know;
    Old Time has leapt another hurdle;

And pauses as he only may
    Who knows he never can be caught.

Brian: The winter solstice, shortest day
    And longest night, was past, I thought.

Basil: Oh yes! but fore-and-aft a week
    Silent the winds must ever be,   30
Because the happy halcyons seek
    Their nests upon the sea.

Brian: The Christmas-time! the lovely things
    That last of it! Sweet thoughts and deeds!

Sandy: How strong and green old legend clings
    Like ivy round the ruined creeds!

Menzies: A fearless, ruthless, wanton band,
    Deep in our hearts we guard from scathe,
Of last year's log, a smouldering brand
    To light at Yule the fire of faith.   40

Brian: The shepherds in the field at night
    Beheld an angel glory-clad,
And shrank away with sore affright.
    'Be not afraid,' the angel bade.

'I bring good news to king and clown,
    To you here crouching on the sward;
For there is born in David's town
    A Saviour, which is Christ the Lord.

'Behold the babe in swathed, and laid
    Within a manger.' Straight there stood   50
Beside the angel all arrayed
    A heavenly multitude.

'Glory to God,' they sang; 'and peace,
    Good pleasure among men.'

Sandy: The wondrous message of release,
                That forged another chain!

Brian: Nay, nay; God help us to be good!

Basil: Hush! hark! Without; the waits, the waits!
                With brass and strings, and mellow wood.

Menzies: A simple tune can ope heaven's gates   60

Sandy: Slowly they play, poor careful souls,
                With wistful thoughts of Christmas cheer,
                Unwitting how their music rolls
                Away the burden of the year.

Basil: And with the charm, the homely rune,
                To early moods our minds incline,
                As when our pulses beat in tune
                With all the stars that shine.

Menzies: Oh cease! oh cease!

Basil: Ay, cease; and bring
                The wassail-bowl, the cup of grace.   70

Sandy: Pour wine, and heat it till it sing.
                With cloves and cardamums and mace.

Basil: And frothed and sweetened round it goes,
                The while we drink the whole world's health.

Sandy: The whole world's health! But chiefly those
                Who grasp the whole world's power and wealth.

Brian: I drink the poor in spirit; theirs
                Is heaven's kingdom.

56 *Menzies*: Glory to God again! 1893.   57 Nay, nay;) Again 1893.
66 Our thoughts like childhood's thoughts are given, *1893.*   67 As when)
When all 1893.   68 that shine) of heaven 1893.   74–96 *See Notes.*

221

Sandy:	Theirs, below,

A bursting granary of tares,
Derison, contumely, woe. 80

Brian: To those who patiently have borne
Sorrow!

Sandy: May joy come soon instead!
I drink the health of those that mourn
And never can be comforted.

Brian: I drink the meek.

Sandy: I drink their foes,
The ruthless heirs of all the earth –
The knaves, the pushing men, and those
Who claim prerogatives of birth.

Brian: I drink the merciful, for they
Shall mercy gain.

Sandy; From usurers? 90

Brian: The pure in heart, and those who pray
And work for peace when faction stirs,

I drink; and all whom men condemn
For righteousness, who never shrink
From persecution.

Sandy: Yes, to them!
To every sinner too, I drink!

Basil: Hush! hark! the waits, far up the street!

Menzies: A new, unearthly charm unfolds
Of magic music wild and sweet,
Anomes and clarigolds! 100

74–96 See Notes.   98 A new, unearthly) A distant, ghostly 1893.

148. ST GEORGE'S DAY

Herbert: I hear the lark and linnet sing;
I hear the whitethroat's alto ring.

Menzies: I hear the idle workman sigh;
I hear his hungry children cry.

Sandy: Still sad and brooding over ill:
Why listen to discordant tones?

1–2 om. YB., SGD.   3 workmen's sighs; YB., SGD.   4 their children's
hungry cries; YB., SGD.   4–5 See Notes.   5 But why keep brooding over
ill? YB., SGD.   6 listen to) hearken such YB., SGD.

Herbert:	We dream, we sing, we drive the quill
	To keep the flesh upon our bones.
	Therefore what trade have we with wrongs,
	With ways and woes that spoil our songs?	10

Menzies:	None, none! Alas, there lies the sting!
	We see, we feel, but cannot aid;
	We hide our foolish heads and sing:
	We live, we die; and all is said.

| Herbert: | To wonder-worlds of old romance |
| | Our aching thoughts for solace run. |

| Brian: | And some have stolen fire from France. |

| Sandy: | And some adore the Midnight sun. |

Menzies:	I, too, for light the world explore,
	And trembling, tread where angels trod;	20
	Devout at every shrine adore,
	And follow after each new god.
	But by the altar everywhere
	I find the money-changer's stall;
	And littering every temple-stair
	The sick and sore like maggots crawl.

| Basil: | Your talk is vain; your voice is hoarse. |

Menzies:	I would they were as hoarse and vain
	As their wide-weltering spring and source
	Of helpless woe, of wrath insane.	30

| Herbert: | Why will you hug the coast of Hell? |

| Brian: | Why antedate the Judgment Day? |

| Menzies: | Nay, flout me not; you know me well. |

| Basil: | Right, comrade! Give your fancy way. |

Menzies:	I cannot see the stars and flowers,
	Nor hear the lark's soprano ring,
	Because a ruddy darkness lowers
	For ever, and the tempests sing.
	I see the strong coerce the weak,
	And labour overwrought rebel;	40
	I hear the useless treadmill creak,
	The prisoner, cursing in his cell;
	I see the loafer-burnished wall;
	I hear the rotting match-girl whine;
	I see the unslept switchman fall;

19 *See Notes.*   26–7 *See Notes.*

I hear the explosion in the mine;
I see along the heedless street
The sandwichmen trudge through the mire;
I hear the tired quick tripping feet
Of sad, gay girls who ply for hire.   50

Basil: To brood on feeble woe at length
Must drive the sanest thinker mad;
Consider rather weal and strength.

Menzies: On what foundations do they stand?
I mark the sable ironclad
In every sea; in every land,
An army, idling on the chain
Of rusty peace that chafes and frets
Its seven-leagued limbs, and bristled mane
Of glittering bayonets;   60
The glowing blast, the fire-shot smoke
Where guns are forged and armour-plate;
The mammoth hammer's pounding stroke;
The din of our dread iron date.
And always divers undertones
Within the roaring tempest throb –
The chink of gold, the labourer's groans,
The infant's wail, the woman's sob.
Hoarsely they beg of Fate to give
A little lightening of their woe,   70
A little time to love, to live,
A little time to think and know.
I see where from the slums may rise
Some unexpected dreadful dawn –
The gleam of steeled and scowling eyes,
A flash of women's faces wan!

Basil: This is St George's Day.

Menzies: St George? A wretched thief I vow.

Herbert: Nay, Menzies, you should rather say,
St George for Merry England, now!   80

Sandy: That surely is a phantom cry,
Hollow and vain for many years.

Menzies: I hear the idle workmen sigh;
I hear the drip of women's tears.

Herbert: I hear the lofty lark,
The lowly nightingale.

49 quick-tripping YB., SGD.   51–7 *See Notes.*   58 rusty) parchment YB.,
SGD.   59 Their seven-leagued limbs and bristled manes YB., SGD.
73 from the slums) in the East YB., SGD.   84–5 *See Notes.*

Basil:	The present is a dungeon dark
	Of social problems. Break the gaol!
	Get out into the splendid Past
	Or bid the splendid Future hail.

90

Menzies:	Nor then, nor now, nor first, nor last,
	I know. The slave of ruthless Law,
	To me Time seems a dungeon vast
	Where Life lies rotting in the straw.

Basil:	I care not for your images
	Of Life and Law. I want to sing
	Of England and of Englishmen
	Who made our country what it is.

Herbert:	And I to praise the English Spring.

Percy:	St George for Merry England, then!

100

Menzies:	There is no England now, I fear.

Basil:	No England, say you, and since when?

Menzies:	Cockney and Celt and Scot are here,
	And Democrats and 'ans' and 'ists'
	In clubs and cliques and divers lists;
	But now we have no Englishmen.

Basil:	You utter what you never felt,
	I know. By bog and mount and fen,
	No Saxon, Norman, Scot, or Celt
	I find, but only Englishmen.

110

Herbert:	In all our hedges roses bud.

Basil:	And thought and speech are more than blood.

Herbert:	Away with spleen, and let us sing
	The praises of the English Spring!

Basil:	In weeds of gold and purple hues
	Glad April bursts with piping news
	Of swifts and swallows come again,
	And of the tender pensive strain
	The bulfinch sings from bush to bush.

Percy:	And oh! the blackbird and the thrush
	Interpret as no master may
	The meaning of the night and day.

120

114 The English Spring, the English Spring! YB., SGD.   121 master) maestro
YB., SGD.

Sandy:	They catch the whispers of the breeze And weave them into melodies.
Brian:	They utter for the hours that pass The purpose of their moments bright.
Basil:	They speak the passion of the grass, That grows so stoutly day and night.
Herbert:	St George for merry England then! For we are all good Englishmen!
Percy:	We stand as our forefathers stood For Liberty's and Conscience' sake.
Herbert:	We are the sons of Robin Hood, The sons of Hereward the Wake.
Percy:	The sons of yeomen, English-fed, Ready to feast, or drink or fight.
Herbert:	The sons of kings – of Hal and Ned, Who kept their island right and tight.
Percy:	The sons of Cromwell's Ironsides, Who knew no king but God above.
Basil:	We are the sons of English brides, Who married Englishmen for love.
Sandy:	Oh, now I see Fate's means and ends! The Bruce and Wallace wight I ken, Who saved old Scotland from its friends, Were mighty northern Englishmen.
Brian:	And Parnell, who so greatly fought Against a wanton useless yoke, With Fate inevitably wrought That Irish should be English folk.
Basil:	By bogland, highland, down, and fen, All Englishmen, all Englishmen!
Menzies:	There is no England now, I say –
Brian:	No England now! My grief, my grief!
Menzies:	We lie widespread, the dragon-prey Of any Cappadocian thief.

130

140

150

148 To make a mob a people, then YB., SGD.   150 Englishmen. YB., SGD.

226

                    In Arctic and Pacific seas
                    We lounge and loaf: and either pole
                    We reach with sprawling colonies –
                    Unwieldy limbs that lack a soul.   160

Basil: St George for Greater England, then!
                    The Boreal and the Austral men!
                    They reverence the heroic roll
                    Of Englishmen who sang and fought:
                    They have a soul, a mighty soul,
                    The soul of English speech and thought.

Sandy: And when the soul of England slept –

Basil: St George for foolish England, then! –

Sandy: Lo! Washington and Lincoln kept
                    America for Englishmen!   170

Basil: Hurrah! The English people reigns
                    Across the wide Atlantic flood!
                    It could not bind itself in chains!
                    For Yankee blood is English blood.

Herbert: And here the spring is queen
                    In robes of white and green.

Percy: In chestnut sconces opening wide
                    Tapers shall burn some fresh May morn.

Brian: And the elder brightens the highway side,
                    And the briony binds the thorn.   180

Sandy: White is the snow of the leafless sloe
                    The saxifrage by the sedge,
                    And white the lady-smocks a-row
                    And sauce-alone in the hedge.

Basil: England is in her Spring;
                    She only begins to be.
                    Oh! for an organ voice to sing
                    The summer I can see!
                    But the Past is there; and a mole may know,
                    And a bat may understand,   190
                    That we are the people wherever we go –
                    Kings by sea and land!

Herbert: And the spring is crowned and stoled
                    In purple and in gold.

Percy: Wherever light, wherever shade is,
                    Gold and purple may be seen.

157 Pacific) Antarctic SGD.

227

Brian: Gold and purple lords-and-ladies
            Tread a measure on the green.

Herbert: In deserts where the wild wind blows
            Blossoms the magic hæmony.   200

Percy: Deep in the Chiltern woodland glows
            The purple pasque anemone.

Basil: And England still grows great
            And never shall grow old;
            Within our hands we hold
            The world's fate.

Menzies: We hold the world's fate?
            The cry seems out of date.

Basil: Not while a single Englishman
            Can work with English brains and bones!   210
            Awaiting us since time began,
            The swamps of ice, the wastes of flame!
            In Boreal and Austral zones
            Took life and meaning when we came.
            The Sphinx that watches by the Nile
            Has seen great empires pass away;
            The mightiest lasted but a while;
            Yet ours shall not decay.
            Because, although red blood may flow,
            And ocean shake with shot,   220
            Not England's sword but England's Word
            Undoes the Gordian Knot.
            Bold tongue, stout heart, strong hand, brave brow
            The world's four quarters win;
            And patiently with axe and plough
            We bring the deserts in.

Menzies: Whence comes this patriotic craze?
            Spare us at least the hackneyed brag
            About the famous English flag.

Basil: I'll spare no flourish of its praise.   230
            Where'er our flag floats in the wind
            Order and justice dawn and shine.
            The dusky myriads of Ind,
            The swarthy tribes far south the line,
            And all who fight with lawless law,
            And all with lawless men who cope
            Look hitherward across the brine,
            For we are the world's forlorn hope.

198–9 *See Notes.*   200 harmony SGD.   212 flame) plane SGD.

228

Menzies:	That makes my heart leap up! Hurrah!
	We are the world's forlorn hope! 240
Herbert:	And with the merry birds we sing
	The praises of the English Spring.
Percy:	Iris and orchis now unfold.
Brian:	The drooping-leaved laburnums ope
	In thunder-showers of greenish gold.
Menzies:	And we are the world's forlorn hope!
Sandy:	The lilacs shake their dancing plumes
	Of lavender, mauve, and heliotrope.
Herbert:	The speedwell on the highway blooms.
Menzies:	And we are the world's forlorn hope! 250
Sandy:	Skeletons lurk in every street.
Herbert:	We push and strike for air and scope.
Brian:	The pulses of rebellion beat
	Where want and hunger skulk and mope.
Menzies:	But though we wander far astray
	And oft in gloomy darkness grope,
	Fearless we face the blackest day,
	For we are the world's forlorn hope.
Sandy:	St George for Merry England then!
	For we are all good Englishmen! 260
Basil:	St George for Greater England then!
	The Boreal and the Austral men!
All:	By bogland, highland, down, and fen,
	All Englishmen, all Englishmen!
	Who with their latest breath shall sing
	Of England and the English Spring!

242 The English Spring, the English Spring! YB., SGD.   243 orctris SGD.
256 gloomy) utter YB.   257 blackest) roughest YB.

149. MAYDAY

Brian:	Late – you are late. And where have you been?
Menzies:	I have been in the woods and the lanes

Brian:	And what have you heard, and what have you seen,
	And what in your fancy reigns?
Menzies:	I have heard the ring-dove coo,
	And the cuckoo toll his bell;
	I have seen the shrieking jay flash blue
	Athwart a wooded dell.

I have heard the chattering streamlet run
In haste to reach the sea;   10
I have watched the golden bee,
Cupid and Hymen in one,
Morn, noon, and afternoon,
Fulfil the tingling hours
With the murmuring sound of his bridal tune
As he married the waiting flowers.

The long, long hedgerows white with May
Bordered the rustling lanes;
And a fragrant wind blew all the day.

Brian: But what in your fancy reigns?   20

Menzies: There reigned, and is regnant still,
A memory, long forgot,
Of a lowland town, a lowland hill,
And a lowland woman's lot.

She shed her tears, and dreamed her dreams,
And wore her sad wan smiles,
Where a wide water winds and gleams

Among its links and isles.
Rock-perched a royal borough towers
High over the highest trees,   30
With crumbling walls and faded bowers
And mouldering palaces.

Near by a hill its dark crest lifts
Sheer from the river bank,
And cloudy shadow broods and shifts
About its russet flank.

The land is stained with purple dyes
Of high-romantic scenes;
The air still quivers with the sighs
Of tragic kings and queens;   40

The very ploughman holds his plough
As proudly as a lance;
The milkmaid bears a dreamy brow,
Inheriting romance.

22 An interwoven thought PMB.

Even in my father's time a crew
Of lads and lasses gay
Would dip their faces in the dew
Upon the first of May.

This joyful mood might not withstand
The age's growing care,   50
When railways hacked and scored the land,
And wires engraved the air.

One woman only, all forlorn,
While twenty summers flew,
Still climbed the hill each May-day morn
Her beauty to renew!

What love, what loss, what hope was hers
No man or maid could tell,
But all the loyal lowlanders
Esteemed her custom well.   60

Dressed in a hat with broken plume,
A cape, and worn black frock,
Before the dawn she left the room,
And climbed by scar and rock.

And so to-day by land and burn,
By scented hedge and shaw,
At many a pause and sudden turn
Her wistful face I saw.

And once as in a waking dream
The whole fair lowland shone –   70
The palaced rock, the hill, the stream,
The softly coming dawn:

And she with sobs and murmured cries
To earth's green bosom laid
Her withered cheek, while from her eyes
Hot dew on cold dew strayed.

Brian: What was her end?

Menzies: Oh, exquisite!
Winter and Spring she lay
Bedridden in a palsy fit;
But on the first of May,   80

When the lark waked the sun, she too
Arose, and in a trance
Went forth to bathe her face in dew,
The martyr of romance.

They found her on the green hill-side
At home, and sleeping fast
Her endless sleep, Death's pallid bride,
Most beautiful at last.

(Singing within)

'Remember us poor Mayers all,
    And thus we do begin 90
To lead our lives in righteousness,
    Or else we die in sin.

'I have been rambling all this night,
    And almost all this day,
And now returned back again
    I bring you a branch of May.'

Brian: An antique minstrel! Hark!

Menzies: It is Basil: I know his note.

(Enter Basil, carrying a branch of hawthorn blossom).

Menzies: Have you been where the night-jar haunts the dark
In outland ways remote? 100

Basil: I have been with the nightingale:
I have learned his song so sweet:
I sang it aloud by wood and dale,
And under my breath in the street.
If the words would only flow –

Menzies: Oh, sing it now!

Basil: No, no!
But it went like this, I think: –

'Where the purple hyacinths grew,
And the campions white and pink,
The jewelled butterflies flew 110
For jewelled cups to drink;
And some were violet-eyed,
Some blue, some rosy-red,
Gold-plumed, or damask-dyed,
Earth-born and heaven-bred;
And every chalice drooped and sighed
When the splendid revellers fled;
But never a flower its cup denied
Though the wine of life was shed.

'The lark from the top of heaven raved 120
Of the sunshine sweet and old;
And the whispering branches dipped and laved
In the light; and waste and wold
Took heart and shone; and the buttercups paved
The emerald meads with gold.

'Now in the forest is night;
The flowers have gone to sleep;
But the stars have opened their eyes of light
Under the brows of heaven deep;

And gentle shadows cross my sight,   130
And murmurs rustle and creep;
And the very darkness is fresh and bright
With the tears the sweet dews weep.

'The wind steals down the lawns
With a whisper of ecstasy,
Of moonlit nights and rosy dawns,
And a nest in a hawthorn tree,
Of the little mate for whom I wait,
Flying across the sea,
Through storm and night as sure as fate,   140
Swift-winged with love for me.'

Menzies: And so you brought home the May
          With the nightingale's song in your ears.

Basil: And sad eyes flashed for a moment gay,
        Or welled with happy tears,
        When they saw my branch and remembered the day,
        And forgot the tedious years.
        And I thought as I tuned my rhyme,
        And waved the branch in my hand,
        Of the famous olden time   150
        When a Maypole stood in the Strand.

Brian: Let the Golden Days return!

Menzies: And let the May-Queen reign!

Basil: When smokeless fires burn,
        And London is born again!

150. MIDSUMMER DAY

Sandy   I cannot write, I cannot think;
        'Tis half delight and half distress:
      My memory stumbles on the brink
        Of some unfathomed happiness –

      Of some old happiness divine.
        What haunting scent, what haunting note,
      What word, or what melodious line,
        Sends my heart throbbing to my throat?

Basil: What? thrilled with happiness to day,
        The longest day in all the year,   10
      Which we must spend in making hay
        By threshing straw in Fleet Street here!

What scent? what sound? The odour stale
   Of watered streets; the rumour loud
Of hoof and wheel on road and rail,
   The rush and trample of the crowd!

Herbert: Humming the song of many a lark,
   Out of the sea, across the shires,
The west wind blows about the park,
   And faintly stirs the Fleet Street wires.   20

Perhaps it sows the happy seed
   That blossom in your memory;
Certain of many a western mead,
   And hill and stream it speaks to me.

Basil: Go on: of rustic visions tell
   Till I forget the wilderness
Of sooty brick, the dusty smell,
   The jangle of the printing-press.

Herbert: I hear the woodman's measured stroke;
   I see the amber streamlet glide –   30
Above, the green gold of the oak
   Fledges the gorge on either side.

A thatched roof shines athwart the gloom
   Of the high moorland's darksome ground;
Far off the surging rollers boom,
   And fill the shadowy wood with sound.

Basil: You have pronounced the magic sign!
   The city with its thousand years,
Like some embodied mood of mine
   Uncouth, prodigious, disappears.   40

I stand upon a lowly bridge,
   Moss-grown beside the old Essex home;
Over the distant purple ridge
   The clouds arise in sultry foam;

In many a cluster, wreath and chain
   A silvery vapour hangs on high,
And snowy scarfs of silken grain
   Bedeck the blue slopes of the sky;

The wandering water sighs and calls,
   And breaks into a chant that rings   50
Beneath the vaulted bridge, then falls
   And under heaven softly sings;

14 rumour) bruit SR., SFSE.   24–5 *See Notes.*   33–4 *See Notes.*

A light wind lingers here and there,
   And whispers in an unknown tongue
The passionate secrets of the air,
   That never may by man be sung:

Low, low, it whispers; stays, and goes;
   It comes again; again takes flight;
And like a subtle presence grows
   And almost gathers into sight.   60

Sandy: The wind that stirs the Fleet Street wires,
    And roams and quests about the Park,
That wanders all across the shires,
    Humming the song of many a lark –

The wind – it is the wind, whose breath,
   Perfumed with roses, wakes in me
From shrouded slumbers deep as death
   A yet unfaded memory.

Basil: About Midsummer, every hour
    Ten thousand rosebuds opening blush,   70
The land is all one rosy bower,
    And rosy odours haunt and flush

The winds of heaven up and down:
   On the top-gallant of the air
The lark, the pressman in the town
   Breathe only rosy incense rare.

Sandy: And I, enchanted by the rose,
    Remember when I first began
To know what in its bosom glows
    Exhaling scent ambrosian.   80

A child, at home in streets and quays,
   The city tumult in my brain,
I only knew of tarnished trees,
   And skies corroding vapours stain.

One summer – Time upon my head
   Had showered the curls of years eleven –
Me, for a month, good fortune led
   Where trees are green and hills kiss heaven.

By glen and mountain, moor and lawn,
   Burn-side and sheep-path, day and night,   90
I wandered, a belated faun,
   All sense, all wonder, all delight.

235

And once at eve I climbed a hill,
   Burning to see the sun appear,
And watched the jewelled darkness fill
   With lamps and clustered tapers clear.

At last the strongest stars were spent;
   A glimmering shadow overcame
The swarthy-purple firmament,
   And throbbed and kindled into flame;   100

The pallid day, the trembling day
   Put on her saffron wedding-dress,
And watched her bridegroom far away
   Soar through the starry wilderness.

I clasped my hands and closed my eyes,
   And tears relieved my ecstasy:
I dared not watch the sun arise;
   Nor knew what magic daunted me:

And yet the roses seemed to tell
   More than the morn, had I but known   110
The meaning of the fragrant smell
   That bound me with a subtle zone.

But in the gloaming when we played
   At hide-and-seek, and I with her
Behind a rose-bush hid, afraid
   To meet her gaze, to breathe, or stir,

The dungeon of my sense was riven,
   The beauty of the world laid bare,
A great wind caught me up to heaven
   Upon a cloud of golden hair;   120

And mouth touched mouth; and love was born;
   And when our wondering vision blent,
We found the meaning of the morn,
   The meaning of the rose's scent.

Ah me! ah me! since then! since then!

Herbert: Nay, nay; let self-reproaches be!
   Now that this thought is throned again,
   Be zealous for its sovereignty.

Basil: And brave, great Nature must be thanked,
   And we must worship on our knees,   130
   And hold for ever sacro-sanct
   Such dewy memories as these.

93–6 *om.* SR. *first reading.*   93 And once at eve I climbed a hill, *corr. from* At shut of eve I climbed a hill SR.   97 The strongest stars in heaven were spent; SR. 98 glimmering shadow) dusky lusture SR.   99 swarthy–) wide-spread SR. 102 Put) Threw SR.   105 I, like a wild thing, closed my eyes, SR. 109–12 *See Notes.*   111 fragrant *corr. from* subtle SR. 112 subtle *corr. from* fragrant SR.   128 zealous for *corr. from* jealous of SR.

Percy: A health, in cider, golden, racy, tough –
        The harvest and the harvesters!

Sandy   I drink
        In amber spirit that enshrines the heart
        Of an old Lothian summer.

Percy: Summers old
        And Gules of August! – to their memory
        I drink, and to the memory of those
        Who wielded shining sickles. Forth they went,
        The gaunt and ragged heralds of the morn:
        Before them spread the sighing leagues of grain;
        Behind, the tardy sun arose and struck   10
        All day on men and women obstinate
        Against the stubborn ranks, the golden horde:
        Silent and set, as their long-sworded sires
        Who fought the crashing rollers on the strand
        And stared athwart the ocean wistfully
        Into the moaning storm, the reapers reaped:
        And they grew lean; and the sun burnt them black:
        A sea of living gold poured round their feet
        And rose in crested shocks; still and anon
        The whetstone shrieked against the curving blade. 20
        I drink the swarthy harvesters of old!

Herbert: To them all honour! But I also drink
        The merry singing wheels that lighten toil.

Sandy: And drive men into cities where they rot!
        Nor do they lighten toil –

Ninian: A truce to this!
        Let us see things and say them. Why debate?

Sandy: Debate? The sergeant-major of the tongue!
        Rather we should invite his discipline.

Percy: Well said, indeed! It is this same Debate
        That overmasters armies; that distils   30
        From rancorous commotion amity;
        It is the proof, sifter and alkahest
        Of all opinion, and the ordeal keen
        Of knowledge, reason and intelligence;
        The arbiter of right; the only source,
        Camp, castle and estate of liberty.
        The sword did never yet perpetuate
        The work it reared – too sharp a trowel, still
        With bloody mortar building on the sand.
        The word alone endures; but prophecy   40
        Being now invalid, we exalt Debate.

Sandy:	The blare of personal and party aims
	In parliaments and journals seems indeed
	No substitute for Sinai; but it serves:
	And from the vehement logomachy
	Of interest and cabal, something humane
	At happy intervals proceeds.

Ninian: How now!
'Something humane at happy intervals!'
A meagre output for your demiurge!

Percy: Debate, like every energy divine,   50
Careless of centuries, elaborates
Events effectual for eternity.
The cavillers, impatient of delay,
Like little boys that violate the earth
To see if seedlings sprout, resent the mode,
When they descry the immaterial
Advancement in a decade; but we know,
We, ponderers devout of secular years,
How this most tedious Cyclops, this Debate,
Laborious long in darkness and distress,   60
Hammered and forged the adamantine chains
That shackle tyranny, and now begins
To smelt the ore from which shall yet be wrought
A kingly crown for every child of man.

Ninian: I see no hope in wrangling. Nations pass
From panic into panic; all men seem
Fools or fanatics.

Percy: Well? . . . Proceed; discuss.

Ninian: Not I; for now you put me on my guard.
Sometimes when I forget myself I talk
As though I were persuaded of the truth   70
Of some received or unreceived belief;
But always afterwards I am ashamed
Of such lewd lapses into bigotry.

Percy: Intolerantly tolerant, I say!

Sandy: This is debauchery: defend yourself!

Ninian: I cannot; I have tried it many a time,
And always failed, because the thing I say
Seems not more just than that which I deny;
Nor would I if I could, because to me
It now appears inept to take a side.   80
I know that silence would become me best,
And I endeavour to be quiet.

Sandy: Oh!

Ninian: Indeed I do. . . . Now I shall say no more.

Herbert: Why do you take offence so readily?

Ninian: I am not well: I am haunted. Lo, I stand
On Arthur's Seat. The chill and brindled fog
That plumed the Bass and belted Berwick Law,
That hung with ghostly tapestry the stones
Of bleak Tantallon, from the windy Forth,
Noiseless and dim, speeds by the pier of Leith,   90
And by Leith Walk, its dreary channel old,
To flood the famous city, Edinburgh.
Then, like the spectre of an inland sea
By wanton sorcerers troubled and destroyed,
It foams with whitening surges through the vale,
The fair green hollow over Salisbury Crags;
And rises clasping every gentle slope,
Uneven scar, and fairy-girdled knoll,
Till with the hungry passion of the dead
It hugs the high earth, frantic to supply   100
Its own lean misty ribs, and live again
Terrestrial, with the mountain for a soul.
I stand and watch. The fog begins to ebb;
And sunset weaves of all the waning wreaths
A veil of lace, investing goldenly
The rock-piled castle – plinth and monolith
Of ruby deep and dark in soaring groups;
The Monument aflame with chrysolite;
St Giles's garland-crown studded with gems.
A bell rings faintly: curled and braided smoke   110
O'erhangs the humming Canongate, and flings
Dusky festoons that wither as they fall
About the wasted towers of Holyrood.
In front the burnished disc of day descends
The ample crimson west; behind, the night
In silent legions troops into the air. –
Masses of vision overwhelm me thus:
I am haunted by the heavens and the earth –
Darkness and light; and when I am addressed
I answer from the point, or petulantly,   120
Or say the opposite of what I would,
And am most awkward, helpless, and forlorn,
Wherefore I shun the company of men,
Not fearing them, but fearful of myself;
Surely to strive to please and still to fail
Is to be wretched in the last degree.

Sandy: Then do not strive to please: contemn contempt,
And trust yourself.

Ninian: But I mistrust myself:
A word, a glance, a cloud, a beam of light,
A perfume from its orbit shakes my soul.   130

239

Sandy: This weakness comes because you look without.

Ninian: I look without: you look within; what then?
You are possessed; I, obsessed: that is all.
I am besieged by things that I have seen:
Followed and watched by rivers; snared and held
In labyrinthe woods and tangled meads;
Hemmed in by mountains; waylaid by the sun;
Environed and beset by moon and stars;
Whispered by winds and summoned by the sea.

Herbert: What do you note now?   140

Ninian: By a Kentish road,
Across the down where poles in ricks repose,
Delivered from the burden of the bines,
And golden apples on their twisted boughs
Illumine ancient orchards, I descend,
Watching and wondering to the Medway's bank.
The alder and the hazel dip their leaves;
The grass-green willow shakes; the spiny thorn,
Embossed and lustrous with its load of haws,
Shines in the water like a burning bush;
And broad and deep, muttering outlandish
      things,   150
The heavy river rolls its umber flood.
Convolvuluses overhang the brink,
Pallid or watchet-hued, and still as bells
That in a trance imagine tuneful chimes
Or virtue to enchant a moonlit mere.
On river lawns with emerald velvet spread
The ewes sedately browse the three-piled nap.
A distant clang of shouts and laughter rings
Across the valley from the gleaming tents
Of sunburnt hoppers at their evening meal;   160
And fainter voices from the roadside inn
Echo about the air, and dwell and die.
Crowned by the yellow oasthouse from whose cowl
Banners and scarfs of fleecy smoke hang out,
And busked with serried, tawny-clustered vines,
Far-reaching slopes lean up along the sky.
The drowsy wind touches a fitful stop;
The Medway mutters dreaming as it rolls;
In bronzing brakes and thickets deeply choired
Autumnal tokens birds at leisure pipe;   170
While the sun, shut within a donjon high
Of massive cloud, through secret loopholes flings
His moted beams that quiver visibly
Broadcast; or seem ethereal lances, stacked
By the celestial watchmen who patrol
The world at night, and on their silent rounds
Move to the ghostly music of the spheres.

Herbert: And whence comes this obsession?

Ninian: Hark! Behold!
The floor is flooded with the tide. I lounge
Upon a shingle bolster. Dimly seen   180
Beyond the weathergleam a pennon'd mast,
A drift of smoke, hover and disappear;
And in the midst dark sails of mackerel boats
Over a reach of water, brown as tan,
Dance, deftly tripping the uneven waves.
Nearer, a yellow width unwinds; between,
A point of emerald glows, and suddenly
Shoots out and burns its way towards the west –
A spark in tinder, then a stripe of fire,
And last a sheet of phosphorescent green   190
Fuming with white waves. Listen! at my feet
The uplifted shuddering rollers headlong fall,
And jangle on the beach as the surf breaks
In silver chains and shekels; while the wind
Out of the southwest sings across the deep.
Straightway, a new sky makes another sea.
Occultly gifted, light upon the waves
Juggles with hidden beams behind a cloud
Bright but impenetrable. Near the shore
A vein of saffron shines; beyond, a band   200
Of olive hue blends with a sapphire zone;
Further away, wine-coloured water heaves
Against a high sea-wall of swarthy fog.
Is it the sea that gleams in merging breadths
Of colour dark and wet? Or do the powers,
That decorate the quarters of the world,
In some vast crucible dissolve and fuse
Virginal mines of ruby, malachite,
Jacinth and chrysoprase to pave the floor
Of ocean rough with wrecks and skeletons?   210
Nature is now about some mystery!
But while I watch, ere I can mark the change,
The passionate sun flames through the shrivelled
       cloud,
And all the crisp and curling water wakes,
Blue as the naked sky that bathes in it.

Herbert: How does it happen you are so beset?

Ninian: I shall attempt to tell you honestly.
It was engraven deeply on my mind
In daily lessons from my infancy
Until I left my father's house, that not   220
Ability and knowledge, beauty and strength,
But goodness only can avail. I watched,
And thought I understood that beauty, strength
And knowledge ought to reign, they being indeed

The trinity of goodness; but I claimed
That this should be revealed to me, that I
Should be directly warned by God Himself
In the old fashion. Strange it seems; and yet
It was not very strange. Each morn and eve,
Year after year, I heard the prophets read,   230
Heard strong believing prayer: the atmosphere
Was not allied more nearly to my breath
Than to my mind the thought of God – no dream
Of deity; a living, active God.
On hill-tops, by the sea, in storm, in calm
I cried to Him to speak to me; with tears
Solicited a sign. Sleepless and pale
I wandered like a ghost, and day and night
Waited upon a message from on high.
Sunset and sunrise came; the seasons past;   240
The years went slowly by; but still to me
The universe was dumb. Books helped me not,
Except for pleasure or to gain command
Of words: I would have God's own voice or none.
At last I ceased to hope and found content
In roaming through the land. The magic sun
Drew pictures on my sight. Wondering I watched;
Nor could the secular fairy ever change
My wonder into curiosity.
All my emotion and imagining   250
Were of the finest tissue that is woven
From sense and thought. No well-thumbed page
     appeared
In the hard book of memory when I woke:
Amazed I trembled newly into life:
I seemed to be created every morn.
A golden trumpet pealed along the sky:
The sun arose; the whole earth rushed upon me.
Sometimes the tree that stroked my window-pane
Was more than I could grasp; sometimes my thought
Absorbed the universe, which fell away   260
And dwindled from my ken, as if my mind
Had been the roomy continent of space. –
My way of life led me to London town,
And difficulties – which I overcame,
Equipped with patience and necessity.
Then suddenly before my thoughts might leap
Resurgent from the living tomb of care
And dip their wings in dawn, about me clung
The slimy folds of sin: its nether coils
Are hidden in the sepulchre of time,   270
The glutted past; the pallid future strains
In travail with its fiery eyes and fangs:
I peer from out the slippery middle wreaths
And see blurred visions of the world, or watch
The flashing scenes that haunt my memory.

When heedfully I viewed my latter days –
Considering for the first time in my life
The naked facts of my affairs and me –
I found that underneath indifference
To every aim saving a livelihood   280
And leisure to enjoy nature and art,
My source of strength, though never to myself
Confessed before, had been the lurking thought
That poison, or a bullet, or the waves
Could stop the unendurable ecstasy
Of pain or pleasure, at whichever pole
Of passion I determined to forsake
The orb of life, on my acceptance thrust
In ignorance and disregard of me,
My temperament and fitness for the gift;   290
But now that refuge of despair is shut,
For other lives have twined themselves with mine.
And yet. . . . How shall I seize you with due
    dread
Of the offensive tide that stifles me,
The worm obscene in whose close coils I writhe? . . .
Now I conceive it clearly; you shall mark
Fate's way with me! A tedious decade hence
My son shall come and pitifully cry,
'Father, why am I weak, outclassed, outcast?
I cannot do the things that others do;   300
I take no place in work or play; my brains
Are unelastic: something in my head
Snaps when I fain would study; visions rise
Unsummoned; phantom tongues mumble strange
    news;
And when I would contend in games, my bones
Grow pithless, and my sinews shrink; my heart! –
Who wore it out with sensual drudgery
Before it came to me? what warped its valves?
It has been used: my heart is secondhand!
Why had I not the force to be born great,   310
Fit for a splendid stage, a noble part,
A crisis in the world? Why must I think
Such things at seventeen? Why think at all
When love should lap me in a constant dream?
I have no faith instinctive in myself;
No reservoir profound of energy;
No fathomless resource; no central fire;
No passionate aroma in my blood
Filling the world with fragrance where I come;
No rapt imagination to transmute   320
All pallor into glory. Life you gave:
Where is my birthright, sir, beauty and strength?'
What can I say to him?

Others: The truth!

243

Ninian: This then: –
'My son, your ancestors supplanted you:
You are my child; hence are your teeth on edge.
Out blood is stale; the tree from which we spring
Fades at the top. Two of our family
Have died insane in my time: one I saw
Go mad. The sounds and sights that visit you
Attend me too, foretellers of our doom.   330
The ultimate iniquity is mine;
But from a root in distant ages sunk
The loathsome filaments entangle you.
And I impeach the smooth conniving world,
The bland accomplice that has made and makes
A merit of defect, a cult of woe,
Sowing exhausted land with seed that's foul,
To harvest tares of madness, impotence,
Uncomeliness in wasteful granaries –
I mean asylums, prisons, hospitals.   340
If only nineteen hundred years ago
A gospel of the pride of life had rung
Our doleful era in; if the device
In nature's choice of beauty and of strength
Had then been shown to man, how had the world
Approved the excellent expedient,
With voluntary euthanasia
Weeded humanity at once, and made
A race of heroes in a golden age! . . .
This helps not. All the blame is mine, my son,   350
Who never should have been' . . . It palsies me;
I cannot comfort him; he stands and stares
Defeated ere he was begot. – Behold
The ancient snake that pinions me! Like one
Chained to a column in a turbid stream,
About my ears a sluggish billow flaps,
And chokes and daubs me with its ropy wash.

Sandy: Escape! I know the manner! Live at speed;
And call your least caprice the law of God;
Disdain the shows of things, and every love   360
Whose stamen is not hate; self-centred stand;
Accept no second thought; in every throb
Your heart gives, every murmur of your mind,
Listen devoutly to the trump of doom.
You are your birthright; let it serve you well:
Be your own star, for strength is from within,
And one against the world will always win!

Ninian: I cannot act. The subtle coils grow tense,
And crush my limbs, my heart, my throat, my head.
I am the sufferer, the endurer, I.   370
Yet God who gives no presage hitherto,
Haply intends hereafter to be heard.

244

I am not thinking solely of myself,
But of the groaning cataract of life,
The ruddy stream that leaps importunate
Out of the night, and in a moment vaults
The immediate treacherous precipice of time,
Splashing the stars, downward into the night.
Meanwhile for me no lulling opiate,
No dream, no mystic solvent: I must watch   380
Hopeless, unhelped, till I go mad or die.

Herbert: But you have hope and help.

Ninian: I? Show me them!

Herbert: You went forth seeking God and found the world
The sounds and sights that haunt, and help and
    please.
The canopy and state of day and night;
The pageant of the year; the changing moods,
The loyal constancy and testament
Of Nature – her asides, her hints, and smiles,
Her clear ideas of repose and toil,
Her covenant and noble ministry   390
Of light and darkness, and of life and death,
Are the true salve for your distempered mind.
Blame not yourself too much; admit no fear
Of madness with the sunrise in your blood;
And hold your own intelligence in awe
As the most high: there is no other God –
No God at all; yet God is in the womb –
A living God, no mystic deity.
With idols in its infancy the world
Deceived itself as maidens do with dolls,   400
And as it grew pretended and believed
That what it should bring forth already reigned.
Now is its hour come, but it only knows
The sick dismay and anguish, ignorant
Of birth-pangs and an offspring more divine
Than man has yet imagined. I have woes,
As you and all men have in their degree;
So let us think we are the tortured nerves
Of Being in travail with a higher type.
I know that I shall crumble back to dust,   410
And cease for evermore from sense and thought,
But this contents me well in my distress: –
I, being human, touch the highest reach
Attained by matter, and within me feel
The motion of a loftier than I:
Out of the beast came man; from man comes God.
Deepest delight is in the certainty
That to the all pervading element
Wherein the universe disports a while,

245

Ethereal oblivion, my deeds   420
And I eternally belong.

Ninian: Yes . . . See,
They throng the room! – no spectres, but themselves:
Sibilant depths of darkness; avenues
Of latticed light; ambrosial, pine-strewn glades;
Ravines and waterfalls; the grass-green turf,
Where primroses by secret alchemy
Distil from buried treasure golden leaves,
And where forget-me-nots above the tombs
Of snow-drops hang their candelabra, trimmed
With azure light – turquoise by magic roots   430
Drawn from the bowels of the earth and changed
To living flame; roses, laburnum, lilac;
Sunrise and sunset like a glowing vice
Bloodstained that grips the world; the restless moon
Swung low to light us; clouds; the limpid sky;
The bourdon of the great ground-bee, athwart
A lonely hill-side, vibrant on the air,
And subtler than the scent of violets;
Sonorous winds, storm, thunder, and the sea.

152. ALL HALLOW'S EVE

Brian: Tearfully sinks the pallid sun.

Menzies: Bring in the lamps: Autumn is done.

Percy: Nay, twilight silvers the flashing drops;
                And a whiter fall is behind.

Brian: And the wild east mouths the chimney-tops,
                The Pandean pipes of the wind.

Menzies: The dripping ivy drapes the walls;
                The drenched red creepers flare;
                And the draggled chestnut plumage falls
                In every park and square.   10

Percy: Nay, golden garlands strew the way
                For the old triumph of decay.

Basil: And I know, in a living land of spells –
                In an excellent land of rest,
                Where a crimson fount of sunset wells
                Out of the darkling west –

                That the poplar, the willow, the scented lime,
                Full-leaved in the shining air
                Tarry as if the enchanter time
                Had fixed them deathless there.   20

In arbours and noble palaces
  A gallant people live
With every manner of happiness
  The amplest life can give.

Percy: Where? where? In Elfland?

Menzies: No; oh no!
  In Elfland is no rest,
But rumour and stir and endless woe
  Of the unfulfilled behest –
The doleful yoke of the Elfin folk
  Since first the sun went west.   30

The cates they eat and the wine they drink,
  Savourless nothings are;
The hopes they cherish, the thoughts they think
  Are neither near nor far;
And well they know they cannot go
  Even to a desert star:

One planet is all their poor estate,
  Though a million systems roll;
They are dogged and worried, early and late,
  As the demons nag a soul,   40
By the moon and the sun, for they never can shun
  Time's tyrannous control.

The haughty delicate style they keep
  Only the blind can see;
On holynights in the forest deep,
  When they make high revelry
Under the moon, the dancing tune
  Is the wind in a cypress tree.

They burn the elfin midnight oil
  Over their tedious lore;   50
They spin the sand; and still they toil
  Though their inmost hearts are sore –
The doleful yoke of the restless folk
  For ever and ever more.

But could you capture the elfin queen
  Who once was Cæsar's prize,
Daunt and gyve her with glances keen
  Of unimpassioned eyes,
And hear unstirred her magic word,
  And scorn her tears and sighs,   60

Lean would she seem at once, and old;
  Her rosy mouth decayed;
Her heavy tresses of living gold,
  All withered in the braid;

247

In your very sight the dew and the light
   Of her eyes would parch and fade;

And she, the immortal phantom dame,
   Would vanish from your ken;
For the fate of the elves is nearly the same
   As the terrible fate of men: 70
To love; to rue: to be and pursue
   A flickering wisp of the fen.

We must play the game with a careless smile,
   Though there's nothing in the hand;
We must toil as if it were worth our while
   Spinning our ropes of sand;
And laugh and cry, and live and die
   At the waft of an unseen wand.

But the elves, besides the endless woe
   Of the unfulfilled behest,   80
Have only a phantom life, and so
   They neither can die nor rest –
Have no real being at all, and know
   That therefore they never can rest –
The doleful yoke of the deathless folk
   Since first the sun went west.

Percy: Then where is the wonderful land of spells,
Where a crimson fount of sunset wells,
And the poplar, the willow, the scented lime
Tarry, full-leaved, till the winter-time,   90
Where endless happiness life can give,
And only heroic people live?

Basil: We know, we know, we spinners of sand!
In the heart of the world is that gracious land;
And it never can fade while the sap returns,
While the sun gives light, and the red blood burns.

153. 'IN HASTE, ERE MY SENSES WITHER'

The Fool: In haste, ere my senses wither,
    I travel and search the night:
    Whence am I? what am I? whither?
    I must have fullest light.

Worldly Wiseman: That is your cry! Take heed;
    Look to your steps, I say.
    Return, for now, indeed,
    Soul-traps beset your way:
    Some man-devouring creed
    Will seize you for a prey –   10

Some engine, baited bright
   With immortality
Will drag you out of sight
   And rend you: know that he
Who must have fullest light
   Plots for his enemy.

In youth we hope; with age
   The bargain seems unjust;
But yet though none engage
   For Death's cold dust to dust –   20
The fixed, the only wage –
   We take our doom on trust.

Such is the gentle rede
   That prudent men embrace –
No fierce, enchanting creed
   To live for in disgrace,
But good enough at need
   In any market-place.

Stare at the darkness, shout
   Your frenzied how and why,   30
No ghost will whet your doubt,
   No echo give reply;
Only the world will flout,
   And fortune pass you by.

The Fool: Let chance sway hither and thither,
    And the world be wrong or right,
  Here, now, ere my sinews wither,
    I wrestle with infinite night:
  Whence am I? what am I? whither?
    I will have fullest light.   40

154. EPILOGUE TO FLEET STREET ECLOGUES

Votary: What gloomy outland region have I won?

Artist: This is the Vale of Hinnom. What are you?

Votary: A Votary of Life. I thought this tract,
    With rubbish choked, had been a thoroughfare
    For many a decade now.

Artist: No highway here!
    And those who enter never can return.

Votary: But since my coming is an accident –

Artist: All who inhabit Hinnom enter there
    By accident, carelessly cast aside,
    Or self-inducted in an evil hour.   10

Votary: But I shall walk about it and go forth.

Artist: I said so when I came; but I am here.

Votary: What brought you hither?

Artist: Chance, no other power:
My tragedy is common to my kind. –
Once from a mountain-top at dawn I saw
My life pass by, a pageant of the age,
Enchanting many minds with sound and light,
Array and colour, deed, device and spell.
And to myself I said aloud, 'When thought
And passion shall be rooted deep, and fleshed   20
In all experience man may dare, yet front
His own interrogation unabashed:
Winged also, and inspired to cleave with might
Abysses and the loftiest firmament:
When my capacity and art are ranked
Among the powers of nature, and the world
Awaits my message, I will paint a scene
Of life and death, so tender, so humane,
That lust and avarice lulled awhile, shall gaze
With open countenances; broken hearts,   30
The haunt, the shrine, and wailing-place of woe,
Be comforted with respite unforeseen,
And immortality reprieve despair.'
The vision beckoned me; the prophecy,
That smokes and thunders in the blood of youth,
Compelled unending effort, treacherous
Decoys of doom although these tokens were.
Across the wisdom and the wasted love
Of some who barred the way my pageant stepped:
'Thus are all triumphs paved,' I said; but soon,   40
Entangled in the tumult of the times,
Sundered and wrecked, it ceased to pace my thought,
Wherein alone its airy nature strode;
While the smooth world, whose lord I deemed myself,
Unsheathed its claws and blindly struck me down,
Mangled my soul for sport, and cast me out
Alive in Hinnom where human offal rots,
And fires are heaped against the tainted air.

Votary: Escape!

Artist: I tried, as you will try; and then,
Dauntless, I cried, 'At midnight, darkly lit   50
By drifts of flame whose ruddy varnish dyes
The skulls and rounded knuckles light selects
Flickering upon the refuse of despair,
Here, as it should the costly pageant ends;
And here with my last strength, since I am I,

Here will I paint my scene of life and death:
Not that I dreamt of when the eager dawn,
And inexperience, stubborn parasite
Of youth and manhood, flattered in myself
And in a well-pleased following, vanities   60
Of hope, belief, good-will, the embroidered stuff
That masks the cruel eyes of destiny;
But a new scene profound and terrible
As Truth, the implacable antagonist.
And yet most tender, burning, bitter-sweet
As are the briny tears and crimson drops
Of human anguish, inconsolable
Throughout all time, and wept in every age
By open wounds and cureless, such as I,
Whence issues nakedly the heart of life.'   70

Votary: What canvas and what colour could you find
To paint in Hinnom so intense a scene?

Artist: I found and laid no colour. Look about!
On the flame-roughened darkness whet your eyes.
This needs no deeper hue; this is the thing:
Millions of people huddled out of sight,
The offal of the world.

Votary: I see them now,
In groups, in multitudes, in hordes, and some
Companionless, ill-lit by tarnished fire
Under the towering darkness ceiled with smoke;   80
Erect, supine, kneeling or prone, but all
Sick-hearted and aghast among the bones.

Artist: Here pine the subtle souls that had no root,
No home below, until disease or shame
Undid the once-so-certain destiny
Imagined for the Brocken-sprite of self,
While earth, which seemed a pleasant inn of dreams,
Unveiled a tedious death-bed and a grave.

Votary: I see! The disillusioned geniuses
Who fain would make the world sit up, by Heaven!   90
And dig God in the ribs, and who refuse
Their own experience: would-bes, theorists,
Artistic natures, failed reformers, knaves
And fools incompetent or overbold,
Broken evangelists and debauchees,
Inebriates, criminals, cowards, virtual slaves.

Artist: The world is old; and countless strains of blood
Are now effete: these loathsome ruined lives
Are innocent – if life itself be good.
Inebriate, coward, artist, criminal –   100

251

The nicknames unintelligence expels
Remorse with when the conscience hints that all
Are guilty of the misery of one.
Look at these women: broken chalices,
Whose true aroma of the spring is split
In thankless streets and with the sewage blent.

Votary: Harlots, you mean; the scavengers of love,
Who sweep lust from our thresholds – needful brooms
In every age; the very bolts indeed
That clench and rivet solidarity.   110
All this is as it has been and shall be:
I see it, note it, and go hence. Farewell.

Artist: Here I await you.

Votary: There is no way out.

Artist: But we are many. What? So pinched and pale
At once! Weep, and take courage. This is best,
Because the alternative is not to be.

Votary: But I am nothing yet, have made no mark
Upon my time; and, worse than nothing now,
Must wither in a nauseous heap of tares.
Why am I outcast who so loved the world?   120
How did I reach this place? Hush! Let me think.
I said – what did I say and do? Nothing to mourn.
I trusted life, and life has led me here.

Artist: Where dull endurance only can avail.
Scarcely a tithe of men escape this fate;
And not a tithe of those who suffer know
Their utter misery.

Votary: And must this be
Now and for ever, and has it always been?

Artist: Worse now than ever and ever growing worse.
Men as they multiply use up mankind   130
In greater masses and in subtler ways:
Ever more opportunity, more power
For intellect, the proper minister
Of life, that will usurp authority,
With lightning at its beck and prisoned clouds.
I mean that electricity and steam
Have set a barbarous fence about the earth,
And made the oceans and the continents
Preserved estates of crafty gather-alls;
Have loaded labour with a shotted chain,   140
And raised the primal curse a thousand powers.

Votary: What? Are there honest labourers outcast here?
Dreamers, pococurantes, wanton bloods
In plenty and to spare; but surely work
Attains another goal than Hinnom!

Artist: Look!
Seared by the sun and carved by cold or blanched
In darkness; gnarled and twisted all awry
By rotting fogs; lamed, limb-lopped, cankered,
   burst,
The outworn workers!

Votary: I take courage then!
Since workers here abound it must be right   150
That men should end in Hinnom.

Artist: Right! How right?
The fable of the world till now records
Only the waste of life: the conquerors,
Tyrants and oligarchs, and men of ease,
Among the myriad nations, peoples, tribes,
Need not be thought of: earth's inhabitants,
Man, ape, dinornis for a moment breathe,
In misery die, and to oblivion
Are dedicated all. Consider still
The circumstance that most appeals to men: 160
Eternal siege and ravage of the source
Of being, of beauty, and of all delight,
The hell of whoredom. God! The hourly waste
Of women in the world since time began!

Votary: I think of it.

Artist: And of the waste of men
In war – pitiful soldiers, battle-harlots.

Votary: That also I consider.

Artist: Weaklings, fools
In millions who must end disastrously;
The willing hands and hearts, in millions too,
Paid with perdition for a life of toil;   170
The blood of women, a constant sacrifice,
Staining the streets and every altar-step;
The blood of men poured out in endless wars;
No hope, no help; the task, the stripes, the woe
Augmenting with the ages. Right, you say!

Votary: Do you remember how the moon appears
Illumining the night?

Artist: What has the moon
To do with Hinnom?

Votary: Call the moon to mind.
Can you? Or have you quite forgotten all
The magic of her beams?   180

Artist: Oh no! The moon
Is the last memory of ample thought,
Of joy and loveliness that one forgets
In this abode. Since first the tide of life
Began to ebb and flow in human veins,
The targe of lovers' looks, their brimming fount
Of dreams and chalice of their sighs; with peace
And deathless legend clad and crowned, the moon!

Votary: But I adore it with a newer love,
Because it is the offal of the globe.
When from the central nebula our orb,   190
Outflung, set forth upon its way through space,
Still towards its origin compelled to lean
And grope in molten tides, a belt of fire,
Home-sick, burst off at last, and towards the sun
Whirling, far short of its ambition fell,
Insphered a little distance from the earth
There to bethink itself and wax and wane,
The moon!

Artist: I see! I know! You mean that you
And I, and foiled ambitions every one
In every age; the outworn labourers,   200
Pearls of the sewer, idlers, armies, scroyles,
The offal of the world, will somehow be –
Are now a lamp by night, although we deem
Ourselves disgraced, forlorn; even as the moon,
The scum and slag of earth, that, if it feels,
Feels only sterile pain, gladdens the mountains
And the spacious sea.

Votary: I mean it. And I mean
That the deep thoughts of immortality
And of our alienage, inventing gods
And paradise and wonders manifold,   210
Are rooted in the centre. We are fire,
Cut off and cooled a while: and shall return,
The earth and all thereon that live and die,
To be again candescent in the sun,
Or in the sun's intenser, purer source.
What matters Hinnom for an hour or two?
Arise and let us sing; and, singing build
A tabernacle even with these ghastly bones.

Urban: Skirting the southern seaboard, overland
The wind tramps from the Atlantic, drums and gongs
Aerial, the music of his march.
The hedges ruffle bravely when he comes,
And shake their branches busked with coral buds,
The pregnant spiceries of leaf and flower;
On this hand and on that the forests bow;
And harvests, newly sprung, a shallow tide –
The emerald down of golden crops to be –
Ripple and press about his shining feet.   10

Eustace: This way – across the valley.

Urban: Look behind!
The sea . . . Be patient, now; and wait! The sea
Leans up along the towering firmament;
In crisp resplendent curves the mail-clad wind
Advances channelward with echoing tread;
Against the silver main your Norman tower
Looms black; with ebony the sharp clouds zone
The belted sun; and shadows overscore
The dazzling waters.

Eustace: Under Erringham,
Up Thundersbarrow Hill, through Mossy Bottom,   20
Past Crooked Moon, and over Truleigh Top,
Behind the tree-shorn Downs, by Small Dole, Beeding,
Bramber, and on to Steyning, where we dine.

Lucian: We range from height to hollow, storm to calm,
And vent our hoarded or our new-come minds.

Eustace: I met a starling yesterday . . . I swear
By Æsop, then, I did! High on a pole,
Above the humming wires he sat; the sun
Adorned his damascened and burnished vest;
He quivered like an artist as he plied   30
His castanets, his yellow, clattering bill:
An ostracised and rebel bird, alone
Where myriads of his friendly kind abide.
'Hello!' I cried, 'What ails you?' 'Who are you?'
He snapped disdainfully. 'I am,' I said,
'Acquainted with the tongues of beasts and birds,
A wandering understander, well-disposed.
Tell me the matter.' 'Oh, its simply this,'
The creature grumbled, flouncing to the hedge:
'I'm more intelligent and capable   40
Than any other starling on the Downs.

---

2 The wind tramps) He tramples ASR.   4–6 See Notes.   10 feet) steps ASR.
11–12 See Notes.   29 Adorned) Gilded ASR.

I proved it to the world in countless ways;
Impressed my unapproached pre-eminence
On every mind, and claimed authority.
They would have none of it! In me behold
A most ill-used, unhappy passerine.'
'But did you, in and out of season, point,
Illustrate and extol your gifts?' said I.
'Oh,' went the bird, 'importunately.' 'Then
You failed, perhaps, on the offensive side.   50
Did you,' I said, 'with resolute assault,
Unflinching hardihood and poignant skill,
Attack, expose, deride and hold to scorn
The faults and foibles of the other birds?'
'Profound observer – for a man! I did,'
The starling cried. ' 'Twas meat and drink to me.
And all day still, though no one hears, I scold
The deep depravity of aviankind.'
'What brought about this ignominy then?'
'My awkwardness,' the bird said; and became   60
More unctuously familiar. 'I'm so wise,
So able, and transcend so far the bounds
Of starling sense, that all attempts to share
The social duties of my kind abused
Opinion, and the stigma stuck: *A gauche,*
Impertinent, disgraceful fowl, they said,
Whom nobody gets on with, beast or bird!
And me a seraph, struggling hard to dwell
On any terms at all with Hottentots!'
'True; gaucherie,' I said, 'is vanity,   70
Quintessence of conceit in man and fowl.'
'Vanity?' said the dubious starling. 'Yes;
A bird abandoned, who conceives himself,
The centre of the universe, records
The highest tide of vanity. You know
You have no soul.' 'No soul?' the starling barked.
'No soul,' I said, 'and hence your gaucherie.
You think yourself of paramount respect,
And like a stranded grayling misbehave,
Having no soul; for soul alone concerns   80
The universe. Now man, of yore enfeoffed
In absolute monopoly of soul,
Without effrontery may claim to be
The core of all creation. What I say' –
'The pot said to the kettle,' croaked the bird,
And sought at once a more secluded perch;
While I began to brood of what and why.

Urban: Of what and why? Nay, here and now, below,
           Among the gables, dip and mount the masts
           Of coasting schooners; from the chimney-tops   90

66 *fowl*) bird ASR.   67 *Whom nobody gets on with*. Man alive, ASR.
68 And me) I was ASR.

256

The smoke, spun-off, and woven by the wind,
Is looped across the harbour.

Lucian: What and why:
Conundrums all men ask, before the world,
Or shamefast and in secret.

Urban: Here and now,
Uncatechizable, the fieldfares, blown
About our ears, like withered foliage whirl.

Lucian: I saw *not* here and now, but in a land
That lies to windward of our crowded sail,
A hero built a palace roofed with gold,
The panel-work of sandal, and the walls   100
Of orient alabaster. Genii,
Obedient to his talisman, adorned
The lofty chambers, galleries, and courts
With beauty fetched from ancient treasuries,
Elaborate looms and caves of earth and sea!
A goddess loved him; left her bower in heaven
To marry him; accomplished all his heart,
And bore him sons and daughters happily.
They lived in sweet contentment with their friends,
Gods, demi-gods, heroes, and men and women;   110
They studied all there was to know; they pleased
Themselves with art; and fought and overcame
Titanic rebels. Yet he dwelt alone.
For in his tower at midnight, 'What,' he said,
'And why?' and many folios filled with words
That never caught an echo of the truth.
One night when he was old an inner power
Bestirred him in his wistful solitude,
And drew him down through all his garnished halls,
His colonnades, and fragrant arbours, out   120
By a little postern where a pit was dug –
For him, he knew at once. Before he laid
Him down to take his ease eternally,
Remembering all his thought, he yearned to speak
A word that might resolve the doubts of men.
So lifting up his forehead to the night
Instinct with stars, he shouted, 'Live to Die!'
That very moment of his upward look,
And anguished utterance, from a wicket-gate
There issued opposite a hermit old,   130
Expelled his poortith by the self-same power
That drew the hero from his pageantry.
Making the pregnant words, inane to him,
The hermit raised his voice and called aloud
With wrathful eyes and gesture, as they fell
Into the pit together. 'Die to Live!'

94 shamefaced ASR.   96–7 *See Notes.*   99 build ASR.   103 lofty *om.* ASR.
127 shouted) cried out ASR.

Urban:	I hate your destitute antinomies
	That paralyze the will; and better love
	The labourer busy in the bottom there,
	Than airy palaces of wiseacres, 140
	Or living tombs of envious eremites.
	He stumbles on behind the plough as stiff
	And rusty as his team; the share, disedged
	And out of date; an elvish urchin jerks
	The bridle; and at either furrow-end
	Perforce he scrapes the clumsy blade, so thick
	And greasily the heavy soil adheres.
	An ancient implement, unhandsome work;
	The numbers of the peasant's poem halt
	A little on the sheet of earth he scores. 150
	But showers and summer sunshine, time and tide,
	Were never known eclectic; golden crops
	When autumn reigns, delight to decorate
	The shaky scrawl of overlaboured hands,
	As well as rigid lines of tireless steam.
Lucian:	Yes; but we cannot fling these questions off;
	They're in the blood, not fashionable wear,
	And drive the simplest and the subtlest mad.
Eustace:	And each of us makes answer as he must,
	In life and death, in every aim and deed, 160
	Unwittingly – and gallantly.
Lucian:	Nay, some,
	Beside themselves, attempt to solve in speech
	What hearted action only can atone.
	Fantastic things men dream and do, distraught
	By rebel sense, usurping soul, remorse,
	Incongruent appeals and challenges,
	Chiefly about the period when begins
	The conflict in the tissues and the blood
	Where age subdues the tyranny of youth.
Urban:	Let youth and sense be tyrants still: accept 170
	The sign – The Fox and Hounds! – What nook is this?
Lucian:	The least of hamlets, all unknown in maps;
	Disdained in country guides; a forge, a store,
	Three dwelling houses and a wayside inn,
	Behind the Downs ensconced.
Urban:	A dingy room:
	The smell of stale tobacco; a cribbage-board
	With pegs of Swedish matches; almanacks;
	And taproom sawdust. Oh, escape, escape!

167 *om.* ASR.

| Lucian: | But taste the Sussex ale before you fly; |
| | And, for a reason, keep the room in mind. |

180

| Eustace: | Why, this is honest malt; and in these times |
| | Of tar and cent per cent, that's something still. |

Urban:	But watch the sky-scape through the drabbled panes!
	The livid clouds, o'errun with glittering light,
	Shrivel and flicker up the firmament
	Like tinder in a chimney, or shadowgraphs
	Against a sheet; and the blue welkin, domed
	And mantling with its watchet dust, the flower
	Of azure, overhangs the world. Out! Out!

Eustace:	The wind has fallen; and not a whisper stirs
	The brimming silence; earth enchanted, waits
	A counter-spell.

190

Urban:	I love that litter, strewn
	About the stithy yard: machines and ploughs;
	Old toothless harrows; rollers, rusty, cracked
	And clotted o'er with tell-tale soil; wheel-tyres
	Of sorts in bunches on the gable: all
	Reposeful, genial and luxurious.

Eustace:	A prying woman opes a door and peeps –
	But not at us, she makes believe. She turns;
	She hesitates, she saunters purposeless,
	Then grasps her gown foothot across the way,
	And puts a period to the silence so.

200

Urban:	A smothered, gurgling sound; a scarf of smoke
	Hung out upon the chimney-stack! The bellows
	Coughs and rumbles, sooty cobwebs blown
	To tatters in its throat; the muttering flames
	Burst from the drenched and close-raked dross; the shoe
	Cries on the anvil as the dull clang rings
	Of dead, on living iron, every blow
	A bruise. A rustle in the hedge; some full,
	Round notes, like water-drops that slowly plunge
	In a deep, mossy well, the blackbird pipes
	With saffron bill; the assembled starlings scold
	In budding tree-tops, and the brazen catch
	And madrigal of fifty chanticleers
	In fifty farms responds and dwindles wide
	From knoll to knoll round Chanctonbury Ring
	That copes with sable crest the silvery air.

210

| Eustace: | Now for your memory of The Fox and Hounds. |

182 tar and) eager ASR. 190 and *om*. ASR. 202 And punctuates the
broken silence so. ASR. 204 stack) stalk ASR. 212 well) fount ASR.

259

Lucian: When first I came on this forgotten den   220
A year ago, I met a savage oaf,
That skulked and tippled in the frowsy room
So little liked by us. His eyes, deep-sunk,
Shifting and fiery, special menace held:
The internecine war of youth and age
Embroiled him, soul and body. 'Sir,' says he,
Waving his tankard, 'did you ever hear
The Cat-call of the Universe?' 'Not I,'
I said. 'A time may come,' he hisses. 'Weeks
And months the beast is silent. Suddenly at night,   230
When the club-bore is doling anecdotes
And pallid waiters yawn; or in the House,
Just on the stroke of twelve, as Mister Smith
"Ventures to think," while a sub-secretary
Sole on the Treasury-Bench for supper frets;
Or on a stair in some perspiring crush,
Where wit and wealth compete for elbow-room
Awaiting all who reach the fabled top,
I hear the Cat-call, and forsake the world.'
'What do you mean by Cat-call?' 'Don't you know? 240
The Cat-call of the Sphinx, the Universe.'
'I know the ancient guess: Four feet at dawn;
At noon, a biped; triple-legged at night.'
'Not to the purpose, sir,' he cried enraged;
'And nothing can compel me to believe
It took a parricide to find it out;
Or that the Sphinx fell down and broke her crown
When Œdipus made answer. Sphinx is now
A symbol of the Universe; her call,
The queries *what* and *why*, intolerably   250
Hurled into my ears at inauspicious
Times, with subtle craft and iteration fell,
More vehement than a tunnel-nearing train,
A factory whistle at the break of day,
Or siren of a liner in a fog.
Here, in this upland public-house I hide,
As you will – mark it – when you hear the Call.
Strange sights you'll see – as I do now! Look there!
On Truleigh Hill a huddled city, built
Of blackest marble; houses, spires and towers   260
Without a door or window; pinnacle
And buttress furred and coated with a nap
Of soot – a rusty black upon the hewn
Or burnished marble's dense or glossy tint.
Between the courses swart smoke coils, crushed through
By stifling pressure. Hark! The city reels
With heavy noise of voices numberless,
Shouting in unison – the muffled roar
As of a thousand bulls of Phalaris,
The bellowing of men in agony.'   270
'Come out,' I said, 'Too much tobacco, beer,

The rancid room' – 'No, here I stay,' he cried,
'Until that roar becomes articulate.
Then will the Cat-call of the Universe
Be shouted down for ever.'

Urban: Mad, I think.

Lucian: A humourist in Hinnom rather; scorned
           By fame; by fortune jilted; flayed and raw
           As to his vanity; bankrupt in love;
           But by a habit soldered into life,
           Transmuting pain to pity, grudge to grin,   280
           And solving all in morbid fantasy.

Urban: Some natures cannot leave the City of Dis.

Eustace: And few escape a bitter sojourn there.

Lucian: But here are we at Steyning – reticent,
           Antique; a tranquil place of oaken beams
           Bow-bent with age; of gables, shingle roofs,
           Of wooden houses, gardens, hanging eaves.
           The railway came, but kept its distance; past
           Is present here; old homeliness, a sense
           Of room, and of an actual ease in life   290
           Deliver and refresh the jaded thought,
           Like a new image or a well-dreamed sleep.
           Nor is an air of mystery wanting: doors
           Withdrawn in shadowed entries, windows broad
           And low, or high and secret, keep account
           Of whispers, vigils, burning glances, tears –
           Known only to themselves, mute witnesses
           With meaning stored and memories of men.
           Oh, towns and houses are your only ghosts!
           Unlaid by Time that tosses ruthlessly   300
           In hallowed bournes his plume of brindled steam,
           Finger on lip, this Steyning haunts the flank
           Of Chanctonbury Ring, a phantom town,
           Forlorn a little, waiting by the way
           With silent welcome for the wanderer.

156. THE IDES OF MARCH

Percy: Where the brimming freshets rush
           And the pebbles chafe and ring,
           The leafless alders flush
           With purple of the Spring.

Herbert: And the crimson osiers burn
           With spathes that swell and split,
           And every bract an urn
           With twinkling catkins lit.

Basil: Where chaos spreads unkempt,
And formless being roves,
I wandered lost
Until I crossed
The ultramundane groves,
And dreamt last night, as Caesar dreamt,
I placed my hand in Jove's.

Ninian: And music sighed and sang,
And voices uttered doom,
And Mars's armour rang
Untouched in Caesar's room.
Most ominous of woe,
A wondering slave appeared,
Whose fingers flamed below –

Sandy: A candelabrum weird!

Ninian: Titanic beings fought,
In fiery arms on high;
The Universe was wrought
To tragic sympathy;
Nor can the years dispel
The awe of that; nor can
The tongues of poets tell
The deed these signs foreran,
For on the morrow fell
The greatest man.

Basil: What cry? what whispered word?

Percy: What music wild and sweet?

Herbert: The listening air is stirred.

Sandy: The sounds are in the street.

Basil: I hear a murmuring flood.

Percy: I hear a trembling string.

Ninian: The sounds are in our blood.

Basil: The sounds are of the Spring.

Herbert: The throstle in the brake,
Alone, and hid away,
Beginning to rehearse
His long-considered lay,

11 I wandered lost until I crossed Ou. 12 *om*. Ou. 34 Hush! not a whispered word! Ou. 35 Hark! music, wild and sweet! Ou.

Because the blossoms wake
On the elms, the first in flower,
Repeats a broken verse
And tunes it by the hour.

Percy: And his cousin thinks him a dunce,   50
            The blackbird, he who sings
            At the top of his voice at once
            While the startled woodland rings:
            He peals his splendid song
            Loud and fluent and clear,
            For echo to prolong
            And all the world to hear.

Herbert: Now like a golden gong;
            Now like a crystal sphere.

Percy: For echo to prolong   60
            And all the world to hear.

Basil: What sound is this that comes
            At sunset lowly pitched?
            The roll of elfin drums
            Or song of things bewitched?
            Perhaps the nightwind strums
            The wires, with news enriched
            Of peace, and silent drums –
            With happy news enriched
            Of silent, sleeping drums,   70
            With war no more bewitched.

Ninian: At least the springtime comes;
            For I hear in a valley I know
            A sound of elfin drums,
            And a shadowy clarion blow,
            As the crimson threads and thrums
            In the twilight sky decay,
            And the wandering beetle hums
            The threnody of day.

Sandy: When the spacious darkness comes,   80
            And the crimson lights decay,
            The ponderous beetle hums
            The threnody of day.

Herbert: The nightwind sighs and sings.

Percy: The darkness deepening comes.

Basil: The antique curfew rings
            To the roll of elfin drums.

Ninian: The flickering threads and thrums,
          The ruddy brands decay;
          And the mournful beetle hums   90
          The threnody of day.

Basil: But soon the wakening comes,
          And darkness dies forlorn;
          And the thunder of the drums
          Of the March wind ushers morn.

Ninian: And woes that wound the sight,
          And spectres disappear.

Percy: And men are men of might.

Herbert: And love is crystal-clear.

Sandy: And I swear by the light,   100
          And the noon and the night,
          It is good, it is good to be here!

157. ST. MARK'S EVE

Basil: Late, Vivian! Midnight stirs
          In the placid bosom of Time.

Vivian: I have been in the wildwood, sirs,
          In the snare of a sovran rhyme;
          Where blossoms and feathers and furs
          Grow rich as a dazzling rhyme –
          With stains of a fragrant rhyme;
          And the very spathes and spurs
          Are tuned to the deafening chime
          Of the larks and the courage that stirs   10
          In the heart of the vernal prime.

Ninian: In the wildwood? Here or beyond?
          At home in the world or afar?
          Where the bracken unfurls a frond,
          Or a nebula loosens a star –
          Where the fern delivers a frond,
          Or a nebula utters a star?

Vivian: At home. In this hermit-nook
          Of conscious pleasure and pain
          I journeyed to listen and look –   20
          With wonder to listen and look
          In the Warren and Honey Lane,
          By the Quicks and the Cuckoo brook
          From Epping to Chingford Plain.

Where the passion of Nature stirs
Undisciplined, up and down
I wandered the wildwood, sirs,
On the margin of London town –
In the forest that's ours and hers
On the threshold of London town. 30

Ninian: Did you see then the blackthorn blaze
Against the empurpled glow
Of the glades and the woodland ways?
Did the violet forest glow
Where the budded leaf delays,
And chaplets pallid as snow
On the twisted blackthorn blaze –
Coronals, garlands, sprays
Like fresh, moon-silvered snow?

Basil: Did you hear from Highbeach tower 40
The mellow quarter-chime –
From the belfry of Highbeach tower
Did you hear the music of Time,
Like silken banners unfurled?
From the ancient and hallowed bower
Of the virginal bride of the world,
Did you hear the melodious hour
Like broidered banners unfurled –
With the dulcet and virginal power
Of Time, the bride of the world? 50

Vivian: I saw the blackthorn blaze
Like wreaths of moonlit snow,
Where the budded leaf delays
And the violet woodlands glow;
From Highbeach steepled tower
I heard the quarter-chime –
From the ancient and hallowed bower
Of the beautiful virgin, Time,
I heard the melodious vesper hour
And the sprightly quarter-chime. 60
Then the blackbird finished his song
On a penetrant, resolute note;
Though the thrush descanted long.
For he knows no tune by rote –
With sighs descanted long
Of the sorrow he aches to tell;
With sobs and shuddering moans,
Like one that sings in Hell,
He laced the phantom over-tones
Of the mellow vesper-bell: 70
Some terror he fain would tell,
But he never can strike the note:

52 moonlit driven) Ou.

So the thrush descanted long,
While the blackbird finished his song.
And the woodwele's laughter ceased
In his ash-green gurgling throat
On the fringe of the tones released
By the vibrant vesper-bell –
The forest laughter ceased
In the wake of the twilight bell,   80
And high, so high, from the dusky sky
The last lark breathless fell.
But the nightingales sang on
Like welling founts of sound,
As the saffron sunset paler shone
And the darkness grew profound;
The nightingales sang on
And the sleepless cuckoos beat
Their dulcimers anon, anon,
In the echoing woodland street –   90
Their golden dulcimers anon
In every forest street.
And lo! from their secret bowers
In the shadowy depths of the chace,
With lanterns jewelled like flowers
In state at a stately pace –
The elfin-folk from their hallowed bowers
In the innermost shrine of the chace,
Came, swinging their fragrant and luminous
    flowers,
To dance in the market-place –   100
Came with their dances and lanterned flowers
To the forest's market-place.
And I watched them dancing for hours
In elfin pomp and state:
I saw the elves and I watched them for hours,
And therefore I come so late.

Basil: How say you? An April tale
        Of the nightingale's song and the lark's;
        Or a vision at best, or a dream?

Ninian: Nay, for enchantments prevail,   110
        And things are as strange as they seem.
        At the mystical Tide of St. Mark's
        A pregnant fantasy stirs,
        And prodigies happen o' nights.

Vivian: And I saw them, I saw them, sirs –
        The elves in their woodland rites!
        When the vesper-bell had rung,
        And the last lark dropped from the sky;
        When the cuckoo's golden tongue,

112 Tide) Eve Ou.

And the nightingale's rhapsody
Full-filled the forest with sound,
From their secret and hallowed bowers
In the woodland depths profound,
From the innermost heart of the chace,
The elves with their lanterned flowers
Trooped forth at an elfin pace;
And I watched them dancing for hours
In the forest's market-place.

158. THE TWENTY-FOURTH OF MAY

Brian: Must this be Empire-Day?

Basil: The date is fixed.

Brian: Forfend
The omen, powers on high!

Basil: Shame, traitor, shame! Amend
So treasonous a sigh.
Empire and Empire-Day –

Brian: I still mistrust them, I! –

Basil: Have come and come to stay!

Brian: I hate the name, the thing!
You know the prophets say,   10
'Empire begins the end:
The loves, the hopes we sing,
Our sweetest common good
Will fade, their source decay,
And fancy's naïve device
Unmourned depart away –
Art and our freer mood
For ever and a day.'
So stiff is empire's price,
The penalty of power.   20

Ninian: But the drama of the woods,
That deepens every hour,
No change in men can change,
While the murmuring cushat broods,
And the restless fern-owls range
The night-winds interstrown
With wonders, jewelled wings
Of moths and chafers – sown
With silken singing wings
Of lost nocturnal things.   30

Lionel: Not fear, not love, not hate,
Not shame, not wounded pride
Can heighten or abate
The jocund summer-tide
That blossoms hour by hour –
The surf and crested tide
Of the fragrant hawthorn flower.

Vivian: No human joy or care,
Not envy, age, or pain,
Not the whole world's despair   40
Can tarnish, taint, or stain
One gold-bossed silver shield
Of the daisies of the field –
The land-wide Milky Way
Of the myriad eyes of day.

Brian: To me the amber studs
Of the kingcups on the leas,
And the fragrant hawthorn buds
Are but the earth's disease;
And the daisies in the grass
A snowy leprosy.   50

Basil: Hush, slanderer, hush! Alas,
How deep your discontent!

Brian: Imperial thoughts for me
Decolour and unscent
The violet and the rose;
For empire is the womb
Of teeming wars and woes,
The enemy of chance
That keeps the world in hope,   60
And the murderer and the tomb
Of art and all romance.

Basil: If that's the only ill,
The source of all your gloom,
No longer need you mope.
Such dire imperial doom
Has been, and shadows still
All landlocked empire, shut
In one unhealthy room;
A drilled mechanic state   70
That jolts in one deep rut –
Whose grave, or soon or late,
Is its habitual rut,
By time and chance and fate
For ever sealed and shut.

39 Not age with envious crutch, Ou.   41 Can tarnish, stain, or touch Ou.

Brian: Infallible rebuke
          That shames imperial pride!

Basil: The doom that overtook
          The empires of the past;
          The doom that must betide   80
          All rule however fast
          Enfeoffed with power and law,
          That makes its interest, first and last,
          To hold the world in awe.
          But England's Ocean-state
          Enthroned upon the sea,
          The armed and equal mate
          Of power and liberty,
          Has this for doom and fate –
          To set the peoples free.   90

Lionel: Nobler than empire – word
          Ill-omened, out of date! –
          What name shall be conferred
          On England's Ocean-state?

Basil: We need no other name;
          Our origin, our fate,
          Our history speaks, our fame,
          In England's Ocean-state.

Vivian: Wherever England comes
          The lowliest has his chance.   100

Lionel: Our English story sums
          The meaning of Romance.

Basil: We bid the poet drink
          Till Hippocrene be dry,
          And the thinker dare to think
          The sun out of the sky.

Lionel: We bid the dreamer, drunk
          With dreaming, dream again;
          And fakir, mollah, monk
          To any heaven attain.   110

Basil: Then though these isles were sunk
          And buried in the sea,
          Our England would remain
          Wherever men are free.

Ninian: Embattled usage falls
          At the beating of our drums;
          All proud originals
          Have scope where England comes.

Vivian:	As free as birds that sing And serenade the morn.
Lionel:	As the swallow on the wing, Or the blackbird on the thorn.
Basil:	Or the throstle, purged of scorn For the music in his heart – That takes such loving pains To school his angry heart, And now at last attains The mastery of his art.

120

159. BAPTIST TIDE

Basil:	Outcast and vagrant, hail! Unhappy, wandering star, You sojourn *here*, unchid; We love you – as you are, Rejected, scorned, forbid, Targe of the world's abuse.
Lionel:	What nectar, dark or pale, To drink your happier cheer in? What brew, what auburn ale, What blood, what golden juice Of Albany or Erin?
Menzies:	The grape, the grape: no malt To deaden soul and sense. Let some illustrious wine My heart and brain exalt, And crowded opulence Of fantasy be mine.
Basil:	Your brain shall teem with sights Desirable as youth; And sense and soul divide The ravished world between them.
Brian:	Bethink you, sirs: in sooth We should be Nazarites, For this is Baptist Tide.
Lionel:	Let formalists demean them As ancient modes provide: We take no oath, no vow; Nor shall our hearts abide In bondage of the past.
Basil:	The adolescent world Is but beginning now; And men are men at last.

10

20

30

Brian:	Yet the sweet heaven unfurled About us like a rose, Nor ending, nor beginning, Nor age, nor ailment knows.
Lionel:	Though that were certain, folk Who cannot make an end Of simple-hearted sinning, Who have their lives to spend, 40 And must endure the yoke Of human joys and woes, Seek still a new beginning, Desire a sweeter song, Expect the compassed close Of misery and wrong.
Basil:	A cup of wine can change Despair to deep delight.
Brian:	An overture that jars Upon our mood! We range 50 The purlieus of the night On thoughts that seek the stars; You drag us down to earth, And urge a vinous mirth!
Basil:	Nay, now; fill, drink, and mark: – A Burgundy mature; Romanée Conti, dark As carmine jewels, pure As Côte d'Or's golden noons, And spiced with dewy scent 60 Of rich autumnal moons.
Brian:	A wine whose virtue's spent Before the lees appear!
Basil:	By Dionysius, no! A mystery slumbers here, A rite, a sacrament, Whose nature I can show. We drink material power; The inmost soul of wine Is adamant, the flower 70 Of carbon: light and heat Long-hoarded in the mine; Mettle of bread and meat; The dawn whose crimson flood Intoxicates the east; The tissue and the heart Of organism; the blood, The seed of man and beast

271

Become by Nature's art
Sterile as candent flame,   80
And yet the stuff, the breath
Of noble strife, of fame,
Of myths that folk invent
To give the past a name;
Ethereal life in death,
Potable ravishment.

Lionel: The naked facts; the truth;
The power, the poetry!

Basil: Now will our outcast see
Some vision of his youth;   90
Of summer's flower and leaf,
Of emprise meetly done;
A happy gleaner's sheaf,
Or love, or battle won;
Some joy beyond belief:
For he has drunk the sun,
Drunk up the night and day,
Drunk down the dregs of grief,
And drunk the world away.

Lionel: He sees us not, nor hears;   100
A glory fills his eyes,
Like one through crystal tears
Beholding Paradise.

Menzies: Not rubies set in gold
Of matchless flame and worth,
But dawn and sunset scrolled
About the emerald earth!
Oh, moon of my desire,
Bend from your heaven above,
A lily sweet, on fire   110
With newly budded love!
Bend from your heaven; be mine
Once more before I die,
And let life's hallowed wine
Empurple earth and sky
In hyacinthine hours,
And dusky midnights hung
With stars and passion-flowers
And ecstasies unsung!

Lionel: Entranced into the street   120
He wanders like a shade!

Brian: He treads on wingëd feet:
I think his grave is made!

272

His soul is bathed in light,
His heart for love athirst:
Were he to die to-night
I scarce should call him curst.

127 curst) cursed Ou.

160. THE FEAST OF ST MARTHA

Brian: Perturbed by wealth, perturbed by want,
    With angered brain and breaking heart,
Why will the world the market haunt?
    If folk would choose the better part!

Lionel: Folk must be troubled; work and think;
    Devote their strength; exhaust their health.
I love St Martha, meat and drink,
    Labour and thrift, and skill and wealth.

Vivian: If exorcism avail not, leave
    The phantom woes you sorrow for.   10

Brian: No phantoms; facts: for facts I grieve,
    Authentic things that dreams abhor: –
Imprisoned clouds that spin and weave
    Complex machinery of war

(Torpedoes, cannon, latent rage
    Impounding peace) as easily
As happy playmates knit a cage
    Of rushes for a butterfly.

Lionel: And chastened lightning, pick and choice
    Of all man's wonder-working might,   20
A public scribe, an airy voice,
    The dazzling conqueror of the night!

Basil: To whisper over heath and holt,
    To herald tidings everywhere,
To travel on a thunder-bolt
    By land, or sea, or middle air!

Vivian: The docile lightning! Jupiter,
    Could no foreboding Proteus see
Your armament celestial wear
    The livery of humanity!   30

Brian: Miraculous; but watch them work –
    Steam, electricity: behold
Iniquity and rapine lurk
    Where'er machinery forges gold!

5 must Ou.   19 Lionel om. Ou.   23 Basil) Lionel Ou.

Basil: I grant the worst: the piston-rod
        Undoes the handicraftsman, seals
    The doom of labour; clad and shod
        In unseen lightning, business steals

    The garnered wealth of rank and power,
        The frugal means of proud content,   40
    The widow's mite, the orphan's dower,
        The toiler's hard-earned increment.

Lionel: And thus the promise darkly given
        Fulfils itself: a child can tell
    In Rich-and-Poor an actual Heaven
        Deep-rooted in an actual Hell!

Vivian: Unhallowed jest! But let me laugh!
        By all the powers without a doubt
    The railway and the telegraph
        Have brought millennium about!   50

Brian: Oh, shame! That one man may be great
        And loll at ease, a god on high,
    Beneath, the castings of his fate,
        A myriad outworn workers sigh.

Basil: But how if that be just? Aha!
        The thing is so; therefore must be.
    Skilled and unskilled automata
        Would all escape from slavery.

    Whoever grasps what all esteem,
        What all desire, wealth, power, renown,   60
    Conceives and dares while others dream;
        And he who wins, deserves the crown.

Brian: Usurious contracts, lawless gains
        That fill the workhouse, stock the haunts
    Of vice?

Basil: The great world's growing pains
        Whose hardy soul no evil daunts!

Lionel: This very lightning you decry –

Brian: Âme damnée by the broker's hearth!
    Promoter's tout, exploiter's spy! –

Lionel: Is yet the angel of the earth.   70

    Not long shall men abuse the sons
        Of men, the tyrant's doom was signed
    When lightning learned to rouse at once
        The righteous wrath of all mankind.

Basil: The earth itself is now inspired!

Vivian: It knows delight, it feels distress!

Lionel: Ten thousand wires and nerves unwired
      Have given the globe self-consciousness!

Basil: Why brood and muse on sordid scenes,
      Why pick and point at faults and flaws?   80
    Ignore uncertain ways and means;
      Regard alone the final cause.

Brian: Who can declare why man was made?

Basil: The lover knows, the children guess;
    War, study, pastime, toil and trade
      Have one sole purpose, Happiness.

Vivian: Only decaying types incur
      Remorse and moral misery!
    Were I a great philosopher
      This should my metaphysic be,   90

    A mighty Will to Happiness.

Lionel: Therefore it is the earth is round
    And speeds through Heaven, a globe express
      For infinite Elysium bound!

Vivian: Therefore the orbs that rule the year
      Establish seasonable times,
    And deck our well-appointed sphere
      In purfled robes of diverse climes.

Lionel: Love therefore sighs with fragrant breath
      For loftier heavens and songs unsung.   100

Basil: And therefore shall benignant death
      Maintain the world for ever young.

Lionel: Therefore were women made divine,
      With beauty, purpose, power to bless
    The overloaded masculine
      Incarnate Will to Happiness.

Vivian: Therefore the all-embracing sea
      Doth with tempestuous voice demand,
    'What power shall keep the golden key
      That opes the gate of every land?'   110

Brian: Therefore we torture heart and brain,
      And cherish neither life nor health!
    We tax the past, the future drain –

Basil: In our divine desire for wealth.

We must be rich: for whom should gold
    Be meant if not for you and me?
In every age the wise and bold
    Have gathered treasure ardently.

Lionel: A health to England's golden rose,
                Her affluence of material stuff!   120

Vivian: A health to all the rich and those
                Who never can be rich enough!

Basil: And health to England's thrifty sons
                And thrifty daughters; health to all
            Courageous, battling, troubled ones
                Who keep St Martha's Festival.

161. BARTLEMAS

Lionel   From an obsolete, festival mood –
                (Ere the people grew wise and aware,
            Transcending the bad and the good,
                How extinct was the Fun of the Fair) –
            Out of Smithfield with vapours endued
                Of the rank Babylonian lair,
            Where Mirth and her fatherless brood
                Carouse it in Bartlemy Fair,
            I come, by the mass, by the rood,
                From the crusted, old Fun of the Fair!   10

Vivian: From the Forest I come whereabout
                The silences, harvested, throng –
            Autumnal the silences throng:
            No throstle, no blackbird devout
                As the seraphim mingle their song,
            With perfume entangle the light
                And powder the woodland with pearl,
            Nor usher the star-stricken night
            With incense and melody rare;
                The song-thrush devout and the merle   20
            No longer enrapture the air
                With concord of ruby and pearl.

Basil: Then you of the Forest shall spin
                A tissue of rhythmical words –
                Of jewelled, diaphanous words;
            And he shall delight in the din
                Of Smithfield and Bartlemas Birds –
            In the venial, carnival sin
                Of Bartholomew's roystering Birds;
            While I as a guerdon prepare   30

276

In our mazer of maple that held
The hydromel, quaffed at the Fair
And older than scriptural eld:
As wassail and guerdon supply,
From a formula ancient as eld
A nectar to drink of and die,
In our mazer of maple, that held
The hydromel quaffed at the Fair
Ere the people grew wise and aware.

Vivian: Alack that the truth must be told!   40
Not once now their dulcimers sweet,
That haunted the Forest of old,
The cuckoos, predominant, beat;
Their echoing pastoral, tolled
In every o'er-canopied street
On dulcimers, dulcet as gold,
Not now will the cuckoos repeat;
Reverberant cantos unrolled,
A thunder of dulcimers sweet,
Through the flower-writhen Forest of old   50
No longer the cuckoos repeat.

Lionel: But yesterday rose on the air,
With the odour of burning entwined,
The breath of an agonised prayer –
But yesterday, braiding the wind
With an incense, nor holy, nor rare
When they tortured the flesh and the mind –
The body as well as the mind;
When the learned and the lewd had to die
For the rights of the tongue and the pen,   60
And martyrdom shrouded the sky
In the smoke of the burning of men;
Where now in the shouldering press
Of the stareabouts destined to stare,
By the booths and the stalls in the stress
Of the tide and the trough of the Fair –
In the narrows and straits of the Fair,
While the cressets, the torches, and links,
Beginning to blossom and flare
As the sun in the occident sinks   70
With phantoms embroider the air –
While the cressets and vaporous links,
As the sun that transfigured the Fair
In his western brazier sinks,
With witchcraft impregnate the air,
Arises the mercantile cry
As of souls in the depths of despair –
Of a people at home with despair,
'What lack you and what will you buy?'
The challenge and lure of the Fair!   80

277

'What lack you, sirs? Buy, will you buy?
    Ripe costard or Catherine pear?
Is it hey for the lust of the eye?
    Will you trip it, coranto or jig?
But first you must eat or you die,
    Of a hallowed Bartholomew pig –
    Of a savoury Bartlemas pig!'
Then hey for the Fun of the Fair,
    The babel of noise and the cry,
The turbulent shows in the glare   90
    Of the cressets that lacquer the sky –
    That fume as they lacquer the sky!
It's ho for the Fun of the Fair!
    And it's hey for the lust of the eye!
Ripe costard and Catherine pear,
    And the yellow gowns fluttering by –
Green sleeves at Bartholomew Fair,
    And the light of a riotous eye!

Basil: Green leaves in the Forest; green sleeves –
        I modulate Lionel's cry –   100
    At the Fair; in the Forest, green leaves,
        And the glance of an innermost eye.

Vivian: No longer the nightingales chant
        To the silvery pulses of night,
    That echo the measure and grant
        Responsal of starry delight:
    No nightingales longer descant
        To the stars as they throb with delight
    Of the passionate answer they grant
        The music that troubles the night –   110
        As they vibrate and bloom with delight
        In the hanging gardens of night.
    For the silences, harvested, throng,
        Though the gold and purpureal dye –
        Though the lacquer, the mordant, and dye
    Of the autumn, like sounds of a song
        Into colour transmutable, lie
    On the Forest – the crystalline tune
        That the spheres were imagined to play
    Into colour transformed in the noon   120
        Of an ever adventurous day;
    Above and within and about,
        The perfected silences throng –
        In the Forest the silences throng:
    No throstle, no blackbird devout
        As the seraphim mingle their song,
    With perfume entangle the light
        And powder the woodland with pearl,
    Nor usher the star-stricken night

87 Bartlemas) Bartlemy Ou.   115 *Om*. Ou.   122-3 *Om*. Ou.

With incense and melody rare;   130
    The song-thrush devout and the merle
No longer enrapture the air
    With concord of ruby and pearl;
Nor now can the nightingale sing
    Expecting a stellar reply;
No fugues intergarlanded ring
    Of the earth and the clusters on high –
Sidereal echoes that bring
    The crystalline tears and the sigh
For the end of a beautiful thing   140
    That soldered the earth and the sky.

134 Nor) Not Ou.

162. OUR DAY

Basil: The chill wind whispers winter: night sets in;
And now, by many a sounding thoroughfare,
Life, like a tidal wave, begins to fill
The theatres and halls and hidden nooks,
Wherein it clangs and seethes and spends itself.

              Enter Lionel.

And whence come you?

Vivian: From wandering to and fro
Somewhere in London – London the unknown;
Which none can ever know, none ever see,
But only wonder at and wander in!

Basil: The City of the World, ancient and proud,   10
Vast, thronged, and awful; richer than the floor
Of ocean and its unsacked treasure-house;
An insolent city and a beautiful;
A place of mirth and sadness infinite:
Of infinite horror, infinite despair,
Infinite courage and felicity.
What! Do we read your thoughts, your eyes
        that speak
Of greatnesses beheld?

Lionel: All day I saw
A greater thing than London; now at night
The ample vision looms more excellent –   20
The vision of a thing that shall endure
When London is a Babylon; shall shine
A jewel in eternal memory;
Shall on the summit of achievement burn,
A challenge and a beacon for the brave:
The perfect battle-pageant of the deep,
Trafalgar.

279

Basil:	You beheld Trafalgar?	

Lionel: Now!
I watch it now!

Vivian: Show us this sight of sights!
Make us behold Trafalgar and the pride
Of England, Nelson!   30

Lionel: Look and see; who looks
With insight, can! A fragile form,
The delicate sheath of valour absolute;
Ambition, daring, honour, constancy,
Prescience, dominion, passion, scope, design,
A woman's tenderness, an infant's awe,
An adamantine courage, mercy, power
Attuned and fateful in an invalid!
Sea-lord, sea-god, his clear, transcendent love
Endowed his friends with lustre of his own,
And saw no blemish for excess of light   40
Which his great spirit shed: his glittering scorn,
His hate for England's sake of England's foes,
Diviner than his love, at England's need
O'erthrew the splendid Titan who essayed
To wrest the loyal sea from English hands,
Holding in trust that greatest gift to Fate.
The Nile, the Baltic, saw his pregnant war;
The palsied navies shrivelled at his touch;
So suddenly he came, so swiftly smote,
So wholly conquered, that his deeds remain   50
The bulwark maritime of England's power.
Nothing could tame his soul: that ocean-hunt
About the Atlantic and about in quest
Of action France and Spain denied,
Whetted his lust of battle; long delay,
That withers enterprise and rots desire
Even of enduring things, augmented all
His purpose and matured the valiant seed
Of utmost victory. Wherefore upon the dawn
Foreknown of battle – for the Admiral said   60
'The twenty-first will be our day' – he paced
His quarter-gallery subtly clad already
In the shadow of his glory; prepossessed
Besides with death; and like a spirit calm
That treads the threshold of eternity.
Now, when the morning brimmed the western world,
And on the weather-gleam a headland rose
Assured of fame, and the confederate fleets
Appeared between, hull crowding hull, five miles
Of armament, our great sea-warrior bade   70
The battle be. Southward the ships of France,
The ships of Spain, northward the English sailed,

As if they meant to pass each other by
In some majestic ritual of the tide.
But Nelson's signals, winged like thought aloft,
Undid that minuet! Twelve sail of his,
The weather line, with Collingwood to lee,
Bore up amain – the wind west by nor'west –
And eastward stood athwart the banded fleets,
That veered unwieldily and headed north   80
With safe retreat on Cadiz, till Nelson's touch
Precipitated battle – he on their van
And Collingwood against their southern flank:
Two columns opportunely; yet to the end
The sailing order held the battle-line –
Our Admiral's prophecy and inspired device.
That happy signal first: 'England expects
That every man will do his duty'; then
Drums beat to quarters: gunners, stripped and girt,
The naked flesh of England against the fire   90
And rending bolt of England's foes, unlashed
Their ordnance: frowning crews, equipped
With linstock, priming-iron, rammer, wad,
Crowbar and handspike, cartridge, wreaths of shot,
Stood by each carronade, each red-lipped gun;
Topman and boarder, trimmer, musketeer,
Marine and powder-boy fulfilled his post,
His deed, his errand, transfigured suddenly.
The ceremonial wind controlled the approach,
Keeping a pageant-pace; and towering sails   100
Of England's navy, sheeted to the sky,
Slumbered at ease, a dulcet, virgin sleep
So placid in their bosoms the breath of heaven
Dwelt like a dream, as every vessel, groomed
For war and marshalled on the vagrant surge
Of coming tempest, rode to victory.
France fired the nuptial gun; the flags broke out
Of every nation, and the battle joined.
In front of England the *Royal Sovereign* first
Achieved the enemy's range. The *Victory* next,   110
Silent against a navy's broadsides, forged
Ahead; and when her double-shotted guns,
One after one, at twenty feet had ploughed
The *Bucentaure* endlong, aboard the doomed
Redoubtable she ran. Forthwith amid
The din of cannon against cannon, mouth
To bellowing mouth, the shriek of timber crashed
And rent, the thund'rous voice of men absorbed
In the wild trance and waking dream of war,
Carnage and agony and the rhythmic swing   120
And travail of the deed, as Nelson paced
His quarter-deck awaiting the superb,

74 tide) sea Ou.   102 *Om*. Ou.   104 Slumbered at ease as every vessel,
groomed Ou.   110 range) fire Ou.

281

Unmatched event his genius had ordained,
The fatal marksman in the enemy's top
Espied his honours and England's hero fell.
Down in the winepress of the war where blood
O'erflowed the orlop, where the wounded strewed
The noisome cockpit and the grimy sweat
Cooled on the labouring surgeons, Nelson died:
The swarthy smoke that coiled from poop to hold   130
Obscured the glimmering lanterns; overhead
The cannon leapt; like a taut rope the hull
Quivered from stem to stern with every shot;
And still above the thunder of the strife,
Cresting the uproar, pealed the great hurrah
Of all the English crews, as ship by ship
The baffled navies struck and Nelson's name
Became immortal.

Vivian: Such a dying deed!

Basil: So great a life, so great a death, so great
A legacy of Empire!

Lionel: All are ours,   140
And will be ours while Nelson's fame endures:
Great lives, great deaths for England and the sea!

131 lanterns) candles Ou.

163. NEW YEAR'S EVE

Cyril: The earth reposes: bird and beast
Are neutral-hued in copse and dell;
The very grass-green turf has ceased
To grow till Spring shall break the spell.

Bertram: From frozen seas the north wind blows,
From sapphire icebergs rooted deep
In Arctic fathoms.

Everard: Ancient snows
About the poles renew their sleep.

Cyril: Old continents of snow – world-old!
How comfortable there to lie   10
Embalmed in everlasting cold
In peace and crystal purity!

Clarence: Let these amenities increase;
But though the north be hoar with rime,
Give me the vineyard's purple peace,
The golden peace of harvest-time;

282

A peace with cannon frankly girt,
   An armament in every sea;
A peace that wears a blood-red skirt
   Deep-dyed in many a victory;   20

The purity of healthy lives,
   Of love that sings both high and low,
Of genial husbands, happy wives,
   Of mothers purer than the snow.

Cyril: Winter's a dream: the fallows feel
      The hope of tilth; each blossom chaste,
  Against the cold in Milan steel
      Of stout hibernacle encased,

Glows with a vision of the Spring,
   The fragrance and the stain of June;   30
And thrushes on a sudden sing
   The motive of their Summer tune.

Bertram: Hush! hark! St Paul's!

Everard: Each vibrant thought,
   An orb of music, fills the ear
With rich harmonics interwrought.

Cyril: The year is dead!

Bertram: Long live the year!

Everard: Now midnight through the city rings;
      A hundred reeling belfries chime,
  With overtones like rhythmic strings,
      The lofty madrigal of Time.   40

Cyril: The world speeds in a trance profound
      From dark abyss to dark abyss
  Across this twelve-arched bridge of sound
      Between the two eternities.

Bertram: Who'll give the dreaming earth a shock,
      Who set its torpid mind aglow?

Cyril: Is there an ink to etch the rock,
      Ethereal lye to blanch the snow?

A cresset to contain the sun,
   A crystal cup to hold the sea,   50
A voice to rouse the dead and done,
   A highway through the galaxy?

Discover these, or things as strange,
   Then shift the earth and turn the year!
Discover these, then seek to change
   The mood of men, the world's career!

Clarence: There is a dish to hold the sea,
   A brazier to contain the sun,
A compass for the galaxy,
   A voice to wake the dead and done!   60

That minister of ministers,
   Imagination, gathers up
The undiscovered Universe
   Like jewels in a jasper cup.

Its flame can mingle north and south;
   Its accent with the thunder strive;
The ruddy sentence of its mouth
   Can make the ancient dead alive.

The mart of power, the fount of will,
   The form and mould of every star,   70
The source and bound of good and ill,
   The key of all the things that are,

Imagination, new and strange
   In every age, can turn the year,
Can shift the poles and lightly change
   The mood of men, the world's career.

Cyril: What cry is this? What mad to-do?
   When and by whom is this great power
That melts and forges worlds anew
   Installed and used? The man, the hour?   80

Clarence: No other time – we understand
   Nor whence, nor whither, why nor how –
Is ever at the world's command
   Than this eternal present Now.

Cyril: You rede the riddle of the earth,
   The ancient rule of all who ride;
And young it is as every birth,
   As new and fresh as time and tide: –

By town and tower, through brake and briar,
   About the world while life shall last,   90
Unbroken horses shod with fire
   The wild-eyed moments thunder past:

Who grasps the flying mane and mounts,
   Indifferent if he fail or thrive,
In happy stride with all that counts
   Arrives where'er the gods arrive.

284

Clarence: 'Tis not enough to mount and ride,
     No saddle, bridle, whip, nor spur;
  To take the chance of time and tide,
     And follow fame without demur.   100

  I want some reason with my rhyme,
     A fateful purpose when I ride;
  I want to tame the steeds of Time,
     To harness and command the tide:

  I want a whip whose braided lash
     Can echo like the crack of doom;
  I want an iron mace to smash
     The world and give the peoples room.

Cyril: We thought we knew you! Who are you
     That talk so loud?

Clarence: One who can tell   110
  That false is false and true is true,
     Alive or dead, in Heaven or Hell.

164. THE FEAST OF ST HILARY

Bertram: Your evolution, still so crude
     In civic life, prefers to sit
  In murky air of muslin stewed
     With soot and sulphur of the pit.

Lionel: Why this is only London's own
     Appurtenance in Janiveer
  And winter months – a want of tone,
     A jaundice of the atmosphere.

Vivian: And every winter cheerful folk,
     Six millions powerless to escape,   10
  Upon this clammy muslin choke
     This filthy air of sodden crape.

Bertram: Expecting no imperial cure
     From any corporate King Log
  They undergo it, *forte et dure*,
     The torture of the London fog.

  And though habitual croakers croak,
     A metaphysical desire
  Not to consume our proper smoke,
     Save when the chimney goes on fire,   20

  Through urban and suburban deeps
     Subconscious in the minds of all,
  Explains the tolerance that keeps
     Our fog a hardy annual.

Lionel: I love the fog: in every street
        Shrill muffled cries and shapes forlorn,
   The frosted hoof with stealthy beat,
        The hollow-sounding motor-horn:

   A fog that lasts till, gently wrung
        By Pythian pangs, we realise   30
   That Doomsday somewhere dawns among
        The systems and the galaxies,

   And ruin at the swiftest rate
        The chartered destinies pursue;
   While as for us, our final fate
        Already fixed with small ado,

   Spills on our heads no wrathful cup,
        Nor wrecks us on a fiery shore,
   But leaves us simply swallowed up
        In London fog for evermore.   40

Cyril: The admirable errantry
        Of London's climate who can sing?
   From fogs of filthy muslin free
        Elastic as a morn of spring,

   The weather like a dazzling bride
        Undid the lonely winter, threw
   The casemate of the orient wide
        And made the enchanted world anew.

   But yesterday, so quick and so
        Chromatic is the climate here –   50
   From russet mud to silver snow,
        From radiant suns to fogs austere.

Lionel: I watched the morning yesterday
        Where from the ample stair you look
   Across the Park beneath the gray
        Ungainly column of the Duke:

   You see him like a stylite true
        Impaled upon his pillar stand; –
   It seems to pierce him through and through,
        The rod that braves the levin-brand.   60

   Sunlit the other column glowed
        Intensely, lifting to the skies
   The admiral who swept the road
        Of empire clear for centuries.

47 casemate *corr. from* casement MS.

Entangled on the Surrey-side
    The eager day a moment hung,
Then struck in haste his ardent stride
    And round the southern chimneys swung.

A silvery weft of finest lawn,
    So thin, so phantom-like, became   70
Ethereal mystery scarcely drawn
    Athwart the morning's saffron flame;

The Palace and the Abbey lost
    Their character of masonry,
Transformed to glittering shadows tossed
    And buoyant on a magic sea;

And park and lake and precincts old
    Of Westminster were all arrayed
In spectral weeds of pearl and gold
    And airy drifts of amber braid.   80

Bertram: Ghastly and foul, as Hecate's ban
    Pernicious are our fogs; but sweet
And wonderful the mists that can
    Imparadise a London street:

The fabrics winnowed sunbeams work
    Of urban dew and smoky air;
The opalescences that lurk
    In many a court and sombre square;

The tissued dawn that gems encrust,
    The violet wreaths of noon, the haze   90
Of emerald and topaz dust
    That shrouds the evening distances;

And gloom in baths of light annealed . . .

      Enter Sandy.

Lionel: From top to toe one travel-stain
    You come! And whence?

Sandy: An outland weald
    I come from, and a dateless reign
That modes and periods never touch.

Bertram: From Epping Forest, I'll be sworn,
    The wilderness you haunt so much!

Sandy: No; from a less familiar bourne: 100

66 eager *corr. from* doubtful MS.   67 Then struck in haste his ardent stride
corr. from In doubt, then struck his measured stride *corr. from* Then struck into
his ardent stride MS.   67 haste) hate FSOP.

A Sussex chace renowned of old
　　Where withering innovation halts;
A tract of mingled wood and wold,
　　Of ragged heaths and ferny vaults.

Lionel:　St Leonard's Forest by your shoes
　　Over the latchet daubed with earth!
I know it well: the Mole, the Ouse,
　　Arun and Adur have their birth

Among its silting springs; and there
　　The nightingale has never sung,　　　　　　110
They say, so humid is the air,
　　So dank the woods with ivy hung.

In summertime you lightly tread
　　On moss as green as emerald,
And soft as silken velvet spread
　　Along the forest chancel, stalled

With bowers of thorn and laurel-tree;
　　And roomier and loftier
Than forest aisles are wont to be,
　　The green groined roof of beech and fir　　120

Admits a dulcet twilight filled
　　With golden motes and beryl hues,
That through the darkling thickets gild
　　Arun and Adur, Mole and Ouse.

Sandy:　When I went out from Horsham town
　　A northern blast of winter's breath
Blew low across the open down
　　As hard as hate, as cold as death.

Close to the land the firmament
　　Like a camp-ceiling clung; and nigh　　　　130
The eaves of the horizon, bent
　　Like frowning brows, the ashen sky.

Through ruined loopholes scattered wide
　　A pallid gleam; but as the path,
Leaving the highway, leapt aside
　　To gain the forest, winter's wrath,

By sheltering hedgerows doubly balked,
　　Became a legendary thing,
And for a while beside me walked
　　The very presence of the spring.　　　　　140

A bridge that spans a pebbled burn
　　The threshold of the forest is;
And there like some daedalian urn,
　　Or sangreal of fragrances,

142 threshold *Corr. from* forest threshold MS.

A deeply sunk, a vaulted dell
   Possessed the summer's inmost soul –
A captive, like the roseal smell
   That haunts a seeming-empty bowl:

Though all the roses, plucked and rent,
   Are squandered yet our essence knows   150
And greets the pure material scent,
   Which is the spirit of the rose.

Within the forest-chancel, stalled
   With bowers of evergreen and laid
With lustrous living emerald,
   As rich a moss as spring displayed,

No green groined roof of fir and beech
   Reflected bronze and beryl hues,
That could through darkling thickets reach
   Arun and Adur, Mole and Ouse: 160

Unthatched, instead of summer's leaves,
   A roof, with ebon rafters bare,
Allowed the light in frosted sheaves
   To silver all the wintry air.

With clapping wings doves wheeled about
   Between the pine-tops and the skies;
And blackbirds flitted in and out
   The underwood with guttural cries;

A throstle had begun to build
   Though still untimed; but loud and long   170
The eager storm-cock sang and filled
   The forest with his splendid song;

While spring, in winter's bosom warm,
   Prologued in bough and bole and root
The pregnant trance of trees that form
   The summer's foliage, flower and fruit.

Bertram: Harvest in winter's bosom sleeps,
         While time his patient vigil keeps.

178 While *corr. from* And MS.

165. ST VALENTINE'S DAY

Julian: Virginia lives in a square;
      I harbour at hand in a street:
    And Spring has begun over there;
      So love like a pestilence sweet
    Envenoms the neighbouring air.

Ernest: No pestilence, Julian! Greet

    The coming of Spring with delight.
      Have done with your modish display!
    The cynic's intelligent spite
      Arrives by the miriest way: 10
    The ferment that works in the night
      Of a prodigal, desolate day,

    A morbid, acidulent scorn,
      Inhabits the vinegared lees
    In bosoms condignly forlorn –

Julian: In bosoms philosophy frees
    From the burden to which we are born!

Ernest: In bosoms that nothing can please,

    Being empty of pleasure and sunk
      In themselves; being wizened and frail   20
    Like vats when the wine has been drunk –
      Being warped and unspeakably stale
    Like vats in desuetude shrunk.
      Let the season and nature prevail;

    Let the winepress of youth overrun; –

Julian: If the valves be corroded with rust,
    And the power and gearing undone!

Ernest: Empurpled with stains of the must,
    My fancy, forestalling the sun –

Julian: In the city we take him on trust!   30

Ernest: Disheartened the fog with a glance,
      And tinctured with opulent dyes
    Of the lily, the rose and the raunce
      The sombre, the tenebrous skies, –
    With the tricoloured blazon of France
      And the light of a paramour's eyes!

    For this is St Valentine's Day,
      And my sweetheart came into the lane:
    As I went by the speediest way,
      Being late for the morning train,   40
    Diana, in sweet disarray,
      The wonder of women, was fain

    To see and be seen of me first!

27 the gearing WG.   33 raunce) paunce WG.

Julian: How happy to love and be loved!
            How wretched is he, how accursed,
               Whom destiny handles ungloved!

Ernest: The highest encounter the worst;
             For they must be sifted and proved,

            While the rabble are shaken with ease
             Through a wide-meshed riddle of fate.   50

Julian: O spare your proverbial pleas
             And the wisdom that wiseacres prate!

Ernest: You said that philosophy frees –

Julian: From a passion I would not abate

            For the wealth of the world all told?
             From the exquisite alchemy pain,
           That tortures the dross into gold?
             I spoke in a negligent vein,
           For I love like the lovers of old,
             Adoring a woman's disdain,   60

            That crushes the doughtiest hope.

Ernest: You speak like a vassal of words,
             The indolent slave of a trope!
             Exalt your irresolute thirds
           Into fifths and their jubilant scope;
             And learn of St Valentine's birds

            That love is the herald of joy.

Julian: The pursuivant rather of care!

Ernest: You must brood on her beauty, and cloy
             Your fancy, extinguish despair   70
           With obdurate visions; destroy
             Yourself in her excellence rare;

            Be buried in dreams of her worth!

Julian: My heart with her excellence bleeds;
            My dreams of her people the earth.
             And the curse is, there's nothing she needs;
           She is rich and a woman of birth,
             While I am the son of my deeds.

Ernest: Achieve then a sire of renown;
             Perform to the height and be great.   80
           You have fought –

45 accurst, WG.

Julian: And defeat was my crown!
                    When, naked, I wrestled with fate
              The destinies trampled me down: –
                    I fought in the van and was great,
              And I won, though I wore no crown,
                    In the lists of the world; for fate
              And the destinies trampled me down –
              The myrmidons trampled me down.

B1